Exploring Dallas With Children

A Guide for Family Activities

Second Edition

Exploring Dallas
With Children
A Guide for Family Activities
Second Edition

Kay McCasland Threadgill

Republic of Texas Press

Library of Congress Cataloging-in-Publication Data

Threadgill, Kay McCasland.
   Exploring Dallas with children : a guide for family activities /
Kay McCasland Threadgill. — 2nd ed.
     p.   cm.
   Includes index.
   ISBN 1-55622-617-9 (pbk.)
   1. Dallas (Tex.)—Guidebooks. 2. Dallas Region (Tex.)—
Guidebooks. 3. Family recreation—Texas—Dallas—Guidebooks.
4. Family recreation—Texas—Dallas Region—Guidebooks. I. Title.
F394.D213T48   1998
917.64'28120463--dc21   98-17587
                                       CIP

© 1998, Kay McCasland Threadgill

All Rights Reserved

Printed in the United States of America

ISBN 1-55622-617-9
10 9 8 7 6 5 4 3 2 1
9804

All inquiries for volume purchases of this book should be addressed to
Wordware Publishing, Inc., at 2320 Los Rios Blvd., Plano, Texas 75074.
Telephone inquiries may be made by calling:

(972) 423-0090

To Whitney, Erin, and Abby, whose input is priceless, and to John for helping to make this happen—KMT

Contents

Introduction xi

Chapter 1: Places to Go 1

African-American Museum 2
Age of Steam Railroad Museum 3
American Museum of the Miniature Arts 5
Bachman Lake 6
Ballpark in Arlington, The 7
Celebration Station 10
Dallas Aquarium at Fair Park, The 10
Dallas Arboretum and Botanical Gardens 12
Dallas Firefighter's Museum: "Old Tige" 14
Dallas Horticulture Center 15
Dallas Memorial Center for Holocaust Studies 17
Dallas Museum of Art 18
Dallas Museum of Natural History 21
Dallas Nature Center 22
Dallas World Aquarium, The 24
Dallas Zoo 25
Fair Park 27
Frontiers of Flight Museum 31
Hall of State 32
Heard Natural Science Museum 34
    and Wildlife Sanctuary
Heritage Farmstead 36
Las Colinas 38
Mesquite Championship Rodeo 40
Old City Park 41
Owens Spring Creek Farm 42

Contents

Palace of Wax and Ripley's Believe It or Not! 44
Samuell Farm 45
Sandy Lake Amusement Park 47
Science Place, The. 48
Six Flags Hurricane Harbor 50
Six Flags Over Texas. 51
Sixth Floor, The 53
Studios at Las Colinas, The 55
Surf 'n Swim. 56
Telephone Pioneer Museum of Texas 57
West End Marketplace. 58
White Rock Lake. 60

Chapter 2: Tidbits: More Good Things To Do . . . 63
More Amusements 64
Nature, Ecology, Science 67
Farmer's Markets and Pick Your Own Food 78
Pets and Wildlife 82
History and Politics 87
Tours of the Working World 105
Underground Dallas/Downtown. 115
Transportation 116
Storytelling, Libraries, and Bookstores. 125
Small Art Museums, Galleries, and Art Centers . . . 131
Outdoor Sculpture and Murals in Dallas. 138
Shopping and Hobbies. 140
Hotel Hiatus 147
Restaurants with More. 149
Community Colleges. 151

Chapter 3: Performing Arts for Children 155
Dance 158
Music and Chorus 159
Opera 166
Opry 167

Puppetry 168
Theater. 169
Annual Concerts and Performance 176
    and Film Festivals

Chapter 4: Sports and Recreation 183
Spectator Sports 184
Individual, Family, and Team Sports 189
Summer Sports Camps. 207
Recreation Centers and Youth Organizations 210
Playgrounds 213
Ranches and Horseback Riding 215
Lakes, State Parks, and Recreation Areas 218

Chapter 5: Festivals and Special Events 225

Chapter 6: Day Trips 247
Bonham 248
Denison 250
Fort Worth 252
Glen Rose 265
Texas State Railroad: Rusk/Palestine. 269
Tyler 272
Waco 276

Chapter 7: Resources 283
Special Events and Ticket/Reservation Hotlines . . . 284
Convention and Visitor's Bureaus 284
State Department of Highways and 285
    Public Transportation
Publications 286
Telephone Services. 291
Top 20 Places to Go 291
Free Activities for Families 292
Birthday Party Ideas 294
Rainy Weather Ideas 297

Index 301

Introduction

Part of our Texas heritage is the spirit of adventure handed down from courageous, pioneer ancestors. The spirit of the West still urges both native Texans and those who have understandably adopted Texas as home to search out exciting and mind-expanding adventures around Dallas and the Lone Star State.

Usually, the major drawback is finding the time to plan ahead and to decide what a family, including a wide range of ages and interests, would find entertaining. That is where this guide will be invaluable, not only to those who live in and around Dallas, but to visitors, youth organizations, and child care institutions as well. The bulk of the legwork (literally) is done. Not only are vital statistics, like addresses and prices, listed, but special hints about things to try, notice, or bring are mentioned to make your visit as comfortable and worthwhile as possible.

I am thrilled to be able to publish this second edition. In three years some favorite "hangouts" have closed their doors, but many new and exciting ones have opened to inform and amuse. Rewriting the guide has enabled me to rekindle friendships made while writing the first and also meet many new, enthusiastic people as well.

In the 1993 edition, my family with children ages five to thirteen, faithful friends, and Girl Scout Troop 956 were invaluable explorers in the quest to unearth and investigate a wide variety of places—some that entertain and excite, some that enlighten, and some that do an exceptional job of both. Having grown up with and in Dallas, I was astonished at what has been available for years that I had not known existed, such as a charming two-story Victorian farmhouse from the early 1900s and a large exhibit of mounted African animals housed in an oil company. Also, many landmark places offer opportunities of which many natives are unaware. Did you know that The Science Place and the American Museum of the Miniature Arts host birthday parties or that a family may have a picnic at the Heard Museum and adopt a raptor? (What's a raptor?)

Dallas continues to grow and change. Because of changing needs and economy, attractions usually stipulate that all prices and hours are subject to change without notice. Some even go out of business without notice. Thus, it's always better to call before an outing to confirm information vital to your enjoyment of the trip. Also, many of the prices listed do not include tax. Unless otherwise indicated, all phone numbers within are prefixed by the 214 Dallas area code. However, on September 14, 1996, the Dallas area was divided into two area codes. After March 14, 1997, when the transition period was over, customers had the option of paying a fee to continue the old area code for up to two and one-half years.

Many of the museums and wildlife centers offer memberships that not only keep members in close touch with programs, but also supply financial support, which is vital to their existence. If your family is interested in science or nature or art or history, inquire about a family membership. Volunteer support is also essential to enable them to offer the range of educational programs and to schedule exhibits that make every visit fascinating.

We have had some wonderful times together compiling data for this guidebook. Few trips were disappointing. One unfailing, remarkable quality was the warm Texas hospitality offered wherever we toured. Everyone wanted us to have a great time. And we did.

1. Places to Go

Family entertainment at its Texas best is described in detail in the following chapter. Turn off the television and the lights, and head out for exciting adventures that may not be far from your own neighborhood but may offer literally acres of fun. Some attractions you seek may be listed in Chapter Two, "Tidbits: More Good Things to Do," because they are smaller or attract a more specialized interest group.

AFRICAN-AMERICAN MUSEUM

P.O. Box 15053
Dallas, Texas 75315-0153 • 565-9026

In 1993 the 38,000-square-foot African-American Museum opened in their new building in Fair Park. The museum is dedicated to research and acquisition of visual art forms and historical documents that relate to the life and culture of the African-American community as well as an outreach program to enable all to understand the African-American experience through exhibits, classes, day camps, and workshops. The building houses both permanent and traveling exhibits.

Architect Arthur Rogers designed a building with a rotunda capped by a 60-foot dome. Four galleries, which represent Africa's quadrants, radiate outward from the central rotunda. The floor tiles are terra cotta, the ceilings are exposed yellow pine, and the effect is light and airy.

On the first floor is a cafe and bookstore, and a balcony is on the second floor. Classrooms, a library, and an amphitheater are in the basement.

The museum is designated by the State of Texas as the official repository for African-American culture, so it houses important historical documents and collections.

- Call for information about group tours.

- Restrooms and water fountains are available.

- The museum is handicapped accessible.

- A cafe is open.

Hours: Tuesday-Friday, noon to 5 P.M.; Saturday, 10 A.M.-5 P.M.; Sunday, 1-5 P.M.

Admission: FREE

Directions: Take the Grand Ave. entrance from Robert B. Cullum Blvd. in Fair Park. Parking is free except during the State Fair and special events.

AGE OF STEAM RAILROAD MUSEUM

Fair Park: 1105 Washington Avenue
Dallas, Texas 75226 • 428-0101
(Mailing address: P.O. Box 153259, Dallas, Texas 75315-3259)

Dallas' oldest train depot, built in 1930, rests at the Age of Steam Railroad Museum alongside an outdoor exhibit of passenger cars, freight trains, and engines that operated from 1900 to 1950. The world's largest steam locomotive named "Big Boy," cabooses, and a 1920s passenger train including sleeping cars are part of this tribute to the glory days of the railroad. Children may observe that these trains have definitely seen better days, but they will come to understand how the engines and cars evolved and catch some of their old spirit.

Arriving from Corsicana on July 16, 1872, the first railroad to reach Dallas was the Houston and Texas Central. The 1905 vintage Houston and Texas Central depot was renovated to house the gift shop as well as other memorabilia of the days when it was a vital part of railroad life. It's the entrance to the museum, except during the State Fair when visitors probably enter at the east end. An extensive booklet is available for sale as well as a souvenir guide. The tour begins at the east end and goes the length of the trains and then back up again. Visitors climb steps to peek in some of the trains, and some of the passenger cars may be boarded.

Look for "Doodlebug," the 1931 Santa Fe Railroad self-propelled railcar that made the rounds between Carlsbad and Clovis, New Mexico. Donations are needed to help restore it. The electric locomotive #4903 that pulled the 1968 funeral train of Senator Robert Kennedy rests in the museum.

- Browse in the gift shop for railroad-related items, including toys.

- There is a soft drink machine outside the depot. Have lunch at the Old Mill Inn located near the Music Hall in the Fair Park grounds, or bring a picnic lunch.

- Guided tours for groups may be arranged with reservations. Tours for children are $1 per child. Adults are $1, and one adult is free with a group of fifteen people. To schedule a tour, call the museum or the Partnership for Arts, Culture, and Education (823-7644).

- The museum is not handicapped accessible. The path between the trains is sometimes rocky or muddy, and stairs lead up to all the doors. Go on a dry day, and wear comfortable shoes.

- Restrooms are available in the nearby Hall of State. A water fountain is in the depot.

- Parking is free except during the State Fair. A parking lot is at the east end of the train yard.

Hours: Wednesday-Sunday, 10 A.M.-5 P.M.; call before going in bad weather. Closed major holidays. Hours change during the Fair.

Admission: Adults, $3; ages 12 and under, $1.50.

Directions: See directions to Fair Park. The train museum is on the north side of Fair Park on Washington east of Parry Avenue.

AMERICAN MUSEUM
OF THE MINIATURE ARTS

2208 S. Routh Street
Dallas, Texas 75201 • 969-5502

Appropriately located in a 1920s two-story Texas prairie home, the American Museum of the Miniature Arts' collection includes fifteen large scale multistory dollhouses furnished to scale in the rural or urban period within the last hundred years that it represents and more than thirty room boxes and miniature vignettes.

Visitors also enjoy the display cases of antique toys and dolls of various sizes. Rotating collections, such as antique miniature china tea sets, puppets, haunted dollhouse, and special collections, give visitors a reason to come back again and again.

- The party room upstairs is a favorite setting for meetings and birthday parties. Catering is available. Birthday parties include a scavenger hunt in which children look for items in the dollhouses and a craft. They can also dress up in "flapper-age" hats, purses, and gloves.

- Except in the case of catered events, there is no food or drink in the museum. The Hard Rock Cafe and many other restaurants are located on nearby McKinney Ave.

- A gift shop offers miniatures, dolls, toys, and craft items.

- There is no handicapped access.

- Restrooms and water fountains are on both floors.

- Parking is free and is located behind the museum.

Hours: Tuesday-Saturday, 10 A.M.-4:30 P.M.; Sunday 1-4 P.M. Closed major holidays.

Admission: Adults, $4; seniors and children under 12, $2. Group rates are available.

Directions: From US 75 (Central) exit Woodall Rodgers Frwy. (Spur 366). Exit on Pearl; go right (toward the Crescent); turn right on McKinney Ave.; turn right again on Routh.

BACHMAN LAKE

3500 W. Northwest Highway
Dallas, Texas 75220 • 670-6374, 670-4100

A popular oasis amid the noises of Love Field Airport and business traffic, the 205-acre Bachman Lake offers a wide variety of entertainment, most of which is good for the body and spirit.

On a 3.08-mile bike/hike trail along the lake, joggers, skaters, and bicyclists pursue fitness and fun. Occasionally, you see the rowing club out on the lake and paddleboats during warm months. Motorboats and swimming are not allowed.

On days when the park is not too crowded, it's a great place to picnic and feed the birds. At Northwest Highway and Lakefield is a covered pavilion that can hold about eight picnic tables available for rent as well as three other sites for rent. One grill for cooking is on the north side, and another is on the south side of the lake.

During the Christmas season, the Park Department organizes a beautiful display of lights at Bachman.

For more than ten years, the **Bachman Lake Recreation Center**, located at 2750 Bachman Drive, has offered special programs for those with special mental and physical needs. Serving ages 6 to elderly, it is therapeutically color coordinated and has rails along the walls. Call 670-6266 for a brochure.

- Paddleboat and skate concession is by contract, so check with the Park Department to see if it is being offered. Try 670-8860.

- Lake traffic is one way, and the driving gate is closed on Saturday and Sunday.

- Always lock your car and do not leave valuables in it.

- Restaurants are nearby on Northwest Highway.

- The trail is handicapped accessible.

- The two permanent restrooms are at the Northwest Highway entrance and the Shorecrest entrance, but they are closed December-March to prevent freezing. Portables are available then. Water fountains are by those restrooms and two are along the trail.

- Parking is free. On weekends, you may want to park at the concession and recreation center parking area.

Hours: Open 5 A.M.-midnight, but staying after dark is not advisable.

Admission: FREE

Directions: Take the W. Northwest Highway (Loop 12) exit off Central (US 75) or off North Dallas Tollway and go west. The lake is on the south side. Or from I-35E, exit Northwest Highway and go east.

THE BALLPARK IN ARLINGTON

1000 Ballpark Way
Arlington, Texas 76011 • tickets 817/273-5100,
executive offices 817/273-5222

"Take me out to the ballgame..." became an even more frequent request in April 1994 when The Ballpark in Arlington opened as the new home of the Texas Rangers. Costing $191 million to build, the stadium complex consists of a sunset red granite and red brick exterior, eight towers, five seating levels, three concourses, and a Home Run Porch. The asymmetrical playing field is natural grass. Entrances to the ballpark are provided at each of the four corners.

The two sections of the main concourse provide many food and beverage concessions as well as the following seating options: lower boxes, corner boxes, left field reserved, and bleacher seating. The upper concourse/upper deck seating offers upper boxes, upper reserved, and grandstand seats. The other levels are suites and club seating. Friday's Front Row Grill is located on the upper suite level behind the Home Run Porch (817/265-5191).

As you walk around the exterior of the stadium, notice the thirty-five cast-stone steer heads and twenty-one Lone Stars as well as ten murals of Texas scenes located between the upper and lower arches that surround the stadium.

Fans may only bring in paper and plastic containers (no cans or glass bottles) and coolers measuring 16 x 16 or smaller that will fit underneath the seats. No alcoholic beverages may be brought in. No flash photography is allowed, but cameras and hand-held video cameras are acceptable. Tailgate parties are allowed as long as they do not take over more parking spaces. Fans may also picnic in Vandergriff Plaza, a park area behind the center-field fence.

In addition to Ranger games, the complex provides the **Dr Pepper Youth Park** baseball facility for ages 12 and under organized youth groups, for birthday parties, or for other occasions 817/273-5269. **Ballpark Sleepovers** may be arranged by calling 817/273-5087.

The **Legends of the Game Baseball Museum** features baseball memorabilia and exhibits from the National Baseball Hall of Fame in Cooperstown, New Jersey. In the third floor Learning Center, interactive exhibits for school-age fans include the Science of Baseball, Baseball History Tunnel, Baseball Geography and Math, and Baseball Communications. Call 817/273-5600 or 817/273-5099 for hours and admission fees.

- If you need help, the Fan Assistance Center is located behind home plate on the main concourse.

- Tours of The Ballpark may be arranged by calling 817/273-5098. Combination tickets for the tour and the museum may be purchased.

- Areas of the stadium are handicapped accessible. Call 817/273-5222 for more information.

- Water fountains and restrooms are provided. Diaper changing areas are in both men's and women's restrooms.

- ATMs are located on all three levels.

- Section 335 is designated as a non-alcohol section. Smoking is prohibited in restrooms and all seating areas.

- The Texas Rangers Grand Slam Shop is on ground level behind center field (273-5001).

- Parking is $7 per car and $14 per bus. Season Parking Pass holders park in a designated area. Everyone else parks in General Parking. The lots open three hours before the game.

Hours: For evening games, the gates open three hours early, and for afternoon games, ninety minutes early. This is subject to change. On non-game days, ticket office hours are Monday-Friday, 9 A.M.-6 P.M., and Saturday, 10 A.M.-4 P.M. Night game hours are Monday-Saturday, 9 A.M.-9 P.M., and Sunday, noon to 9 P.M.

Admission: Tickets may be purchased at the ticket office or by phone 817/273-5100 and may be charged on Visa, MasterCard, or American Express. Tickets may also be purchased at metro Dillard's stores or by phone, 800/654-9545. Ticket prices depend on selection of seating. There are some discounts for ages 13 and under.

Directions: From Dallas, take I-30 west and exit at Six Flags Drive. Take Six Flags Drive to Randol Mill Road and turn right. Continue to the parking lots. Another route is to take I-30 to Ballpark Way exit. Go right on Ballpark Way and continue to the parking lots.

CELEBRATION STATION

4040 Towne Crossing Boulevard
Mesquite, Texas 75150 • 972/279-7888

"Daniel and the Dixie Diggers," animated hounds with musical talent, steal the show at Mesquite's newest family entertainment park. Indoors in the 16,000-square-foot facility is a restaurant downstairs offering great pizza, hot dogs, and more. On the first level are games that give tickets, which may be redeemed for prizes, and on the second level are more challenging video games.

Go-carts, bumper boats, batting cages, a few kiddie carnival rides, and two miniature golf courses are offered for more fun outdoors in the six-acre park.

- Group rates (fifteen or more) are available. Birthday parties (minimum of eight) are welcome. Call for reservations.

- Miniature golf courses are handicapped accessible.

- Restrooms and water fountains are available.

- Parking is free.

Hours: Open daily, weather permitting. Hours change seasonally.

Admission: No entrance admission fee. Purchase tokens for games.

Directions: Going east on I-30 toward Mesquite, take the Gus Thomasson Rd. exit. Pass Gus Thomasson, stay on the service road to Towne Crossing, and turn right. From I-635, exit at Town East Blvd. and go west. Turn right on Towne Crossing.

THE DALLAS AQUARIUM AT FAIR PARK

1462 First Ave. and Martin L. King Blvd. at Fair Park
Dallas, Texas 75226 • 670-8443
(Mailing Address: P.O. Box 150113,
Dallas, Texas 75315-0113)

Newly renovated, the Dallas Aquarium building, which dates from the 1936 Texas Centennial at Fair Park, houses thousands of species of freshwater and marine fishes. In addition, there are amphibians, reptiles, various invertebrates, and cases of beautiful shells and other nonliving material.

New exhibits include other fish from the Gulf, Red Sea, Caribbean reef, and Australia Great Barrier Reef. The new little Australian scavengers, cleaner wrasses, actually clean the parasites off of other fish. A 10,500-gallon Amazon flooded forest tank has been added as well as a breeding lab for species such as the Texas blind salamander, Barton Springs salamander, and endangered desert fish.

The walking batfish, a fish that actually walks on legs (modified fins), will catch the attention of children as well as the five-foot electric eel, piranhas, seahorses, and a 135-pound alligator snapping turtle.

- The Education Center at the Dallas Zoo coordinates summer classes at the Aquarium. Call 670-6832 for the schedule.

- In the Adopt-an-Animal program, for $15-$100 your family, Scout group, or business can select from a list of aquatic friends one to "adopt." "Parents" receive an Adoption Certificate, color photo, adoption party invitation, and other benefits. Call 942-3678 weekdays for a brochure and details.

- There are no concessions, but the Old Mill Inn is within walking distance in Fair Park (open Tuesday-Sunday, 11 A.M.-3 P.M.). They do have candy and soft drink machines. On a nice day, you may wish to bring a blanket and have a picnic. Picnic tables are usually between the Aquarium and the Planetarium building.

- The building is handicapped accessible. Restrooms and water fountains are availble.

- Parking is free except during the State Fair.

Hours: Open daily 9 A.M.-4:30 P.M. Closed Thanksgiving Day and Christmas Day. Hours extended during the State Fair.

Admission: Ages 2 and under, free; 3-11, $1; 12-adult, $2. Educational group rates are available. Call 670-6832.

Directions: From the Robert B. Cullum Blvd. side of Fair Park, enter at the Martin L. King Blvd. gate and park. The Aquarium is just past the Garden Center to the left, very close to the Texas Star Ferris wheel. See directions to Fair Park.

DALLAS ARBORETUM AND BOTANICAL GARDENS

8617 Garland Road
Dallas, Texas 75218 • 327-8263

Even before arriving at the entrance, some of the gorgeous, lush gardens of the 66-acre Dallas Arboretum may be seen from the road, but that is only a glimpse of the acres of beauty to come. Located on the eastern shore of White Rock Lake, the Arboretum provides education in horticulture, a haven for wildlife, vibrant flower displays, and numerous special events for families. Children not only love the trees and flowers, but also the winding paths and fountains. Here, they really have room to stretch and enjoy the outdoors. In 1996 the $1.4 million **Women's Council Garden**, which is behind the Degolyer House, was opened to the public. The 1.8-acre garden incorporates water as a symbol of strength and unity. Don't miss the frog sculpture, an interactive fountain in which four bronze frogs shoot twenty-foot streams of water.

Favorite times to visit include Dallas Blooms in March and April and Autumn at the Arboretum in October. During 1991 Dallas Blooms, the **Lydia Bunker Hunt Paseo de Flores** and the **Fogelson Fountain** were opened.

The **Jonsson Color Garden** features more than 2,000 varieties of azaleas while over 30 varieties of ferns grow in the Palmer Fern

Dell. More than 200,000 flowers bloom during this festival, and children's activities are scheduled on weekends. Children also look forward to the annual Easter Egg Hunt.

Autumn at the Arboretum is painted with countless colors of chrysanthemums and other plants with fall blooms. A spooky "Haunted Gardens" evening invites young goblins under 12 in costume to visit "Little Goblin Land" for special activities. Ghosts and ghouls appear along the paths for older children.

- Tours of the **DeGolyer's Spanish Colonial Revival Mansion**, now a museum, include the oilman's study and other rooms filled with interesting art and furniture. Tours leave every 30 minutes. One room is a gift shop.

- Garden hunt sheets are available daily and change seasonally.

- Picnics are encouraged, but food service is offered only at special events.

- Christmas at the Arboretum in December includes a holiday market and many festive decorations and activities.

- Children's Nature Club events are usually held in May and June for ages 4-12. Classes last two to three hours.

- In June through August are family focus summer events with special activities for kids during each event.

- Call the Horticulture Hotline for gardening tips at 327-8263, Ext. 134.

- The gift shop sells in-season plants and bulbs as well as gardening books and equipment.

- An annual tour for special needs children and adults called "Gardens for Everyone" is held in the spring. Call for specific dates. Most of the paths are handicapped accessible.

- Restrooms and water fountains are available.

- Parking is $2.

Hours: Open daily, year round. March-October, 10 A.M.-6 P.M.; November-February, 10 A.M.-5 P.M.

Admission: Adults, $6; seniors (65+), $5; ages 6-12, $3; members and children under 6, free. Friday, from 3 P.M. until closing, free for all ages. Memberships are available.

Directions: Located on the north side of Garland Rd. at Whittier, just west of the intersection of Garland Rd. and Buckner Blvd. Signs direct visitors to the parking area.

THE DALLAS FIREFIGHTER'S MUSEUM: "OLD TIGE"

3801 Parry Avenue
Dallas, Texas 75226 • 821-1500

Located in the 1907 Old No. 5 Hook and Ladder Co. Station, the Dallas Firefighter's Museum houses a collection of wonderful retired fire trucks. "Old Tige," named after then-mayor W. L. Cabell, is the 1884 horse drawn steam pumper.

Recapture the early days of fire fighting in the alarm office complete with clanging bell and in the old firehouse setting with its wood burning stove. Visitors see the progress in the last 100 years in fire fighting equipment through the collection of photos, fire tools, helmets, suits, and extinguishers. Sometimes, you can hear today's Dallas Fire Department radio as dispatchers conduct business. A favorite of most children is the hook and ladder truck that they can climb on as well as the collection of toy fire trucks. Pieces of wooden water main unearthed from the Farmer's Market area, which date around the 1880s, are on display.

The museum is dedicated to firemen who fell in action, a tribute to their courage and devotion to duty.

• Tours are available with reservations.

- There is no food or drink in the museum, but the Old Mill Inn just across Parry in Fair Park is open for lunch Tuesday-Sunday.

- Only the lower floor is handicapped accessible.

- Restrooms and water fountains are provided.

- Parking is available in front or on the side street. During the State Fair, park at the Fair Grounds and walk across Parry.

Hours: Monday-Friday, 9 A.M.-4 P.M. Open daily during the State Fair. Closed major holidays.

Admission: FREE. Donations are very appreciated.

Directions: Located on the northwest corner of Parry at Commerce. If on I-30 going west, take Fair Park First Avenue exit and circle under the bridge to Exposition. Take it to Parry and turn left. If on I-30 going east, take the Fair Park Second Avenue exit to Parry. Turn left and go three blocks.

DALLAS HORTICULTURE CENTER

3601 Martin Luther King Blvd. at Fair Park
Dallas, Texas 75226 • 428-7476
(Mailing Address: P.O. Box 152537, Dallas, Texas 75315)

The Dallas Horticulture Center, the second oldest botanical institution in Texas, serves the community as a free-admission public garden and as a resource for environmental and horticultural education. Annually, more that 300,000 visitors enjoy the 7.5 acres of gardens that feature colorful floral displays and rare Texas native plants.

- The Visitor Center features *The Plants of Africa* collection in the William Douglas Blachly Conservatory. The first conservatory in the Southwest, this 6,800-square-foot glass garden houses more than 250 species of rare and exotic African plants. A magnificent specimen of the Traveler's Palm is in a setting of waterfalls and natural rock surrounded by dramatic aloes, graceful ferns, and beautiful orchids.

- During the State Fair of Texas, the Blachly Conservatory also houses the largest butterfly exhibit in North Central Texas. *Butterflies in the Blachly* provides a wonderful opportunity for families to experience butterflies in a total immersion exhibit. Butterflies emerge from their chrysalises and then fly around visitors as they search for nectar and roosting spots. An admission fee is charged. Other nature exhibitions are displayed in the Visitor Center throughout the year. Call for topics and times.

- Gardens include the Benny J. Simpson Texas Native Plant Collection, Faerie Blanton Kilgore Rose Garden, a Physic Garden to touch and smell, a Butterfly Garden that provides habitat for native butterflies, an Earthkeepers Garden that demonstrates environmentally sound gardening practices, and the Grand Allee du Meadows with a 50-foot geyser fountain in the midst of a "Fan of Color" landscape.

- Areas of the center may be reserved for parties and meetings.

- The DHC offers *Earthkeepers Education Workshops* for groups of children. Topics include "Life in a Compost Pile," "Gardening for Children," "Terrarium Worlds," "Bugs and Other Garden Critters," "Butterflies and Botany," and more. Call for more information on these and summer day camps.

- There is no food service, except sometimes during the State Fair. The Old Mill Inn, across from the Music Hall, is within walking distance (Tues.-Sun., 11 A.M.- 3 P.M.).

- Handicapped access is available.

- There are restrooms and water fountains.

- Parking is free except during the State Fair and Fair Park special events.

Hours: Open Tuesday-Saturday, 10 A.M.-5 P.M.; Sunday 1-5 P.M. Grounds are open until dusk. Closed major holidays.

Admission: FREE to the grounds. Donations are welcomed. Call to inquire about any changes in this. Memberships are available. Children under 13 must be accompanied by an adult.

Directions: Enter Fair Park through the Martin L. King entrance off Robert B. Cullum Blvd. Parking is to the right. See directions to Fair Park.

DALLAS MEMORIAL CENTER FOR HOLOCAUST STUDIES

7900 Northaven Road
Dallas, Texas 75230 • 750-4654

Dedicated as a tribute to the memory of the six million who died during the Holocaust and as a hope that such an atrocity will never occur again, the Dallas Memorial Center for Holocaust Studies was conceived by a group of Holocaust survivors who wished to tell their stories and help others understand the impact of the Holocaust on themselves and world history.

Poems and paintings are exhibited in the entry stairwell with a boxcar at the bottom of the stairs that actually transported Jewish victims to the death camps. Upon leaving the boxcar are the museum and exhibition rooms. Here, visitors see a pictorial history, items from the camps, and a video screen. An extensive library of 2,500 books, periodicals, and European government record books are available for use by the public on site. An audio-visual materials catalog on Holocaust topics is available.

The Memorial room includes a symbolic sculpture and plaques that list the names of victims, survivors, and courageous people who risked their lives to save others. Some of these people have videotaped their memories, and visitors may ask to view the tapes.

- Museum personnel recommend that only children fifth grade and up should tour. Some knowledge of the Holocaust prior to the tour is advisable.

- Books and postcards are for sale.

- There is no food or drink.

- Handicap access is through an elevator in the Jewish Community Center.

- Restrooms and water fountains are in the Jewish Community Center.

- Parking is free.

Hours: Monday-Friday, 9:30 A.M.-4:30 P.M.; Sunday, 12 P.M.-4 P.M.; from September-May, open Thursday, 9:30 A.M.-9 P.M. Closed on Jewish and most national holidays.

Admission: Suggested donation of adults, $2 and students, $1. Memberships are available.

Directions: From US 75 (Central), exit Royal Lane and go west. Turn right on Freda Stern and right again into the parking lot.

DALLAS MUSEUM OF ART

1717 North Harwood
Dallas, Texas 75201 • 922-1200

One of the finest ways for families to develop and share a love of art is at the Dallas Museum of Art's Gateway Gallery, a 3,200-square-foot informal exhibition area that has magnetic appeal for everyone with its interactive permanent and temporary exhibits.

"Stories in Art" was installed in the Discovery Room in February 1998. Another favorite area for children, especially those who need to stretch, is the outdoor sculpture garden with its cascading wall fountains and sculptures in a maze-like layout. They cannot be climbed on, but you can take your lunch out there to enjoy the garden. The nearby Trammel Crow building has more sculptures encircling it. Raymond Nasher is planning an outdoor sculpture garden across the street from the DMA.

- An Orientation Theater familiarizes visitors with special exhibitions and permanent collections. One fascinating collection on long-term loan from Boston is "Eternal Egypt: Objects of the Afterlife," which includes both funerary objects and objects from daily life of ancient Nubia. Other major collections include Post-World War II Contemporary and African, Asian, and Oceanic art objects; American and European paintings, sculptures, and decorative arts; and the Wendy and Emery Reves Collection in which they re-created six rooms of their Mediterranean villa featuring prized impressionist paintings.

- The DMA has opened the new 140,000-square-foot Hamon Building which includes larger exhibition areas, the Museum of the Americas, the Atrium Cafe, and performance space for jazz and classical music on Thursday evenings. The new museum offers art from the Western Hemisphere.

- Other Thursday activities include Art Talk by docents and staff at 7 P.M. On Wednesday at 12:15 is a 30-minute Gallery Talk.

- An information desk, which has maps and information about current exhibits, is at the entrance.

- The Gateway Gallery offers both free and fee-based art activities, classes, and tours. Call 922-1251 for registration. Free drop-in art is usually planned on Saturday from mid-September through mid-May from 1-1:30 P.M. Ask about free family art activities in which parents participate with their children in activities that often relate to an exhibition. The activities change monthly. In summer, drop-in art days are Tuesday through Saturday 1-3:30 P.M. and change about every two weeks.

- The museum shop invites youngsters to select art-related books, puzzles, calendars, games, and toys.

- Free public tours are at 1 A.M. on Tuesday-Friday and at 2 P.M. on Saturday and Sunday. Meet in the Barrel Vault. School tours are free but require three weeks notice. Call 922-1313.

- The DMA has a non-circulating library and teacher resource room. Call for details about use. The GTE Collection Center offers computers with more than 2,000 images. For $1, visitors can make a print of an object with some information about it. There is no charge for just using the computer.

- The second floor Seventeen Seventeen Restaurant prepares lunch Tuesday-Saturday from 11 A.M. to 2 P.M. A Sunday brunch is offered with reservations (880-0158). The Atrium Cafe is open during museum hours until 30 minutes before closing.

- The museum is handicapped accessible.

- There are restrooms and water fountains.

- Underground parking is available from Harwood or St. Paul. Surface parking is located across Harwood from the museum. A fee is charged for parking. The trolley route brings you to St. Paul and Ross, right by the museum.

Hours: Tuesday, Wednesday, Friday, 11 A.M.-4 P.M.; Thursday, 11 A.M.-9 P.M.; Saturday, Sunday, and all holidays, 11-5 P.M. Closed Mondays, New Year's Day, Thanksgiving, and Christmas Day.

Admission: FREE, except for special exhibitions. Memberships are available.

Directions: Located downtown in the Arts District on Harwood between Woodall Rodgers Frwy. and Ross Avenue. From US 75, exit Woodall Rodgers. Take the St. Paul exit if traveling from Central toward I-35. Coming from the west, exit Field-Griffin in the right-hand lane.

DALLAS MUSEUM OF NATURAL HISTORY

3535 Grand Ave. at First in Fair Park
Dallas, Texas 75210 • 421-DINO
(Mailing Address—P.O. Box 150433, Dallas, Texas 75315)

Parents may have problems getting their children into the Dallas Museum of Natural History because they have discovered the giant mammoth sculpture and want to stay out on the lawn and play on it. They will notice the exterior walls of shellstone in which fossils of early Texas ocean life are embedded. This Art Deco building was built by the WWPA for Texas Centennial in 1936 and has intrigued its visitors ever since with its collections of Texas fossils, mounted native birds and animals in more than fifty lifelike dioramas, land and freshwater mollusks, and Texas pollinating insects.

Over 400,000 visitors every year stand in awe of the remains of a 31-foot Heath Mosasaur found at Lake Ray Hubbard and the 20,000-year-old, 13-foot tall skeleton of a mammoth. Look for the giant prehistoric sea turtle and live insect zoo. A hands-on interactive discovery center called City Safari for ages 4-10 is now on permanent exhibit.

An annual event is Dino Day focused on those creatures of long ago.

- The DMNH offers classes and workshops for children ages 4-12. Summer family programs include taking nature walks and discovering critters in the creek. Once each month, usually on Saturday, is Family Festival Day from 11-4.

- Tours for classes are available with reservations. Call 823-7644 for group reservations.

- The DMNH sponsors a naturalists' lecture series which includes famous speakers, such as Jean Michel Cousteau.

- Nature Presents, the gift shop, stocks books, tapes, toys, and more of interest to young naturalists. Open Monday-Friday, 10 A.M.-4 P.M.; Sunday, 11 A.M.-5 P.M.

- An amphitheater is available for rental for community cultural performances.

- No food is available in the museum, but the Old Mill Inn is a short walk within Fair Park. Call for hours. You could bring a blanket and picnic by the lagoon. A McDonald's is located across the street from Fair Park museums.

- Handicapped access is available.

- Water fountains and restrooms are provided.

- Parking is free except during the State Fair.

Hours: Daily 10 A.M.-5 P.M. Closed Thanksgiving, and Christmas. Hours subject to change.

Admission: Adults, $4. Children 3-18, $2.50. Under 3, free. FREE on Monday for all from 9 A.M. to 1 P.M. Additional fee for some special exhibits. Memberships are available.

Directions: Enter Fair Park through the Grand Ave. gate from Robert B. Cullum Blvd. The museum is to the right of Grand.

DALLAS NATURE CENTER

7171 Mountain Creek Parkway
Dallas, Texas 75249 • 296-1955

Just 20 minutes south of downtown Dallas, the Dallas Nature Center encompasses 650 acres of environmentally rich land on the White Rock Escarpment.

Families enjoy hiking on seven miles of trails through prairie and woodlands where native animals and birds live in a protected environment. Many of the animals are nocturnal, so night hikes and private campouts are very popular. Visitors may spot native plants, such as yucca, sunflowers, and orchids.

In spring the brilliant flowers attract the butterflies, and the orchards of peach, apple, and plum trees bloom.

In addition to night hikes, the Center's calendar includes craft days, trail walks with special themes, and nature workshops. Trail hikes are available during the week for school groups, and the center works with Scouts on badge programs.

Home for various raptors such as owls and hawks, On The Wing Again sometimes presents programs on the Nature Center grounds.

- Special events include a Spring Wildflower Festival, a Christmas program, Haunted Hayride, and Haunted House.

- The gift shop hours vary by season. The nursery sells native plants, seeds, trees, and food items.

- Picnic tables and a soft drink machine are provided. Birthday ideas include a scavenger hunt and picnic at the Nature Center. An amphitheater is available for rental.

- The trails are not handicapped accessible. Call about the buildings.

- There are accessible restrooms and water fountains.

Hours: Grounds open daily 7 A.M. to dusk. Call for calendar of special events.

Admission: FREE. Donations of $3 per vehicle are suggested. Fee for programs and guided trails. Memberships are available.

Directions: Go south on I-35 to Hwy. 67 South (sign says Cleburne); take I-20 West (sign says Ft. Worth); exit Mountain Creek Parkway and go south (under the highway). Drive 2 miles to the Center's gate on the right.

THE DALLAS WORLD AQUARIUM

1801 North Griffin
Dallas, Texas 75202 • 720-1801, 720-2224

Something "fishy" is going on at Daryl's By Design catering company, located at Hord and North Griffin in the West End Historic District. Owner Daryl Richardson is combining business and his hobby of observing marine life by bringing in a 22,000-gallon tank with a tunnel visitors can walk through and thirteen 2,000-gallon tanks in which he beautifully displays aquatic life from all over the world. Each tank represents a different area, such as the Red Sea exhibit, and the corals and other plants are also from that region. It doesn't take long for visitors to discover the lively penguins that were used in a Batman movie and an Ace Ventura movie.

- The 40,000-square-foot five-story rain forest building houses Peruvian squirrel monkeys, snakes, frogs, toucans, and jaguars. A waterfall adds to the atmosphere, which was inspired by the Venezuelan Oronoco River Basin.

- Self-guided tours are available with a brochure that explains each tank and provides a list of feeding times. Group tours with a guide may be requested.

- A restaurant, eighteen-O-one, is open for lunch.

- Two gift shops offer nature-related gifts.

- The aquarium offers education programs to study rainforest and marine life for children ages four and above. Classes have interesting names, such as "Romancing the Reef" and "Class Act, Fish Colors—Not Just for Looks," at a cost of $5.41 per student. Try "Culture and Cuisine" for $8-$12. Call 720-2224 on Monday-Friday to schedule. Classes are held Monday-Friday from 10:00 to 1:00 and last about 30 minutes, but schedule around 1½ hours at the aquarium. Sack lunches are available at an additional cost.

- Small Talk program is for ages 4 and 5.

- During the summer, the education department offers "keeper talks" and hands-on fun every half hour between 10 A.M. and 2:30 P.M.

- The group rate for 15 or more people is $6.50.

- The West End Marketplace and restaurants are within easy walking distance.

Hours: Aquarium is open daily, 10 A.M.-5 P.M. Restaurant is open 11:30-2:30 daily. Closed Thanksgiving and Christmas.

Admission: Adults, $11.85 Children (3-12) and seniors (60 and above), $6.50. These prices include sales tax.

Directions: From Central (US 75), exit onto Woodall Rodgers. Take the Field exit and turn left. Stay in the right-hand lane, which will curve to Griffin. The first right is Hord. You can see the fish sculptures on the front of the building. The DART rail station at the West End is just a couple of blocks from the aquarium.

DALLAS ZOO

650 South R.L. Thornton (I-35E)
Dallas, Texas 75203 • 670-5656

Since 1888 the Dallas Zoo has been fascinating families with its collection of exotic and endangered species. In 1997 a 67½-foot giraffe sculpture, the largest sculpture in Texas, was installed at the new Marsalis entrance to welcome visitors. The Lemur Lookout exhibit is located at the end of the entry plaza.

A family favorite at the zoo is "The Wilds of Africa" exhibit in which zoo visitors travel through six habitats on a one-mile monorail ride with a narrator. More than 86 species of mammals and birds roam freely in this 25-acre exhibit.

This safari continues as visitors then walk along a wooded quarter-mile nature trail. Of further interest is the two-acre Jake

L. Hamon Gorilla Conservation Research Center where gorillas may be viewed without them realizing that they are being observed. A rain forest is simulated, and everything in it is edible.

The Chimpanzee Forest, a $1.9 million exhibit of these endangered animals, opened in 1997. It features naturalistic terrain, a waterfall and stream, natural climbing structures, trees, and rocks that are heated in winter and cooled in summer.

In addition there are more than 40 edible plants and a giant termite mound in which the chimps can "fish" with long sticks for special treats, such as peanut butter and honey. The chimps also have 3,000-square-foot indoor quarters.

- The Reptile Discovery Center has 10-12 interactive modules that are informative and help people to be less afraid of reptiles. Check the schedule (April-September) for the Rainforest Puppet Theater for ages 3-8.

- The Children's Zoo also has hands-on exhibits. It is open year round from about 10 A.M.-5 P.M. Visit the Tom Thumb Pet Pal Central exhibit and learn from the SPCA how to select a family pet that will suit the needs of both pet and family.

- The animals are more active in cooler weather and at feeding times. Babies are adorable in the spring.

- One adult is required for every seven children on the monorail.

- The zoo sponsors special events, such as the Big Cat Weekend, Boo at the Zoo, and Family Fun Weekend. There may be a separate admission charge for special events.

- Summer classes are offered for children. Call 670-6832. A popular volunteer program for ages 11-12 is Junior Zookeeper. Applications must be in by mid-January. The zoo also appreciates adult volunteers, ages 18 and older.

- The zoo has an "adopt-an-animal" program.

- The zoo gift shop located at the main entrance offers a variety of souvenirs, books, and toys related to birds, reptiles, and mammals.

- The Flamingo Food Court offers hamburgers, etc., and picnic tables are provided. It may be closed during construction.

- The paved pathways are accessible to wheelchairs, but the area is hilly. Parts of The Wilds of Africa and Zoo North are hard to negotiate.

- Restrooms, benches, and water fountains are available.

- Parking is $3.

Hours: Daily, 9 A.M.-5 P.M. Closed Christmas Day. Monorail rides begin at 10:00 A.M.

Admission: Ages 12-64, $6; ages 3-11, $3; seniors $4; ages 2 and under, free. Monorail rate: ages 3 and over, $1.50. Group rates and memberships are available.

Directions: Three miles south of downtown off I-35 South. Take the Marsalis exit, go north on the service road, and turn right at the base of the giant giraffe statue into the Zoo parking lot. A separate entrance for DART riders is available on Clarendon Drive, just across the street from the new DART light rail Dallas Zoo station.

FAIR PARK

1300 Robert B. Cullum Blvd.
Dallas, Texas 75226 • 565-9931 (State Fair) 670-8400 (Fair Park)
Fair Park mailing address (Nov.-Aug.):
P.O. Box 159090 Dallas, Texas 75315
State Fair Mailing Address:
P.O. Box 150009, Dallas, Texas 75315

Fair Park, location of the outstanding State Fair of Texas, has been close to the hearts of native Dallasites and those who visit from around the state since 1886. R.L. Thornton Sr. persisted in the selection of Dallas as the site of the Texas Centennial in 1936. The largest historical landmark in Texas, this 277-acre park is well known for its major museums, Music Hall, Cotton Bowl stadium, Starplex Amphitheater, and Coliseum, which are active year round.

Fair Park at its finest should be visited during the State Fair, which lasts for three weeks beginning at the end of September. During that time young children pet furry animals in the Petting Farm, giggle at puppets in the Midway Puppet Show, and try Midway rides designed especially for them. The 212-foot Texas Star Ferris wheel and 78-year-old carousel are yearly favorites. Museums prepare fascinating exhibits for the Fair, and the Texas-Oklahoma football classic is a thrill for all fans. Families look over prime livestock brought from area farms and ranches and attend free shows in the Coliseum, watch amazing free-flight bird shows in Kings of the Wind at the Bandshell, select the car of their dreams in the Automobile Building, puzzle over exotic displays of wares in the International Bazaar, and admire prize-winning crafts in the Creative Arts Building.

Those who love the night lights of the Fair stay for the Starlight Parade and the Cotton Bowl Laser Show where lasers and familiar tunes create dazzling special effects. Honest families must confess that, although the shows and exhibits alone are worth the trip and putting up with the crowds, the real draw is the tantalizing aroma and anticipation of foods, such as corny dogs and greasy fries followed by giant cinnamon rolls, cotton candy, and ice cream. Indoors at the Tower Building and outside at Cotton Bowl Plaza and other locations are foods for every palate. The blend of these aromas, the tumultuous sounds of the Midway, and the welcoming voice of a 52-foot tall cowboy named Big Tex invite everyone to relax and have a wonderful time.

Families are advised to arrive early enough to park in well-lighted areas inside the Fair grounds and walk in groups. Do not wear expensive jewelry. Police are highly visible on raised stands, on horses, and in small vehicles. Their headquarters are southeast of the Cotton Bowl. At the entrances, there are usually identification tags that children can wear as necklaces. Their names should not be written where a stranger could easily read it and call to them. Families should agree on a meeting place in case they are separated.

- The *Dallas Morning News* reports special events daily during the Fair, and the Fair provides a map and guide to activities upon entering the gates.

- The Magnolia Lounge has a theater for rent near the Grand Avenue entrance. The Friends of Fair Park present a documentary film and offer free films on Dallas and Fair Park as well as walking tours. Open Monday-Friday, except holidays. For information, call Friends of Fair Park, 426-3400.

- Talented family members might enjoy entering one of the arts and crafts or food contests in August. Winners are displayed during the Fair.

- Children especially love climbing on the orange serpentine sculpture between the Museum of Natural History and The Science Place. Picnics in this area are fun. There may be some ducks to feed.

- Museums at Fair Park are listed individually. They include The Science Place with its IMAX Theater and Planetarium Building, Museum of Natural History, Dallas Aquarium, Dallas Horticulture Center, Age of Steam Railroad Museum, Hall of State, D.A.R. Building, and the African-American Museum. A new women's museum is to open during the State Fair in October 2000.

- Most of Fair Park is handicapped accessible. Midway rides during the Fair will vary.

- Restrooms are not plentiful, but there are some in the major exhibition buildings, outside the Cotton Bowl steps, near the Magnolia Lounge, and in the livestock area. All major museums have restrooms, and most have water fountains. Outdoor water fountains are turned off during the winter.

- The Old Mill Inn, which was once a flour mill, is a restaurant located near the Magnolia Lounge and the Music Hall. Call 565-1511.

- Flea markets are scheduled as well as special events, such as football games, ethnic celebrations, and Senior Citizens Craft Fair.

- Starplex Amphitheater and Dallas Summer Musicals provide wonderful summer entertainment. Special concerts featuring popular artists, such as Garth Brooks, are held during the Fair at the Miller Stage. The Dallas Opera also performs in the Music Hall.

- Another museum kids love is the Firefighters Museum located across Parry from Fair Park.

- For current information, call the 24-hour English/Spanish information line at 890-2911.

- Parking for about 10,000 vehicles is available on the grounds. A fee of around $5 is charged during the Fair. Call DART, 979-1111, for information about State Fair Flyers bus service and ticket combinations.

Hours: The grounds are open daily. The museums are listed under individual headings in this text. Their days and hours of operation vary.

Admission: Some of the museums are free, and some have a fee. State Fair admission is approximately $9 for adults; children ages 3 and over, $5. Discount tickets are usually available at Kroger.

Directions: Fair Park is two miles east of downtown. From Central Expressway (US 75), exit Fitzhugh or Haskell. From I-30W, exit Barry or Carroll and head southwest. From I-45 North, exit MLK Blvd. and proceed northeast. Scyene Rd. going west becomes Robert B. Cullum Blvd. and leads to Fair Park. Or take Abrams Rd. south which changes name to Columbia, turn left on Carroll, and then right on Parry which goes in front of the park.

FRONTIERS OF FLIGHT MUSEUM

Love Field Terminal, LB-18
Dallas, Texas 75235 • 350-1651

The biplane hanging from the ceiling just inside the main entrance of Love Field airport greets visitors on their way to the second floor Frontiers of Flight Museum. Take the escalator or elevator on the left upstairs where a collection of rare aviation artifacts will guide you from "Early Concepts of Flight" through "The Space Age."

Eras in aviation history are illustrated through mounted newspaper and magazine articles; personal items such as uniforms of famous aviators and the fur parka belonging to Rear Admiral Richard Byrd; and items used during flights of various airships, such as remnants of the dirigible *Hindenburg*.

As visitors look at models of the *Kitty Hawk Flyer*, the Red Baron's favorite triplane, and large replicas of modern passenger planes and the space shuttle, they can hear the Love Field Control Tower and watch the planes load, take off, and land outside the long wall of windows.

The museum presents special Focus Nights programs with authors and specialists in fascinating aspects of the aviation field from pre-World War II to today's "stealth" aircraft. The museum also hosts the Fina Dallas Air Show each September, which offers families wonderful opportunities to see and touch aircraft from biplanes to jets.

- Group tours are available with reservations. A meeting room will hold 50-100 people.

- Children who read well and have some knowledge of major figures in aviation would benefit most from the tour.

- A brochure is available.

- A gift shop carries books, videos, and toys related to aviation, as well as freeze-dried food for astronauts.

- No food or drink is in the museum, but on Level One in the main lobby is food service.

- The museum is handicapped accessible.

- Restrooms and water fountains are available in the terminal.

- Park in the garage in front of the main entrance. Bring the ticket to the museum for validated discount.

Hours: Monday-Saturday, 10 A.M.-5 P.M.; Sunday, 1-5 P.M. Closed some holidays.

Admission: Adults, $2; ages under 12, $1. Memberships are available. Children must be accompanied by an adult.

Directions: Exit Mockingbird Lane going west from US 75 or North Dallas Tollway. Enter Love Field at the main entrance, Mockingbird and Cedar Springs.

HALL OF STATE

Fair Park: 3939 Grand Avenue
Dallas, Texas 75226 • 421-4500
(Mailing address: P.O. Box 150038, Dallas, Texas 75315)

Operated by the Dallas Historical Society, the Art Deco-style Hall of State residing at the end of the Esplanade in Fair Park is the home of both permanent and temporary exhibits which reflect the history of Dallas and Texas. As part of the 1936 Centennial, the Hall of State was built of Texas limestone in a T-shape for $1,200,000. A statue of a Tejas warrior occupies the niche above the entrance, and the blue background represents the state flower, the bluebonnet. The symbols in the bronze grills on the entry doors, cotton bolls, spurs, and oil wells, are representative of Texas agriculture and industry. The statue out front is of R.L. Thornton, who was largely responsible for bringing the Centennial to Fair Park, for his 41 years of service to Dallas.

Just inside is the Hall of Heroes where bronze statues of heroes of the Republic of Texas reside. The four-story Great Hall to the back has an Aztec motif in its hand-stenciled ceiling. A gold-leafed medallion with a five-pointed star and the six figures around it represents the rulers over Texas. The large murals on each side tell the story of Texas history and industry. The shafts of light indicate changes in time. Notice native wildlife in mosaics on the floor.

The other four exhibit rooms, two on each side of the Hall of Heroes, represent East, West, North, and South Texas through murals, figurines, frescos, photographs, and mosaics.

- Guided tours for groups are available with reservations. A fee of $2 per person is charged. Call 823-7644. Educational programs are available to teachers and students.

- The G.B. Dealey Library is housed in the West Texas Room. Open Tuesday-Friday, 9:30 A.M.-4:30 P.M.

- A history book about Dallas can be bought through the library.

- There is no food or drink in the museum.

- Handicapped access is available.

- Restrooms and water fountains are on the lower floor. A water fountain is on the upper level.

- Parking is free on Washington Avenue except during the State Fair. The Hall of State is near the Age of Steam Railroad Museum.

Hours: Tuesday-Saturday, 9:00 A.M.-5:00 P.M.; Sunday, 1-5 P.M. Closed Christmas Day and New Year's Day.

Admission: Free entrance, $2 per person for a scheduled tour. Memberships are available.

Directions: From Parry Avenue, go east on Washington in Fair Park past the railroad museum. It's the large building across from the parking lot at Grand and Nimitz inside Fair Park.

HEARD NATURAL SCIENCE MUSEUM AND WILDLIFE SANCTUARY

One Nature Place
McKinney, Texas 75069 • 972/562-5566

The 274-acre wooded wildlife sanctuary, the legacy of Miss Bessie Heard, is dedicated to preserving and encouraging native wildlife and vegetation as well as educating the community to appreciate and conserve nature. Around 100,000 visitors wander each year along the nature trails, spotting rabbits, raccoons, and hawks as well as favorite wildflowers and native trees. Self-guided trails and guided trails are available. Groups, such as Scouts or bird watchers, may take special guided tours. The "Hoot Owl Trail," the basic three-quarter-mile trail, takes about an hour to cover. Outings in canoes as well as bird and flower walks are sometimes offered.

In addition to the looping, beautiful trails is the 16,250-square-foot museum, which has added another 8,000 square feet for classrooms. On the upper floor are exhibit halls, and live animal displays are on the lower floor. Visitors marvel at the collections in the Natural Science Hall, Seashell Room, and the Rock and Mineral Hall. Artwork is displayed in the Print Gallery and Activity Hall. In the Live Animal exhibit, families may see the grandeur of an eagle or sharp eyes of a hawk close up.

More than 5,800 students, ages 3 through junior high, each year take part in the education program, which includes subjects such as animal families and astronomy, with related arts and crafts. A nature photography contest is also held each year for community entries.

Around 100,000 injured or orphaned birds of prey are treated and released in the Heard Raptor Center. If an injured raptor is found, call the museum for assistance (972/652-5560). Support for this program and the live animal exhibit partially comes from the Wild Child Adoption Program in which supporters may "adopt" a creature, such as a golden eagle for $100, a tiger salamander for $25, or a three-toed box turtle for $20.

- Consider bringing binoculars or a camera.

- Ask about special events, such as Family Fun Festival (second weekend of September), Wild Bird Seed Days, and Native Plant Sale in April.

- The Heard museum offers birthday parties. Overnight programs are planned for Scouts.

- Volunteer opportunities are available for ages 14 and up.

- Call the Wildflower Hotline at 542-1947.

- The Nature Store offers a variety of nature-oriented gifts. They will also special order some things.

- A small picnic area is available. A soft drink machine is on the outside balcony. School groups sometimes picnic at Finch Park on Kentucky St. or Town Lake Park in McKinney.

- A paved trail and the museum building are handicapped accessible.

- Restrooms and water fountains are in the museum.

- Parking is free.

Hours: Open Monday-Saturday, 9 A.M.-5 P.M. with self-guided trails, 9 A.M.-4 P.M.; Sunday, 1-5 P.M. with self-guided trails, 1-4 P.M.; guided trails on Saturday, 11:30 A.M. and Sunday, 1:30-3:30 P.M. on every half hour (register with receptionist); groups contact the Education Dept. Closed some holidays.

Admission: FREE for the museum building; self-guided trail, adults $3, and children $2; free on Monday; group fee for guided tours; memberships are available. Donations are appreciated.

Directions: From US 75 (Central), take Exit 38 (Hwy. 5) north where there is a sign. Proceed 1 mile, turn south on Hwy. 5, and go another 3/4 mile. Turn left on FM 1378. Drive east on

FM 1378 1 mile to the museum, which is located on the north side. It's located south of McKinney about 25 miles from downtown Dallas.

HERITAGE FARMSTEAD

1900 West 15th Street
Plano, Texas 75075 • 972/424-7874

Behind a bank of trees, which shields it from the noises of progress, lies a two-story Victorian blackland prairie farm home and twelve outbuildings. One step onto its wrap-around porch, and visitors step back in time to 1891 when it was located on a 360-acre working farm owned by Dudley and Ammie Wilson.

A short film in the Orientation Center explains what farm life was like at the turn of the century through the advent of the tractor and what farm families did to survive. As the tour goes into the main house, the rooms, such as the two parlors, music room, Ammie's sewing room with its loom, Dudley's farm office, and the kitchen with a wood-burning stove, come alive. Check under the beds for chamber pots and in the children's bedrooms for period toys. On the second floor, look for the framed hair wreath.

Some items in the rooms are changed periodically to reflect the way it would have looked during a particular season or holiday. Adult visitors will likely find items they remember from their grandparents' houses, a way of life that would be lost to the younger generation if not for the efforts of preservationists.

Other favorite buildings are the smokehouse, corn crib, broodhouse for chickens, and livestock area with its donkey, sheep, pigs, and rabbits. Look under a shelter for a horse drawn carriage, Model T truck, and Fordson tractor. In spring, cotton, sorghum, and various vegetables and herbs are planted. The pole barn has picnic tables and a small stage that may be rented for outdoor meetings, such as wedding receptions. Children also find interesting the cistern, windmill, and storm cellar.

Opened as a museum in 1978, the four-acre museum is listed on the National Register of Historic Places, and tour guides dressed in period costumes explain life as it once was on a Collin County farm.

- Special events include the Lantern Light Tour, Christmas exhibit, Scout Day, and Blackland Ball. Usually only the house's lower floor is toured on event days. Call for more special events.

- Tours leave on the hour with the last one hour prior to closing. Going on a dry day is recommended.

- Handicapped access to the lower floor. Pictures of the upstairs are by the first floor telephone. Pathways are accessible.

- Group tours of ten or more are asked to preregister six weeks ahead. Spanish-speaking docents may be available.

- There is no concession.

- The Country Store has farm-related children's books, stuffed toy animals, dolls, and other toys as well as gifts with historical emphasis and items made on the farm by crafters.

- Restrooms are located in the altered hen houses. Bottled water is in the Orientation building and a water fountain is outside.

- Parking is free.

Hours: November 1-July 31: TWTF 10 A.M. and 12 noon. August 1-October 31: Thursday and Friday 10 A.M. and 12 noon. Year round: Saturday and Sunday 1 P.M. and 2:45 P.M.-5 P.M. Closed Monday and major holidays.

Admission: Under 3, free; ages 3-17 and senior citizens, $2.50; adults 18 and over, $3.50. Fee includes guided tour. Memberships are available.

Directions: Take the 15th St. (FM 544) exit off Central (US 75) and go west. Turn south on Pitman, which is between Alma and Custer. Look for signs and two-story house on the left.

LAS COLINAS

204 Mandalay Canal
Irving, Texas 75039 • 972/869-1232, 972/556-0625

Las Colinas is a carefully planned 12,000-acre development of attractive office buildings, homes, recreational businesses, and retail stores. Boy Scouts of America, Kimberly-Clark, Exxon, GTE, and others have their world headquarters there.

If you enter the Las Colinas Urban Center on O'Connor Rd. from the south, be sure everyone looks to the right for the beautiful **flower clock** with the words "Las Colinas" spelled out in shrubs just before driving under Highway 114 (Carpenter Freeway).

On the west side of O'Connor just past Las Colinas Blvd. is a parking garage and then the West Tower of Williams Square. Between the West and East towers is a plaza larger than two football fields on which nine larger-than-life Spanish horses called the **Mustangs of Las Colinas** appear to be galloping across a "stream." Fountains under the horses' hooves give the look of splashing water. Families can climb steps along the water and cross it on granite stepping stones. In the lobby of the West Tower is the **Mustang Sculpture Exhibit** which explains the process used to sculpt and install the horses through photographs, models, and a slide presentation. Other African wildlife sculptures by mustang sculptor Robert Glen are also on display. The exhibit is open Tuesday-Saturday (869-9047). If your family is hungry after this visit, try the Mustang Cafe or Velma's Cookies and Ice Cream located in the building.

Within walking distance just southeast of O'Connor and Las Colinas Blvd. is the **Mandalay Canal**. The canal itself winds around the Urban Center into Lake Caroline and back again. As you walk or drive down Las Colinas Blvd., you will pass the Caltex House building and another parking garage on the right. Between them are stairs leading down to the canal walk. The water taxis that cruise the 1.5 miles may be boarded at several locations, basically wherever you see their moorings. The ticket booth is by The

Landing and Texas Bar and Grill. The 12-passenger boats, made of mahogany and fiberglass, may be enclosed and heated in winter. Look for mallards and seagulls on the lake. Call 972/869-4321 for transportation schedule information. Three electric boats are available for charter. They are closed on major holidays.

A pink granite path will lead you to retail stores along the canal, giving the area an Old World, European flavor. Families will enjoy browsing through Safari Book and Coffee Company and Little Rebel's children's clothing and eating at one of the restaurants, such as the Texas Bar and Grill, The Landing, Wendy's, or Victor's Mexican Cafe. Call for days and hours open. Some may not be open on weekends.

- Near the Urban Center on the east side of Highway 114 at Rochelle Road is the **Marble Cow Sculpture**, which includes five large marble cows atop Bluebonnet Hill. A sidewalk goes up the hill, and kids love running from cow to cow. There are benches under the trees. It is across the street from the Texas Commerce Tower.

- North of Las Colinas Urban Center on O'Connor Rd. are the **Las Colinas Equestrian Center** and the **Dallas Communications Complex** which includes tours of the Studios at Las Colinas.

- A bike trail runs through Las Colinas. Call Las Colinas Bike and Fitness located at Northgate and N. MacArthur about in-line skate rental at 972/541-2665.

- Williams Square is handicapped accessible. The canal is accessible through an elevator in the Tower East parking garage elevator on Las Colinas Blvd.

- Restrooms and water fountains are located inside restaurants. Portables are brought in for events.

Hours: Call the transportation office or particular store or restaurant you would like to visit. The hours may vary by season. Most retail stores are open Monday-Saturday, 10 A.M.-6 P.M.; Sunday, 12-6 P.M.; Thursday evening until 8 P.M.

Admission: Mustang exhibit and Mandalay Canal walk, FREE. Water taxis: seniors, $2.75; adults, $3.25; ages 4-15, $1.75; ages 3 and under, free.

Directions: Located in Irving, the Urban Center is at O'Connor Road and Highway 114.

MESQUITE CHAMPIONSHIP RODEO

LBJ at Military Parkway exit,
1818 Rodeo Drive
Mesquite, Texas 75149 • 972/285-8777

Don your Wranglers and Ropers and recapture the thrilling days of the Wild West with its daring cowboys and powerful livestock at the Mesquite Championship Rodeo. Families can experience the true flavor of Texas beginning with hickory-smoked barbecue at the 300-seat Pavilion. Pony rides and the Kiddie Korral barnyard entertain young buckeroos awaiting the exciting prelude to rodeo events, the majestic Grand Entry.

Eyes widen and pulses race as the crowds watch calf ropers, steer wrestlers, and bronc and bull riders brush with danger and conquer it with courage and skill. Lovely barrel racers, crazy clowns, and country music add to the entertainment. Even the young'uns have their turn in the arena for the Kids' Calf Scramble for ages eight and under.

The $8 million covered Mesquite Arena has grandstand and reserved box seating as well as the luxurious Texas Suite, which can hold 18 people. The $850 rental price includes dinner.

- Call for the date of the Mesquite Rodeo Parade, which kicks off the rodeo season the first weekend in April.

- Discount coupons are sometimes in Friday newspapers.

- A gift shop and emporium are on the rodeo grounds.

- Concessions sell food and beverages.

- The arena is handicapped accessible.

- Restrooms and water fountains are available.

- Lighted and paved parking.

Hours: April-September, Friday and Saturday nights, 8-10 P.M. The gates open at 6:30 P.M.

Admission: General admission: adults, $10; seniors, $7, ages 12 and under, $4. Reserved box seats: $16, $14, $12. Group rates available for 25 and up. Barbecue: adults, $8.50; ages 12 and under, $5.50. Parking is $2.

Directions: Exit Military Parkway off I-635 (LBJ Freeway) in Mesquite. Twenty minutes from downtown Dallas. Arena visible from freeway on west side.

OLD CITY PARK

1717 Gano
Dallas, Texas 75215 • 421-5141

One of Dallas' historical and architectural treasures is Old City Park, thirteen acres on which rests thirty-six restored nineteenth-century homes, buildings, and preserved arts.

The tour may begin with a short film at the 1887 MKT Railroad Depot and continue to the Drummer's Hotel, Flower Garden, General Store, and Miller Log House. Children will love the Miller's Log Playhouse. The Barn often serves as a potter's workshop. Notice that the Gano cabin "dog trot house" has an open breezeway with rooms on each side to allow for circulation. A windmill stands nearby. The Renner School, Victorian George House, Pilot Grove Church, and Brent Place (a house that could be ordered in a kit) will also be of interest.

With younger children, the best days to visit are the special event days. On the first Saturday in June, the park has Dairy Day. In honor of the Texas dairy industry, free samples of ice cream and yogurt are given away, there are games and calves to pet, and a cow may be available for milking. Other highlights are the July 4 celebration, "Treat Street" at Halloween, and the Candlelight Christmas Tour.

- A one-hour mini-tour is scheduled Tuesday-Saturday from 10 A.M.-3 P.M. and Sunday from 12:00 to 3:30 P.M. Group tours are offered.

- McCall's Store, a Victorian gift shop, carries some interesting toys, especially at Christmas.

- Outside McCall's is a soft drink machine and popcorn wagon. Brent Place Restaurant is open Monday-Friday 11-2. To the west on Griffith is a Ramada Inn with a dining room on the top floor. Visitors may bring a picnic lunch.

- There is handicapped accessibility to the grounds but not to some of the buildings.

- Restrooms with wheelchair access are located in the Fisher Road House and Stone House behind the church. There are water fountains.

- Parking is free.

Hours: Grounds are open Tuesday-Saturday, 10 A.M.-4 P.M.; Sunday, noon-4 P.M. Tours are self-paced and self-guided.

Admission: Adults, $5; seniors, $4; and ages 3-12, $2.

Directions: From the west on I-30, exit at 46B Ervay. Turn left at St. Paul and left again at Gano. From the east, exit 46A Downtown Central. At Harwood, turn right. The first right is Gano.

OWENS SPRING CREEK FARM

1401 East Lookout Drive
Richardson, Texas 75082 • 972/235-0192
(Mailing address: P.O. Box 830249, Richardson, Texas 75082)

Rolling green hills and white buildings complete the home of Owens Country Sausage at Spring Creek Farm. The Owens Museum located near the entrance takes visitors 100 years back in time in the Butcher Shop, Country Store, Country Kitchen, and Farmer's Workshop.

Outside the museum are farm animals and the Antique Wagon Showroom. What children remember most about the farm are the stables which house the Owens "Gentle Giants," four blonde magnificent Belgian draft horses which weigh about 2,300 pounds each. They also have an eight-horse pony hitch with matched miniature horses that pull a variety of miniature wagons. Both are favorites in area parades.

Just inside the gates is a two-story farmhouse dated about 1887 and called **Miss Belle's Place** after the spinster schoolteacher who held classes in her home. Tours of the home may be arranged through the Junior League of Richardson, 644-5979.

- Free guided tours are available with reservations. Call 972/235-0192.

- There is no food or drink at Owens, but at the intersection of Plano Road and Campbell are Purdy's and The Feed Bag for burgers.

- Handicapped access is available.

- Restrooms and water fountains are provided.

- Parking is free.

Hours: Open daily, 9 A.M.-4 P.M.; closed 12-1 P.M. for lunch. Tours on the hour from 9 A.M.-3 P.M. with reservations. Closed major holidays.

Admission: FREE

Directions: Exit Campbell Road east from US 75 and go north on Plano Road. Or take Plano Road north from I-635. The farm is on the right.

THE PALACE OF WAX AND RIPLEY'S BELIEVE IT OR NOT!

601 East Safari Parkway
Grand Prairie, Texas 75050 • 972/263-2391

Two unique attractions located together just five minutes east of Six Flags are The Palace of Wax and Ripley's Believe It Or Not! Lifelike figures of the famous and infamous have eyes that seem to follow visitors as they go from one vignette to the next. Those remembered in wax vary from Jesus Christ to Hollywood's stars and starlets to Mother Teresa. Walk through "Behind the Scenes" to a working wax studio and costume shop to see how these amazing wax figures are created.

Bring a camera to capture the collection of incredible oddities in Ripley's Believe It Or Not! museum. Eight major theme galleries invite visitors to experience tornadoes and earthquakes and walk across coals of fire. On display is an enormous collection of curiosities that Robert Ripley collected on his tour of 198 countries. Visitors marvel at his strange treasures, such as a leaning Tower of Pisa made of matchsticks, and "The Lord's Prayer" handwritten on one fourth of a postage stamp. Many hands-on exhibits challenge guests to "Believe It Or Not!"

- Singe Halloween a favorite Halloween event. Families might call for more information before taking young children.

- Facilities include a gift shop, snack bar, and game area.

- Wax Hands allows you to create a replica of your own hand in wax. Fantastic Fotos creates a picture of your head on someone else's body.

- Birthday packages are available.

- The museums are handicapped accessible.

- Restrooms and water fountains are available.

- Parking is free.

Hours: Open daily year round except Thanksgiving, Christmas, and New Year's Day. Memorial Day-Labor Day: 10 A.M.-9 P.M. Remainder of year: Monday-Friday, 10 A.M.-5 P.M.; Saturday-Sunday, 10 A.M.-6 P.M. Ticket office closes one hour before listed closing time.

Admission: To see only one of the two museums: ages 13 and up, $9.95; ages 4-12, $6.95; and 3 and under, free. To see both museums: ages 13 up, $12.95; ages 4-12, $9.95; 3 and under, free. Discount rates are for groups of twelve or more.

Directions: From I-30, exit north at Belt Line Road. The museums can be seen from the highway.

SAMUELL FARM

100 East Highway 80
Mesquite, Texas 75149 • 670-7866 or 800/670-FARM

The vintage tractor at the entrance gives visitors an idea of what is to come. Children love to climb all over the preserved farm equipment at Samuell Farm, a 340-acre farm operated by the Dallas Parks and Recreation Department. It is operated much like a farm would be during 1840-1930.

Once they have tried all the tractors, swings, and slides, children then notice the barnyard. There, patient sheep, goats, cows, pigs, and other farm friends allow plenty of petting. Ducks and geese glide around the pond, and horses and more sheep and goats graze behind fences.

Catch "the big one" at one of five stocked ponds, but bring your own equipment, including insect repellent. Beautiful wooded trails invite horseback riding on your own horse, hiking on 4½ miles of trails, and bike riding.

Food has never tasted so good as when eaten at one of the picnic tables under ancient oaks. Grills are available.

- Twenty-five-minute hayrides for groups of fifteen or more are available for $2 each. Ages 2 and under are free. Call two weeks in advance for reservations. Deposit required.

- For groups of fifteen or more, the farm offers barnyard tours which could include a barnyard tour and/or candle dipping, and demonstrations. Call for reservations and information.

- Ask about special events such as Halloween Haunted Barn held on the weekends before Halloween, Civil War Weekend, Family Farm Festival, and Easter Egg Hunt.

- Day camps are held in June and July and Fin and Feathers, a preschool program, in the spring and fall.

- Birthday party packages are available on weekends.

- Cold drink machines are located near the entrance. Ask about concessions on special event days.

- Rules include no smoking in restricted areas, no dogs on premises, no collecting of plant or animal life, and no cutting of firewood.

- One adult should chaperone each group of ten children.

- Animals may be fed plain, unsalted popcorn, chopped apples or chopped carrots, or bread. Treat them kindly.

- Adventures at Samuell Farm is located nearby for those who would also like to horseback ride for $12 per hour. 670-8551.

- The Bird Rehabilitation number is 670-8257.

- Handicapped access is available.

- There are restrooms and water fountains.

- Parking is free.

Hours: Open daily, 9 A.M.-5 P.M. Closed Thanksgiving and Christmas. Closed weekends Thanksgiving through March 1 each year.

Admission: Adults, ages 12 and over, $3; ages 3-11, $2; under 3, free.

Directions: Located 14 miles east of downtown Dallas on the south side of Highway 80. Exit Belt Line service road.

SANDY LAKE AMUSEMENT PARK

I-35E North at Sandy Lake Road (Exit 444)
Carrollton, Texas 75006 • 972/242-7449
P.O. Box 810536 • Dallas, Texas 75381

A favorite swimming hole of Dallasites for more than twenty-seven years, Sandy Lake continues to delight families with its large pool designed for all ages, slides, and sunning areas.

A hilly miniature golf course, paddleboats, and nineteen amusement rides add to the fun. Screened in along the lake area in the Bird Barnyard are peacocks, ducks, geese, guineas, and turkeys to watch.

A very special event is held Easter weekend when 40,000 eggs to hunt are dropped from a helicopter onto the grounds. During April and May local school bands, orchestras, and choirs compete there. In August is the Back-to-School Family Fair, a safety program.

- Tickets are bought for the attractions, and discount books are available.

- Birthday party packages, which may include a meal, are offered.

- Paddleboat riders must meet height requirements or ride with an adult. Small children wear life jackets.

- Four concessions with hot dogs and snacks are convenient. Families may bring only home-prepared food with no glass bottles for picnics. Picnic tables are provided, but groups of fifteen or more need a reservation and there is a fee.

- Most areas are handicapped accessible, but the miniature golf course is too hilly.

- Restrooms and water fountains are available.

- Parking is free.

Hours: April-September. Hours and days vary from month to month.

Admission: General admission at the gate is ages 4 and up, $2; 3 and under, free. Swimming, $4; paddleboats and miniature golf, $2; and amusement rides, $1-1.50.

Directions: Take I-35E north and exit at Sandy Lake Road (Exit 444) in Carrollton. Go west a short distance to the park on the right.

THE SCIENCE PLACE

1318 Second Avenue
Dallas, Texas 75210 • 428-5555
(Mailing address: P.O. Box 151469, Dallas, Texas 75315)

Housed in two buildings in Fair Park, The Science Place has been fascinating children with scientific marvels for over thirty-six years. Exciting traveling exhibits, such as "Whales: Giants of the Deep," which has five active, full-sized robotic whales, and "Treasures from the Vatican: The Etruscans," regularly team up with permanent exhibits to challenge the minds of onlookers. Hands-on activities and demonstrations allow families to become active participants in the world of scientific discovery. The TI Founders **IMAX Theater**, which has a 79-foot domed screen, opened in 1996. Visitors who bring small children may want to ask about the intensity of the programs.

Permanent exhibits include **Kid's Place**, which delights children up to age seven with the Number Forest, Building Things, Senses, and Waterworks. The basics of math and physics may be explored in Hands-On Physics, and Looking at the Light explains illusions and raises new questions about what you see. The importance of environmental concerns are addressed in the display Crash Test. Look also for Language World and Dino Dig.

- Demonstrations such as the Electric Theater explain electricity. Call for times and news about other current demonstrations.

- The Science Place **Planetarium** in the SP Planetarium Building (formerly called Science Place II) presents programs which often coincide with current exhibits. Look for the annual program about the Christmas Star. Call 428-5555 for programs and times. There are special show times during the State Fair.

- Lectures given by experts in fields of science are scheduled often.

- The SP Preschool Program offers an exciting curriculum for children during the week and special weekend workshops for preschool through eighth grade year round. Summer classes and family workshops are also scheduled. Call for a brochure.

- Imaginature by Kid's Place has critters, bees, and fish.

- Birthdays may be celebrated after 2 P.M. daily with a staff person to assist. Call for information and reservations.

- The Science Plays Store offers books, toys, games, costumes, and other science-related items.

- The Science Place Cafe offers light lunch fare from soups to sandwiches and a variety of snacks. Open daily, 11 A.M.-3 P.M. Picnic tables are usually located behind the museum by the lagoon.

- Handicapped access is available.

- Restrooms and water fountains are provided.

- Parking is free except during the State Fair.

Hours: Sunday-Thursday, 9:30 A.M.-5:30 P.M.; Friday and Saturday, 9:30 A.M.-9:00 P.M. (Kids Place closes at 6:00 P.M.). Closed Christmas Day. Planetarium hours are Monday-Friday, 9:30-5:30; Saturday, 10:30-5:30.

Admission: Adults, $6; ages 3-12 and seniors, $3; members and ages under 3, free. Planetarium is $1 with admission to The Science Place or $3 for the show only. Memberships are available.

Directions: Enter Fair Park through the Grand Avenue gate off of Robert B. Cullum Blvd. Parking is available in front of the museum.

SIX FLAGS HURRICANE HARBOR

1800 East Lamar
Arlington, Texas 76006 • Metro 817/265-3356

Aptly named, Hurricane Harbor water park offers an exhilarating way to cool off during the hot Texas summertime. Whether taking a leisurely inner tube cruise around Arlington's Lazy River ride or dropping into a free fall from 76 nautical feet of Der Stuka, family members will find nonstop entertainment during their stay at Hurricane Harbor.

Young children are first drawn to the water toys in the shallow waters of Pepsi Park's play pool. Next they may want to grab an inner tube and try the Surf Lagoon wave pool, a million-gallon lagoon with a gradual beach-like slope ending in eight feet of water, which periodically rocks swimmers with four-foot waves. The more adventuresome may try the Bubba Tub in which four ride in a rubber tub from a six-story height. The white water rafting of Colorado is replicated in the inner tube ride on Ragin' Rapids of a man-made river with slides and waterfalls to add to the experience. Rides like Banzai Banzai and the Black Hole live up to their names in thrilling speed and splashing finales.

- Lifeguards are professionally trained and are very visible. Some rides have height requirements or caution those with heart problems or those who are pregnant.

- Adults must accompany young children, who must use approved flotation devices. Watch children very carefully in the wave pool, especially on very crowded days.

- Tubes for the wave pool are available for rent, but you will probably want to bring your own.

- Picnic tables are available. Visitors may bring their own food and nonalcoholic drinks. No glass containers are allowed. Concessions provide drinks and fast food.

- Lockers may be rented for $4 and a $1 deposit.

- Shower facilities, an arcade, gift shop, volleyball courts, and lounge chairs are available.

- Handicapped access to the pool area is provided.

- There are restrooms and water fountains.

- Parking is $5.

Hours: Open from mid-May through mid-September. Hours vary. Call for specific days and times.

Admission: Over 48 inches, $24.75; under 48 inches, $17.19. Both prices include tax.

Directions: The Arlington park is just off I-30, directly across from Six Flags Over Texas. Exit the Hwy. 360 service road. The park is on the north side.

SIX FLAGS OVER TEXAS

2201 Road to Six Flags
Arlington, Texas 76010 • Metro 817/530-6000

As children see the bright, waving flags and dancing fountains of Six Flags Over Texas, excitement and anticipation of the thrills to come overflows. For over thirty years, this 205-acre family theme park has entertained all ages with a variety of rides, shows, and special events.

Young children are drawn to the antique Silver Star Carousel, Looney Tunes Land, and Yosemite Sam's Gold River Boat Ride.

Older children brave the roller coasters, which range from the tamer Mini-mine Train to the legendary 14-story wooden roller coaster called The Texas Giant. For those who need a cool-down, a liberal drenching is promised by the River Rapids and the Log Flume.

Everyone loves the shootouts between Six Flags cowboys, the shows at the Crazy Horse Saloon and Southern Palace, as well as special concerts at the 10,000-seat Music Mill Amphitheater. The lush landscaping, cheerful employees, and cleanliness are always appreciated. Emporiums with T-shirts and other souvenirs are plentiful.

- Discount coupons and information about special events are often available at local restaurants, in grocery stores, or through or other promotions. Special prices are sometimes offered for bringing designated soft drink cans.

- Special events include September's Heritage Craft Fair, Fright Fest in October, and Holiday in the Park in November and December.

- There are diaper stations and Lost Parents headquarters in Looney Tunes Land. Stroller rental at the main gate is about $7.

- Admission to the park includes all rides and shows, except some special concerts in the amphitheater. Some rides have a height requirement. Food, arcade games, and souvenirs are not included in the fee but may be needed in the budget.

- The Arlington Hilton and Arlington Marriott hotels by Six Flags may offer packages for overnight stays and two-day tickets. Many other hotels are nearby for the budget-minded.

- Restaurants serve fried chicken, Mexican dishes, burgers, and pizza as well as other fast foods at food stands with picnic-type outdoor seating. A shaded family picnic area with tables is located in the parking lot between rows 25 and 30. Get your hand stamped at the gate for re-entry.

- There is handicapped access to the park. Rides vary. A guide to ride accessibility is available at the gate.

- Restrooms and water fountains are available throughout the park and are noted on the park map. Lockers are provided near the entrance.

- Parking is about $7. Trams transport visitors from the remote parking to the entrance and back. A park map is distributed at the entrance to the parking lot.

Hours: Open weekends in spring and fall; daily in summer. Special schedule for Holiday in the Park. For specific hours and information, call Metro 817/530-6000, Ext. 517.

Admission: A one-day pass is adults, $32.95; children under 48 inches and seniors, $26.91; ages 2 and under, free. Two-day passes and individual and family season passes are available. Discount rates for groups of 15 or more may be purchased in advance.

Directions: Located between Dallas and Ft. Worth off I-30 on the south side. Exit at Highway 360 in Arlington. The orange Observation Tower can be seen for miles.

THE SIXTH FLOOR

411 Elm Street
Dallas, Texas 75202 • 747-6660

The Sixth Floor Exhibit: John F. Kennedy and the Memory of a Nation is a permanent collection of historical information regarding the assassination of President John F. Kennedy on November 22, 1963. Located on the sixth floor of the former Texas School Book Depository, photographs, 40 minutes of documentary film, and significant artifacts are presented to help visitors understand the events leading to and following this tragic event. New in the museum are items from the estate of Mrs. Jacqueline Kennedy Onassis. Museum personnel believe all materials are appropriate for viewing by families.

An audio tour is available, and about 75 minutes should be allowed to cover the exhibit adequately. The museum brochure recommends a walking tour around Dealey Plaza following a map that notes points related to the motorcade and theories about the gunman. As visitors leave the Sixth Floor, they are invited to write their own memories of the assassination in books that will always be part of historic record.

- No photography is allowed.
- The Visitor Center has a small bookstore. You may write or call for a free brochure.
- Oliver Stone's movie *JFK* was filmed here.
- On Market between Commerce and Main is the **John F. Kennedy Memorial Plaza.**
- Restaurants are located in the nearby West End Historic District. A DART rail station is located there.
- The handicapped accessible entrances are on the north side of the building at Pacific and on the west side.
- There are restrooms, water fountains, and some vending machines.
- Paid parking is available to the north of the Visitor Center. Ample parking is available next to the Visitor Center on the west side of the building. Enter off Houston or Elm Street. Visitors might check the DART bus schedule.

Hours: Open daily, 10 A.M.-6 P.M.; Last ticket sold one hour prior to closing. Closed Christmas Day.

Admission: Exhibition only: adults, $4; seniors, $3; ages 6-18, $2; under 6, free. Add $2 to each to include the audio tour. There is an audio tour for ages 6-12 as well as adult audio tours in seven languages. Group rates are available.

Directions: The Visitor Center faces Dealey Plaza on Houston Street between Elm and Pacific in the old Texas School Book

Depository Building, which is now called the Dallas County Administration Building.

THE STUDIOS AT LAS COLINAS

Dallas Communications Complex
6301 N. O'Connor Road
Irving, Texas 75039 • 972/869-FILM

Housed in the 112-acre Dallas Communications Complex at Las Colinas, The Studios tour takes visitors behind the scenes to a working motion picture and TV sound stage. You'll see sets and memorabilia from movies and TV shows, such as *Star Trek*, *Forrest Gump*, *Hunt for Red October*, *Wayne's World*, *Gerbert*, *The Sound of Music*, and *Robocop*. A tour of The Studios lasts about 1½ hours.

Fascinating displays illustrate special effects, make-up, and costumes.

While at The Studios, you can also tour the **National Museum of Communication**.

- The Hollywood Company Store is open for movie and TV fans.

- The Studios is handicapped accessible.

- Water fountains and restrooms are available.

- Group tours may be arranged by calling 972/869-7752.

Hours: June-August: Monday-Saturday, 10 A.M.-6:30 P.M., Sunday, noon-6:30 P.M. September-May: Monday-Saturday, 10 A.M.-4 P.M., Sunday, noon-4. Tours are at 10:30, 12:30, 2:30, and 4:00.

Admission: Studio tour, which includes museum: adults, $12.95; seniors, $10.95; ages 4-12, $7.95.

Directions: The Studios is located at Royal Lane and O'Connor Road north of Northwest Highway in Irving.

Surf 'n Swim

440 Oates Road
Garland, Texas 75043 • 972/686-1237

Nestled in a shady greenbelt area, this large wave pool is operated by the City of Garland in Audubon Park. Excited whoops go up as the surf is turned on, producing rolling waves that lift and lower raft and inner tube riders.

Lifeguards carefully monitor the area and can push a button to stop the waves if necessary. Only soft flotation devices are allowed.

Plenty of shaded and unshaded grassy areas are provided for spreading out beach towels. Picnic tables are provided and food may be brought in, but glass bottles and alcoholic beverages are not allowed. Ice chests are checked at the entrance.

- Inner tubes may be purchased, or a swimmer's own tube can be aired up for 50 cents. A tube makes the waves more enjoyable.

- Very young children should be watched carefully, especially on crowded days, to see that they do not get caught underneath some rafts. The waves will lift them off their feet, and their heads go under water.

- Audubon Park has a wonderful shaded playground area east of the pool. Passes are honored all day, so swimmers may leave and return on that day.

- Call ahead if the weather has been stormy. The pool is closed if the water is clouded. Even in summer it can be cool there on a cloudy, windy day.

- Rental after closing time is offered for groups.

- The concession sells fast foods and snow cones.

- The pool area is handicapped accessible.

- Restrooms, an open shower, water fountains, and a pay telephone are available.

- Parking is free.

Hours: Open from Splash Day about mid-May on weekends to daily while school is out until Labor Day, 11 A.M.-7 P.M. Open Tuesday and Thursday until 9 P.M. Crowd thinnest early morning and late afternoon.

Admission: Adults, $4.50; ages 5-17, $3.25; seniors, $3; ages 4 and under, free. Twilight discount Tuesday and Thursday from 6 to 9 P.M.: adults, $4; youth (5-17), $3; and seniors, $2.75. One adult must be present for every two children under age 7. Free use of life vests is available for all ages.

Directions: Take the Oates Exit off LBJ Freeway (I-635) and go east. The pool is past the baseball fields on the right at Audubon Park, which is at the corner of Oates and O'Banion.

TELEPHONE PIONEER
MUSEUM OF TEXAS

One Bell Plaza: 208 South Akard
P.O. Box 655521
Dallas, Texas 75265-5521 • 464-4359

The many unique and entertaining venues explaining the history and operation of the telephone at the Telephone Pioneer Museum of Texas attract all ages. In the theater, an audio-visual presentation explains how far communication has come and where it is going. Alexander Graham Bell, as a life-like figure, is diligently pursuing his new invention, the telephone, while a huge bright red telephone with a face in its receiver explains telephone etiquette to all who will listen.

A Norman Rockwell print reminds visitors of the diligence of the cable repairman perched at the top of a pole. A number of telephones and similar inventions are displayed. In one exhibit, visitors may dial and watch the call being completed. At the Party Line display, children may listen in on lively dialogue between characters, such as Ma Bell, Big Tex, Superman, and Thomas A. Edison. Don't leave without listening to the talking bear who explains the services of the Telephone Pioneers. The Pioneers and the telephone company worked together in assembling this museum which is open only with reservations, so call ahead for your group.

- Browse in the gift shop for T-shirts, toys, and telephone-related items.

- The museum does not allow food or drink.

- The museum is handicapped accessible.

- There are restrooms and water fountains.

- Call about parking before coming to the museum. DART buses stop within walking distance. Call 979-1111 for the bus schedule.

Hours: Open Tuesday-Friday, 9:30 A.M.-2:30 P.M. Tours available by reservation only. Call at least two weeks in advance. Closed holidays and weekends.

Admission: FREE

Directions: Located downtown Dallas in One Bell Plaza between Commerce and Jackson with Browder on the east. Second floor.

WEST END MARKETPLACE

603 Munger Ave. at Market Street
West End Historic District
Dallas, Texas 75202 • 748-4801, 720-7107

Always festive any time of year, the West End Marketplace entertains families on five floors of the former cracker factory.

Located in the 55-acre **West End Historic District**, the Marketplace houses more than 50 retail shops and push-carts, including Star Toons, Wild Bill's Western Store, and Elusive Image with holography. A Dallas Tourism Information booth is located on the first floor.

Children are happy to spend the day on the Fountain Level at Tilt in Dallas Alley with more than 100 electronic video games. When hunger strikes, take the escalator to the fourth floor for a variety of casual eateries.

While on this floor, duffers may want to compete in miniature golf at **City Golf**, a 27-hole indoor miniature golf course. Murals make golfers feel like they are out on the course. It's a favorite place for year-round birthday parties. Another welcomed addition is a ten-screen **movie theater.**

The West End hosts several festivals and special events, such as Hoop It Up and Taste of Dallas. Call for a calendar of events or watch for newspaper announcements on Friday. Many other restaurants, such as Spaghetti Warehouse and Sonny Bryan's, serving a variety of foods are located just outside the Marketplace. Visitors enjoy **Planet Hollywood**, a restaurant and movie memorabilia museum.

- The West End is near the Dallas Arts District and Sixth Floor Museum.

- The Dallas Surrey Service and Max A Million provides horse-drawn carriage rides around the West End and downtown, weather permitting. Call 946-9911 or 914-8600 for information.

- The Marketplace is handicapped accessible.

- Restrooms and water fountains are available.

- Variety of parking lots with fees; some metered street parking; six-story West End Parking Garage at Munger and Lamar, one block east of the Marketplace; better not to travel alone or wear flashy, expensive jewelry after dark.

Hours: Monday-Thursday, 11 A.M.-10 P.M.; Friday and Saturday, 11 A.M.-midnight; Sunday, noon-6 P.M.; closed Thanksgiving, Easter, and Christmas Day.

Admission: FREE to enter and look around. Fee may be charged to participate in special events.

Directions: From I-35 (Stemmons Freeway), exit Continental, which changes name to Lamar and passes by the Marketplace and garage. From US 75 (N. Central Expressway), take Woodall Rogers to Field St. Turn right on Munger to pass parking garage. The DART rail line stops at the West End.

WHITE ROCK LAKE

Bath House Cultural Center
8300 Garland Road
Dallas, Texas 75218 • 670-4100

Built for water supply in 1910, White Rock Lake is now operated as a public park that consists of over 1,000 acres of lake and 1,000 acres of park land. Main avenues surrounding White Rock include E. Northwest Highway, Buckner Blvd., Mockingbird Lane, Garland Road, and Lawther Drive. On sunny days, the shaded park is highly populated with sailors, fishermen, joggers, bicyclists, skaters, and picnickers.

On a 9.33-mile trail around the lake, those jogging, skating, and bicycling get their exercise while protected from city traffic. An eight to ten station parcourse is between Emerald Isle and Poppy Drive on the lake's east side. The 7.3-mile White Rock Creek Trail continues north through the greenbelt area to Valley View Park. A pretty ride is from Greenville Avenue and Royal Lane to Lawther Drive.

Boats with motors of ten horsepower or less as well as sailboats, kayaks, canoes, and paddleboats are welcome on the lake. The three sailing clubs sometimes hold regattas that are beautiful to watch. Fishermen line the creek banks and piers, hoping for white crappie, largemouth bass, and catfish. They should have a fishing license and follow length and limit regulations. White Rock provides twelve fishing piers and five boat ramps, two on the east side and three on the west.

At one time, visitors could take Lawther all around the lake, but the crowds were unpopular with residents of the area. Now it is divided into four sections with entrances at Emerald Isle, from Poppy to the Dreyfus Club building off Buckner, by the spillway on Garland, and at Lawther off Mockingbird. Visitors can drive the entire length of the west side.

Shaded picnic areas with nearby playgrounds are plentiful. Covered pavilions and buildings may be rented for large groups. The old Pump House at the south end is now a historical site and management office for the Water Department. A sculpture is in front of the building.

Perched on the hill on the southeast corner of Mockingbird and Buckner is a small, pretty playground with covered picnic table that overlooks the lake. Another picnic/play park is just a little further north beside the baseball fields on Buckner.

Flag Pole Hill, with its playground, covered pavilion for picnics, and wonderful hill to climb, is also a great place to fly a kite, throw a frisbee, or listen to special outdoor summer programs by the Dallas Symphony.

Since swimming has not been allowed for many years, the old 1930s bath house is now the **Bath House Cultural Center** which is used as a gallery, center for performing arts, and educational center for various workshops. From Buckner Blvd., go west on Northcliff to E. Lawther. Call 670-8749 for a calendar of events.

- Bikes, including tandem, may be rented from Jack Johnston's Bikes (328-5238). Canoes may be rented from High Trails Canoe in Garland. Call 972/2-PADDLE. Both businesses are near the lake on Garland Rd.

- Call the Park Department about building and pavilion rental at 670-8748.

- The Dallas Arboretum is near the spillway on Garland Rd. The White Rock Yacht Club restaurant is just a little further down Garland where it splits to the left on East Grand.

- Portable restrooms in winter are not handicapped accessible. After April 1, five permanent restrooms are opened that are accessible. Water fountains are located nearby. Eight water fountains are along the trail.

- Free parking. Lock car. Do not leave valuables in sight.

Hours: Daily, 6 A.M.-midnight. It is not advisable to be there after dark.

Admission: FREE

Directions: Access to the park is on Garland Road, E. Northwest Highway, Lawther Drive, and N. Buckner Blvd. Signs direct visitors.

2. Tidbits: More Good Things to Do

The first chapter just scratches the surface of the many things to see and do in and around Big D. The listings in this chapter may be a little smaller or appeal to a certain age or interest group, but they still offer entertaining and educational activities to explore and enjoy. As Dallas grows, sometimes getting off the beaten path is the most rewarding.

MORE AMUSEMENTS

There is always something to do around town no matter how old one is or what the ever-changing Texas weather is doing. In addition to these listed, many shopping malls also have an arcade, such as Aladdin's Castle or Tilt, to entertain family members who had rather play than shop. Look under "Individual and Family Sports" for activities such as skateboarding, go-carting, rock climbing, and miniature golf.

AIR COMBAT SCHOOL
921 Six Flags Drive #117
Arlington, Texas 76011 • Metro 817/640-1886

To get the feeling of being a real "Top Gun," attend Air Combat School. For this experience, the aviator must be at least 4 feet, 8 inches tall, and he may want to bring other family members or friends with him because they can communicate with each other on radios while they fight in this intense simulated flying experience.

From ground school, the pilot goes to the equipment room for the flight suit, helmet, and other necessities. An F-106 Delta Dart egress trainer will test the trainee's survival skills and strap him into a motion base flight simulator. From this jet fighter cockpit, he will be pitted against all kinds of threats. Other experiences are in an A-4 Skyhawk, F-8 Crusader, F-111 Raven, and F-16

Flying Fox. This is not recommended for anyone who is claustrophobic or has heart or breathing problems. Someone who has a severe problem with motion sickness might consider taking some preventative medicine that his doctor approves. A parachute repelling training program is also offered.

The price for each person is $39.95 plus tax, and birthday parties are welcomed. Gift certificates are available. Call for operating hours or to schedule a flight. To reach Air Combat School, exit Highway 360 from I-30.

DISCOVERY ZONE
15240 Dallas Parkway • Dallas, Texas 75248
1233 N. Town East Blvd. • Mesquite Texas 75150

Discovery Zone is a colorful indoor play park for ages 1-12. Children climb, slide, fall into balls, crawl through tubes, and have a great time in this active form of entertainment. Pizza and other snacks are available, and parties are very popular here. Ages 3-16, $7.99; under 38 inches, $4.99.

FUN FEST
3805 Belt Line Rd.
Addison, Texas 75244 • 972/620-7700

The daily fun at Fun Fest includes bowling, billiards, laser tag, and Virtual Reality. Children must be accompanied by an adult in the evening.

MALIBU SPEEDZONE
1130 Malibu Dr. (I-35E at Walnut Hill) • 972/247-RACE

The focus is on racecars of various types at 12-acre Malibu. In addition to the racecars, which are primarily for adults, Malibu also has two miniature Putt'n Fun golf courses, a restaurant, and the Electric Alley game room that has 100 simulator and skill redemption games.

Hours are Friday-Saturday, 11 A.M.-2 A.M.; Sunday-Thursday, 11 A.M.-midnight (18 years and older only after 9 P.M.).

PLANET PIZZA
3000 Custer Road at West Parker, Unit 310
Plano Texas 75075 • 972/985-7711

Ferrari Bumper Cars, a swinging Pirate Ship, and a large soft play area with tunnels, balls, tubes, and slides are only part of the fun at Planet Pizza, an indoor play park. Arcade games with a ticket redemption center and a fast food menu add to the entertainment for children ages 2-10. Individual tickets or unlimited rides and soft play hand stamps may be purchased. The unlimited play is about $5-7.

Birthday party packages are available for a minimum of six children.

RONALD'S PLAYPLACE
14770 Preston Road • 972/233-8788
Plano Rd. at Forest Lane • 343-9609

Both of these McDonald's have entertaining indoor play parks with tunnels and slides and toddler areas.

WHIRLYBALL
3541 W. Northwest Hwy. at Webb Chapel
Dallas, Texas 75220 • 350-0117 or 350-0129

Whirlyball is a unique team game that combines jai-alai, basketball, and hockey. Team members ride in bumper cars while they try to score points. There is a video arcade, two courts, and two party rooms. Teams must have a minimum of ten players, and the courts rent for $140/hr. daily, and $160/hr. after midnight.

NATURE, ECOLOGY, SCIENCE

As the metroplex grows in population and the natural areas are developed to accommodate new and expanding families and businesses, preservation of those natural areas and their wildlife in preserves and parks has become a priority of both state and local park departments and organizations such as the Texas Committee on Natural Resources and Sierra Club, as well as families who wish to escape city life to undisturbed settings. Even though "The stars at night are big and bright deep in the heart of Texas," sometimes city lights obscure all but the brightest stars. If you can't get out of town, local planetariums offer celestial programs day and night. Of further interest to naturalists is the progress in recycling and other conservation efforts in the Dallas area. Some local businesses are specializing in products to encourage and equip families who are interested in science and outdoor activities.

About a two-hour drive southwest of Dallas is Comanche Peak Nuclear Plant. Area colleges and businesses are offering courses, such as computer science, to help youngsters understand this field. Although some of the Dallas area's science museums and nature centers were listed in "Places to Go," the following should be of special interest.

NATURE

CONNEMARA CONSERVANCY

Located along Rowlett Creek north of Plano, Connemara Conservancy is a 72-acre nature preserve featuring outdoor sculpture and presenting performances of music and dance at various times beginning in March. Cars must be left outside the preserve. It is very popular for hiking and informal picnicking on the rolling, grassy terrain. From US 75 North, take exit 34 (McDermott Drive) and proceed west for 1.6 miles. Turn south and go 1 mile to a stile with fence at left on the east side of the road. Call 521-4896 for details.

DALLAS COUNTY AUDUBON SOCIETY, INC.
P.O. Box 12713
Dallas, Texas 75225 • 972/283-5216

Woods, Wings, and Water is a publication of the active Dallas County Audubon Society, Inc., and the title is descriptive of their activities. Their monthly meeting is held at Clark Auditorium in the Scottish Rite Hospital on the second Monday of each month September-November and January-April. The guided birding field trips to places like Hagerman Wildlife Preserve and Woodland Basin are wonderful outdoor experiences, and beginners are welcome. The society is involved in wildlife preservation and helps injured birds. Annual dues are $35 or $10 for local chapter membership only. Birdwatchers may call 817/329-1270 to hear a tape on rare bird sightings in the North Texas area.

For information on current monthly programs and field trips, phone the Dallas County Audubon Society InfoLine, 972/283-5216. Bring along binoculars and a field guide.

Wild Birds Unlimited, 4300 Lovers Lane, sells a wide variety of bird-related products (891-9793)

DALLAS COUNTY PARK
AND OPEN SPACE PROGRAM

Beginning in 1977, Dallas County and various private interests have been working together to acquire natural areas to preserve as public open space park land. The terrains vary from grassland to wetlands to woods, and they all welcome visitors free of charge. Most are suitable for hiking and informal picnicking. Insect repellent would be handy to have along. Remember to bring water and something to store trash in to leave the area undisturbed. These areas are maintained by the cities in which they are located. For more information, call the city's park department or Dallas County Park and Open Space Administrator, 653-6653. You might ask for a brochure that outlines all of the preserves.

Cottonwood Creek Preserve is known for its beautiful display of wildflowers in the spring. It includes 220 acres of natural land with some 200-year-old pecan trees along the creek. Points of interest are noted along the creek trail. It's recommended for hiking, nature study, and informal picnicking. To reach this preserve in Wilmer, go I-45S and turn east on Belt Line. Turn north on Goode and then east to the end of Cottonwood Valley Road.

Elm Fork Preserve is 22 acres of heavily wooded land used for hiking and nature study. Take Sandy Lake Rd. west from I-35 to R.J. McInnish Park and go south through the park entrance to the preserve at the southeast corner of the park. Park at the back by the softball complex in McInnish Park. There are restrooms and a picnic/playground area. A three-quarter-mile trail has been cleared. Call Carrollton Parks and Recreation Dept., 972/466-3667.

Escarpment Preserve covers 41 acres of wilderness in Cedar Hill next to City of Dallas Escarpment Park and **Dallas Nature Center** which offers nature education programs. It's suitable for study of plants and animal habitats and hiking. Go south on I-35 to Hwy. 67 South (sign says Cleburne) and take I-20 West (sign says Ft. Worth). Exit Mountain Creek Parkway and go south (under the freeway). Drive 2½ miles to the Nature Center, 296-1955. Restrooms and picnic areas are at the Nature Center.

Grapevine Springs Park Preserve in Coppell is the latest acquisition in the Open Space program. Originally established as a park in 1936, it was abandoned after a few years and became very overgrown. Now, it is again part of the park system and the subject of interest to both archaeologists and historians. In 1843 it was the temporary capital of Texas for about three weeks while Sam Houston tried to sign a treaty with a delegation of Cherokee Indians. The treaty was to be executed at the full moon, but it was a blue moon month with one at the beginning and one at the end of the month. Sam Houston was at the site for one moon and the Indians at the other. They met at another place later.

The fifteen acres of this park are said to look like a sunken water garden when it rains, for the WPA built man-made channels in a drainage pattern along the creek. The park is being cleaned and picnic tables and paths added. To reach the park, go north on Denton Tapp Rd. to Bethel Rd. and turn west. Go about one mile to Park St. and turn south. It dead ends into the preserve.

Lemmon Lake Preserve includes a 142-acre lake along the Trinity River which is surrounded by 133 acres of prairie woodland. A footpath is suitable for hiking and nature study. Picnicking near the park entrance and bank fishing are popular. Take Old Central Expressway-Texas 310 south from Loop 12 (Ledbetter Dr.) to River Oaks and go east to the preserve. Call Dallas Parks Department, 670-4100 or 670-0967.

McCommas Bluff Preserve covers 111 wooded acres on the Trinity River's east bank. It's also the site of a historical marker called "The Navigation of the Upper Trinity" concerning the barge commerce and the locks on the Trinity during 1900-1910, as well as the river way for the *Sally Haynes* steamboat. But the area was just as famous because it contained the spring where notorious characters like the Daltons, Jesse James, and Belle Starr watered their horses. It is being surveyed by archaeologists because it was also the site of the abandoned Trinity City from 1871-1911. Now it has a nature trail and is used for hiking, fishing, nature study, and informal picnicking. From Loop 12 in Dallas, go south on Longbranch (which becomes Riverwood at the dead end) and west to the preserve. Or from Longbranch go west at Fairport to the dead end.

North Mesquite Creek Preserve encompasses 22 acres of native grasses and trees adjacent to North Mesquite Creek at the southeast corner of Dallas' Samuell East Park, which includes Samuell Farm. No formal trails are here, but it is used for hiking, nature study, fishing, and informal picnicking. The closest facilities are at Samuell Farm. To reach the preserve, take Hwy. 352 (Collins/Main St.) south to Wheatfield and then go west to the cul de sac. Call Mesquite Parks and Recreation Dept., 972/216-6260.

DUCK CREEK GREENBELT

For those who prefer some development in their nature areas, Duck Creek Greenbelt offers three miles of concrete trails that loop along Duck Creek in Garland. In February 1992 a Garland girl found a bison bone that was more than 500 years old beside Duck Creek and donated it to the Museum of Natural History. Visitors often enter the area at Audubon Park at 342 Oates Road, east of I-635 where there is paved parking, picnic tables, and a playground as well as Surf 'N Swim wave pool. Call 972/205-2750.

EARTH DAY

Every year more families in Dallas and the surrounding areas join together on April 22 to celebrate the Earth and dedicate themselves to bettering its condition through efforts such as preservation of natural environments and wildlife, elimination of hazardous products, and recycling. Activities range from planting begonias in the front yard to cleaning a local park to attending a city festival. Watch local newspapers *Dallas Family* or *dallas child* for announcements of activities or call the **U.S. Environmental Protection Agency** at 665-6444.

The Sierra Club or the Texas Committee on Natural Resources may also know of other family-oriented Earth Day events. The Heard Museum, the Nature Center, and the Museum of Natural History plan special events in honor of the Earth. The state parks also participate with special activities. Call to find out what they have planned at the ones near Dallas. If your neighborhood is interested in obtaining federal funds to plant trees and create a "pocket park," call the Dallas Urban Office of the Texas Forest Service at 977-6670.

HOME AND GARDEN SHOW

Begin watching newspapers the last week of February for announcements about the Dallas Home and Garden Show, a favorite event for over fifteen years. It's usually held on the first weekend in March at Market Hall. The entrance gardens have colorful spring flowers, and beautiful designer gardens are located inside. Usually The Science Place has exhibits to educate and inspire young gardeners, and children will also enjoy the exhibits about hobbies and ecology. Kids under 12 are free, and discount coupons may be available. Parking is free. You may want to bring your camera.

L.B. HOUSTON NATURE AREA

More than 300 acres on the Elm Fork of the Trinity River make up the L.B. Houston Nature Area. It is near the area where gold seekers crossed the Trinity in the 1800s to reach California. Trails with names like River Trail, Beaver Trail, and Wilderness Way Trail vary from a half-hour walk to a two-and-one-half-hour walk. Restrooms and picnic facilities are at California Crossing Park north of the preserve. Birding and spotting animal tracks are popular activities here. Wait at least two days after a rain. Enter L.B. Houston from Tom Braniff Parkway north of Highway 114 near Irving. Call 670-6374 for details.

THE NATURE COMPANY
317 Northpark Center
Dallas, Texas 75225 • 696-2291

Children will be fascinated with the collection of nature-related books, toys, and other items in The Nature Company. They also have a catalog.

PLANETARIUMS AND OBSERVATORIES

Richland College Planetarium has special programs such as laser concerts and holiday programs that are open to the public. On the first Friday night of each month is a program and telescope observation. A planetarium program is presented on the second and third Saturday at 2 and at 3 P.M. Contact the planetarium director at 238-6013 for dates and times. The campus is located at 12800 Abrams at Walnut.

St. Marks School of Texas Observatory is open to the public occasionally for special programs. A program about the Star of Bethlehem is a Christmas favorite. Call 363-6491 for specific dates. The address is 10600 Preston Road.

The Science Place Planetarium is located in the Planetarium Building at Fair Park. Programs are changed periodically and often coincide with Science Place exhibits. It's a public planetarium for Dallas residents and visitors and times are extended during the State Fair. The building has a snack bar and permanent and changing exhibits. Also, Planetarium birthday parties may be arranged. Buy tickets at The Science Place just west of the Planetarium Building: adults, $6; ages 3-12 and seniors, $3; add $1 for the Planetarium. The Planetarium-only show is $3. Enter Fair Park through the Grand Avenue gate off Robert B. Cullum Blvd. Parking is available in front of the museum.

University of Texas at Arlington Planetarium opens its planetarium to the public at 8 P.M. on the first Friday of each month, except January and possibly the summer months. Cooper St. in Arlington goes through the middle of the UTA campus. At the middle bridge is Science Hall. Enter here and go to the planetarium at Preston Hall. To park, from Cooper go east on Border and park on the south side. Admission is adults, $2, and UTA students and children under 12, $1. Call 817/273-2266 for more information.

ROWLETT NATURE TRAIL

Rowlett Nature Trail is a 1.3-mile path following the shore of Lake Ray Hubbard in Rowlett. As visitors enter the greenbelt, there is a parking area, picnic tables under ancient pecan trees, and a fishing pond. It's also great for birdwatching as well as hiking and other nature studies. Take I-635 to I-30 East. Exit at Belt Line and go left under the overpass. Turn right on Rowlett Rd. and travel about 5 miles. Turn left on Miller, going about $1\frac{1}{2}$ miles to the trail located on the right side of the street. For further details, call 972/475-2772.

SIERRA CLUB

The Sierra Club is a national organization which was founded about a hundred years ago by naturalist John Muir. It is dedicated to preserving, studying, and enjoying the environment and plans activities for all ages to achieve these goals. They have a catalog and newsletter. The newsletter, *ENVIRONmentality*, includes notice of environmental issues and activities by nature centers, such as the Heard and Dallas Nature Center, as well as a calendar of hiking and canoeing outings. Meetings are held the second Wednesday of each month at the Richardson Civic Center at Central and Arapaho. For information about the local chapter call 369-5543.

TEXAS COMMITTEE ON NATURAL RESOURCES
5934 Royal Lane, Suite 223
Dallas, Texas 75230 • 368-1791

This nonprofit membership organization works with state and local government agencies to acquire and preserve natural areas. Their task forces present programs to school children and other groups on a variety of subjects such as recycling, water and air quality, wildlife, pesticides, forests, and wetlands. Each March they host the Texas Buckeye Trail, a walk in the Great Trinity Forest to see Buckeyes in bloom, as well as numerous species of shrubs and flowers. One of their favorite activities is the annual **Texas Wilderness Pow Wow** which is usually held on an April weekend and includes activities for all ages.

TURTLE CREEK GREENBELT

Turtle Creek Greenbelt is also for those who like their trail a little less woolly. Both paved and unpaved paths in Dallas and Park Cities begin at Reverchon Park, 3535 Maple Avenue, with $2\frac{1}{2}$ miles of paved trail to Stonebridge. It continues along the creek beside Lakeside and St. John's in an affluent area in Highland Park.

WHOLE EARTH PROVISION CO.
5400 East Mockingbird Lane
Dallas, Texas 75206 • 824-7444

Exploring the Whole Earth Provision Co. is the next best thing to being outdoors. Provisions include clothing and shoes designed for outdoor activities and travel tools, including an excellent selection of guidebooks for outdoor activities in Texas and elsewhere. Technical gear includes sleeping bags, tents, compasses, mess kits, and telescopes. Children love the stuffed wild animals, animal masks, backpacks, bug kits, puzzles and books, and many other nature games and toys.

WILDFLOWERS

Spring in Texas is gorgeous as the state flower, the bluebonnet, begins to bloom alongside other hardy favorites. Certain areas along highways are seeded and designated non-mowing areas. Towns, such as Ennis, often create festivals around the bluebonnet in April and feature trails that are great for photography. Contact the Ennis Chamber of Commerce, 214/87-VISIT. Bardwell Lake is near the festival.

The Texas Department of Transportation provides recorded information updated weekly in the spring about where to find the best wildflowers, 374-4100, and they have published a pamphlet called "Wildflowers of Texas." Richardson also hosts an annual wildflower festival, and Palestine has the annual Dogwood Trails, which is a popular time to ride the Texas State Railroad between Palestine and Rusk.

WOODLAND BASIN NATURE AREA

Located in a marshy area on Rowlett Creek at Lake Ray Hubbard in Garland, Woodland Basin Nature Area has a 1,000-foot boardwalk lined by cattails and sedges that extends out into the lake. This is a popular area for fishing and bird watching, and it is wheelchair accessible. There is paved parking. From I-635, go east on Centerville, and turn east on Miller. Follow Miller about one-half mile to the park at 2323 E. Miller Rd. Call the Garland Park and Recreation Department at 972/205-2750.

——————— ECOLOGY ———————

RECYCLING AND CONSERVATION

Families and businesses are becoming very involved in recycling efforts in their communities from sorting materials at home and using natural alternatives to hazardous house and garden products to buying recycled paper products for home and office uses. The **Dry Gulch Recycling Center** is a nonprofit recycling collection center initiated by the Texas Committee on Natural Resources and many others with the City of Dallas to benefit the Downtown Dallas Family Shelter. Call 353-9986 for hours or to arrange a tour. You may also want to visit the Lewisville Landfill (972/315-4500) or the Rock Tenn mill in Oak Cliff (941-3400). Curbside recycling has been initiated in several communities. After Christmas, ask the Parks Department for places to drop off your Christmas tree so it may be recycled as mulch for park gardens and trails. For more information about recycling in Dallas, call 670-4475.

Each March for many years, the Dallas Water Utilities has sponsored the **Water Conservation Poster Contest** for students in first through eighth grade. A $50 savings bond is given to each winner, and the posters are displayed at City Hall during Drinking Water Week. The water education program of DWU includes tours of water and wastewater treatment plants for grades four and above, a speaker's bureau, and curriculum aids. Call 670-4022 for more information, and see the "Tours of the Working World" section of this guide.

——————— SCIENCE ———————

COMANCHE PEAK NUCLEAR POWER PLANT
Visitors Information Center
Texas Utilities Generating Company
P.O. Box 2300
Glen Rose, Texas 76043 • 254/897-5554

Located about a two-hour drive southwest of Dallas, the Comanche Peak Nuclear Power Plant generates electricity through the nuclear fission process. The plant has two Westinghouse-built reactors. At the visitors information center, families may watch a video presentation, look over exhibits and displays that explain the operation of the first nuclear power plant in Texas, and take a van tour of the plant. See "Day Trips" for other places of interest around Glen Rose. Call or write for visitor center hours or group tour information.

COMPUTER SCIENCE

Since Dallas area elementary schools and some preschools have incorporated computer literacy into their curriculum, today's children are growing up with computers and see them as useful tools and toys in their daily lives. Dallas libraries and museums allow children to use them to gather information and create artwork. For further instruction in computer science, contact local universities' and community colleges' continuing education departments for courses and summer day camps. **St. Mark's School of Texas**, **Greenhill School**, and **Hockaday** offer summer day camps centering on science and computer science.

NATIONAL SCIENCE BALLOON CENTER

From the end of April to the end of August is the best time to see this NASA contractor near Palestine launching high-altitude balloons for scientific experiments. The 45-minute tour may be arranged by calling 903/723-8002 seven to ten days in advance.

SCIENCE FAIR AND INVENTION CONVENTION

Dallas area school children participate each February and March in the Science Fair and the Invention Convention. Winners are selected at each school, then go on to regional competition. An excellent way to foster curiosity, problem-solving skills, and an interest in science is to be a participant and, win or lose, visit the Fair and the Convention at the regional competition level. Check with your local school for dates and locations in March or April.

In addition to The Science Plays store at The Science Place in Fair Park, area businesses that aid in science-related projects are the following:

Science Projects in the Tower Shopping Center 267 Hickerson in Cedar Hill (972/291-3345)

Science Projects 13440 Floyd Rd. near Texas Instruments (972/470-0395)

The Science Shop 1750 Alma Rd. in Richardson (972/437-3600)

GEOscience 3610 Greenville Avenue at Martel (821-6493)

FARMER'S MARKETS
AND PICK YOUR OWN FOOD

—— FARMER'S MARKETS AND NURSERIES ——

Stopping by the Farmer's Market can be a wonderful experience each week for your family. First, they are outdoors, and you can meet the farmers themselves. You are supporting your local economy and encouraging your family to select fruits and vegetables that are so good for their health. Children learn to compare prices among the vendors, to look for ripeness and quality in the produce, and to learn in which seasons certain fruits and vegetables are harvested. Often, the markets make holidays even more special with truckloads of pumpkins or Christmas trees grown in East Texas. Some markets include beautiful plants, crafts, country music, and sometimes barnyard animals. The *Dallas Morning News* Wednesday "Food" section lists local markets and what seasonal produce is in good supply. Call the market for hours.

BIG TOWN FARMER'S MARKET
U.S. 80 at Big Town Blvd.
Mesquite • 972/319-8093

TOM McCURDY'S FRUIT STAND
111 N. Interurban, Richardson
(one block east of North Central Expressway)

CITY OF DALLAS FARMER'S MARKET
1010 S. Pearl
Dallas, Texas 75201 • 939-2808

Serving Dallas for more than 50 years, the City of Dallas Farmer's Market has row after row of beautiful fruits, vegetables, and house and garden plants. They also publish an informative yearly calendar. The Fall Harvest Festival at the end of October is a favorite event.

NURSERIES

A relatively free (unless like most you can't resist buying some plants or seeds) nature excursion is one to your local nursery. Children can learn a great deal about identification and care of flowers, trees, and vegetables from this visit. They usually carry supplies for birds as well as books on gardening, such as Neil Sperry's *Texas Gardener*. Popular nurseries include Nicholson-Hardie, Calloway's, Northhaven Gardens, and Plants N Planters. Southwest Landscape Nursery Company at 2220 Sandy Lake Rd. in Carrollton has 40,000 square feet of greenhouse growing space on 10 acres.

PICK YOUR OWN FOOD &
—— CHRISTMAS TREES, COMMUNITY ——
SUPPORTED AGRICULTURE

One of the most rewarding family experiences is to leave early before the Texas sun heats up the air and drive out to a **Pick Your Own (PYO)** farm to hand pick fruits and vegetables that could not be any fresher. Not only can children see on what kind of tree, vine, or bush the produce grows, but they have the experience of doing something for themselves and will be more likely to enjoy it served later at a meal. Blueberries, peaches, and a variety of vegetables are most often offered at the farms. Usually, the farm provides a basket, but ask about containers, restrooms, and picnic areas as well as hours. Do not wear perfume or hair spray because it attracts insects. A hat or visor, insect repellent, and sunscreen would be wise. The Texas Department of Agriculture compiles a list of PYO farms and roadside sales yearly called *Texas Fresh Produce Guide*. To receive a copy, write them at 1720 Regal Row, Suite 118, Dallas, Texas 75235, or call 631-0265.

DENTON COUNTY
Smith's Pumpkin Patch and Katie's Country Market
708 Rockhill Rd.
Aubrey, Texas • 940/365-2201 in October

FANNIN COUNTY
Walker's Blueberry Farm
(NW of Bonham Rt. 1, Box 174 FM 274 - Mulberry Rd.)
Ravenna, Texas 75418 • 903/583-4739

Jenkins Fruit Farm
Rt. 1, Box 278A
Bonham, Texas 75418 • 903/583-2220

HENDERSON COUNTY
Blueberry and Blackberry Basket
12462 FM 2588
LaRue, Texas 75770 • 903/677-3448 (near Athens)

SMITH COUNTY
Barron's Blueberries
16478 Co. Rd. 431
Lindale, Texas 75771 • 903/882-6711 (near Tyler)

Deep Creek Blueberry Farm
Tyler, Texas 75704 • 903/877-3221

O.L. Rozell's Peach Orchard
14278 SH 64 W
Tyler, Texas 75704 • 903/592-2074

Plantation Pines Berry Farm and
Peach Farm/Plantation Pines Christmas Tree Farm
9628 CR 429 Tyler, Texas 75704
903/595-2046, 903/592-2041, 903/595-6860 (peaches)
(picnic tables, wheelchair accessible, brochure available)

Trail Creek Christmas Tree Farm
FM 2710/Iron Mountain Rd.
Lindale, Texas OWNER: Earl Hollingsworth
P.O. Box 40412
Ft. Worth, Texas 76140 • 817/293-9000 or 817/478-3222

VAN ZANDT COUNTY
Blueberry Hill Farm in Edom
Rt. 1, Box 527A
Edom, Texas 75756 • 903/852-6175

Holiday Plantations Christmas Trees
Rt. 1, Box 171
Ben Wheeler, Texas 75754 • 903/852-6817

COMMUNITY-SUPPORTED AGRICULTURE

One area organic farm sells shares of about $495 each year to families who drive out once a week to pick up their shares of the harvest of pesticide-free produce in baskets or boxes which amounts to around 600 pounds over nine months. Children are usually welcome to check on the progress of crops. The farm also has produce dropoff places in Lakewood and Richardson. Tours may be arranged. Call or write Good Earth Farms, Rt. 2, Box 343, Celeste, TX 75423, 903/496-2070.

PETS AND WILDLIFE

—————— PETS ——————

Bonding between a child and his pet is a very important part of childhood, providing a child with a loyal friend and teaching him about kindness and responsibility. A trip to a pet store can be very educational and entertaining whether or not you plan to adopt. A highly recommended place to find a family friend is your local animal adoption center/shelter. Check your city's offices or look up "Humane Societies" in the *Yellow Pages* for their number and call for hours. Then go by for a visit. Most will arrange tours for groups and also mention opportunities for volunteers. They can give you information about low cost spay/neutering surgery for pets you already own. Each March the Texas Kennel Club presents its **All-Breed Dog Show and Obedience Trial** with more than 130 breeds and 3,000 dogs. What better way to learn about different breeds and perhaps talk to owners to help make a pet selection for your family than to attend this weekend event held in the Exhibits Hall of the Dallas Convention Center, and it is free (606-3638). The Dallas **INCATS/City Kitty Cat Show** is usually on an April weekend at Dallas Market Hall.

CITY OF DALLAS PET ADOPTION CENTERS

The City of Dallas operates two centers where citizens may bring homeless animals or adopt a pet. A homeless animal without a collar or tags is kept for 72 hours and then checked for adoptability. If not adoptable, it is euthanized. Adopting a pet may cost about $19 if sterilized and $30-$60 if sterilization is necessary. The **Dallas Coalition of Animal Owners** rescues purebred dogs that are not adopted and tries to find them a home. Call 349-4897 if interested in these pets.

The two shelters are open for adoption or the search for lost pets Monday-Saturday, 8 A.M.-4:30 P.M. and closed holidays. Located behind the Dallas Zoo, the Oak Cliff location is 525 Shelter Place (670-6800), and the Pleasant Grove location is 8414 Forney Rd. (670-8226).

THE SOCIETY FOR THE PREVENTION OF CRUELTY TO ANIMALS OF TEXAS
362 S. Industrial Blvd.
Dallas, Texas 75207 • 651-9611
McKinney, Texas Shelter • 972/562-7297

The SPCA was established in 1938, and volunteers have been active ever since in finding homes for homeless animals, offering low cost spay/neutering surgery, investigating complaints of cruelty, locating lost pets, and gathering stray animals for their safety and the safety of citizens.

The dogs are divided into rooms according to whether they are large or small, male or female, or puppy or full grown. Cats usually occupy a separate room. The SPCA does almost everything your family vet would do, including spay/neutering, and offers the pets for about $39 minimum. They ask families questions about the animal's new home and length of time he will be left alone. They answer your questions about health care, behavior, and feeding.

To help this nonprofit organization cover operating costs, personalized bricks for the "Petwalk" are being sold for $50. Two owner and pet fun runs are held each year, the annual fall walk-a-thon and the spring Lakewood Love Run. **Repeats** is the name of their resale store at 14350 Marsh Lane at Spring Valley where the SPCA accepts donations of clothes, furniture, and household items that are still in good condition (972/241-8066). If you lose a pet or find a lost one, call the SPCA's computerized lost and found service at 651-WAGS. **Operation Kindness** is another rescue and adoption group (972/418-PAWS). They also sponsor a fall family pet festival.

If your family would like to adopt a pet, the SPCA is usually at Northpark Center before Christmas, and the Pet Center at 6721 Preston Road sometimes exhibits adoptable cats and dogs (520-7387).

ANIMAL ADOPTION CENTER
117 North Garland Avenue
Garland, Texas 75040 • 972/494-KIND

This NO-KILL animal welfare organization receives homeless animals and cares for them until they are adopted. They operate on donations of money and volunteer time. Visitors may come by Monday-Tuesday, 11 A.M.-4:30 P.M.; Wednesday-Saturday, 11-5:30; and Sunday, 1-4:30. They offer flea dips from April through October at low cost.

PETMOBILE PET HOSPITAL
608 W. I-30 at Beltline
Garland, Texas • 972/423-PETS, 972/427-VETS

The Petmobile Pet Hospital offers city pet registration, low-cost vaccinations, dips, nail clipping, and other services at Dallas city parks and various locations year round.

EMERGENCY ANIMAL CLINIC
12101 Greenville Avenue
Dallas, Texas 75243 • 994-9110

The Emergency Animal Clinic is a veterinary clinic offered as a service by more than 50 veterinarians. Hours are Monday-Friday, 6 P.M.-8 A.M., and Saturday, noon-Monday, 8 A.M.

FRITZ PARK PETTING FARM
312 E. Vilbig
Irving, Texas 75060 • 972/721-2501, 972/721-2640

Offered by the Irving Parks and Recreation Department only in June and July, the Fritz Park Petting Farm opens with a neighborhood parade and special events at the park. Cows, horses, goats, sheep, chickens, and more graze and nap among admiring children. The Little Red School House is home to smaller critters. The farm also has an incubator where children can watch chicks hatch right out of the egg. Tours are available and volunteers are appreciated at the farm, which is open Tuesday-Saturday from 10 to 6 and on Sunday, 2 to 8 if the weather permits. Free admission.

———————— WILDLIFE ————————

Texas has abundant wildlife in spite of development, and environmentalists are working diligently to protect it as well as exotic wildlife imported from other lands. In addition to Dallas Zoo, the Dallas World Aquarium, the Museum of Natural History, Dallas Aquarium, and the raptor center at the Heard Museum that was discussed in "Places to Go," wildlife may be studied at some other museums, zoos, and wildlife refuges and parks near Dallas. See "Day Trips" for wildlife areas in Ft. Worth, Tyler, Gainesville, Denison, Waco, and Glen Rose. One of the best places to see local wildlife is in the open space preserves listed earlier in this chapter. The purchase of a Texas Parks and Wildlife Conservation Pass allows you access to many places that are closed to the general public, and offers a variety of field trips.

Fairfield Lake State Park has begun a bald eagle sighting tour in the winter beginning in November. The eagles like to eat tilapia, which grows near the power plant hot water discharge. The park is about 100 miles south of Dallas, 15 miles east of I-45 at Fairfield. Visitors see approximately six to thirteen eagles.

BOLIN WILDLIFE EXHIBIT
1028 North McDonald
McKinney, Texas 75069 • 972/562-2639

Located inside the Bolin Oil Company, this exhibit of preserved animals from Africa and other areas of the world was a delightful surprise. Perry Bolin, rancher and oil distributor, collected these animals on big game hunts and organized them in the museum as an educational experience. Upon entering the large exhibit room, the push of a button begins an audio tape that explains the nature and habitat of each group of animals as you go around the exhibit.

Across the hall from the wildlife exhibit is a collection of vintage cars and oil-related items, and upstairs are displays of furniture and other items from life in Collin County in the early 1900s. Admission is free. Take US 75 to Exit 40/Virginia St. in McKinney and go east to McDonald. Turn left and the oil company will be on the right. They are open Monday-Friday from 9-4 and closed for lunch from 12-1. It's about a 40-minute drive from Dallas. The lower floor is wheelchair accessible, and the stairway to the second floor has a lift chair attached to the stairway.

LAKE MINERAL WELLS STATE PARK
I-20 to US 180
Mineral Wells, Texas • 817/596-7731

Texas Treks offers half-day and full-day treks on trails in Lake Mineral Wells State Park. What makes this unusual is that children ages 10 and older may lead (not ride) a llama on the trail. Younger children may go along, but they cannot have their own llamas.

The half-day trip spans two miles and costs about $35, while the full-day trip covers five miles and costs $60. Overnight trips will soon be possible on a twenty-two-mile recreational trail. These unique walks may be scheduled from October through May. The park is located two miles beyond Cool, Texas, between Weatherford and Mineral Wells, and park admission is included in the fee.

WILDSCAPES

Texas Parks and Wildlife offers suggestions for creating a landscape in your yard that will attract wildlife. Patterned after the National Wildlife Federation's Backyard Wildlife Habitat program, Texas Wildscapes' $15 information packet includes lists of native plants, brochures on butterfly and hummingbird gardening, information on feeders and nest boxes, and an application. Make checks payable to "Nongame Fund." Send in the completed application after implementing your habitat design, and they will send you an achievement certificate and a sign designating the site.

Address inquiries to Nongame and Urban Program, 4200 Smith School Road, Austin, Texas 78744, or call 512/389-4974. Demonstration sites in the area include Cedar Hill State Park on Joe Pool Lake and White Rock Lake. For information about the sites, call the Urban Fish and Wildlife Program Leader at 972/293-3841.

WILDLIFE SUCCESS STORIES

"Wildlife Success Stories and Endangered Species" is a popular wildlife program used by elementary schools. Developed by the Texas Agriculture Extension Service, the interactive computer program and accompanying exhibit include four Mac computers and an 8x10 display board. "Something's Fishy" is an aquatic science module that is available. Call 904-3051 for information about scheduling.

HISTORY AND POLITICS

———— HISTORIC ARLINGTON ————

ANTIQUE SEWING MACHINE MUSEUM
804 West Abram Street
Arlington, Texas 76013 • 817/275-0971

"A stitch in time" by owner Frank Smith has saved more than 150 antique sewing machines dating from 1858-1930. The Antique Sewing Machine Museum, located in a house built in 1905, is dedicated to the invention, production, and advancement of sewing machines. This collector began in 1963 as a salesman for New Home Sewing Center, but started to see both history and art in the old treadle machines that would come in occasionally. He began to search antique stores and flea markets to save and preserve the old machines. He also collects old parts and restores machines that belong to individuals. The walls are covered in memorabilia related to sewing, such as an 1880 McCall pattern and a picture of Elias Howe.

Frank Smith has an eclectic souvenir shop and can give tours for up to thirty people in America's only sewing machine museum. Families and students who are learning to sew would enjoy this collection. It is open Monday-Saturday, 9:30-5, and closed Sunday. Admission is adults, $3; seniors, $2.50; ages 4-14, $2; and ages 3 and under, free.

ARLINGTON HISTORICAL SOCIETY
1616 West Abram
Arlington, Texas 76013 • 817/460-4001

The **Texas State Museum of History** at the Fielder House and the **M.T. Johnson Plantation Cemetery and Historic Park** are operated by the Arlington Historical Society, which is dedicated to preserving the historic landmarks of Arlington and educating the public about their heritage.

Built as a private residence in 1914, the home has served since 1978 as the **Texas State Museum of History**, a place where the history of Arlington comes to life through exhibits such as "Treasures of Native Americans" and "Metroplex: Then and Now." The quilt exhibit is a favorite annually as well as exhibits of other Arlington crafters and artists. The upstairs rooms are furnished to represent an early barbershop and a bedroom and nursery. A general store is downstairs. The basement houses a collection of irons and other tools of daily life, a root cellar, and a steam engine train handcrafted to 1/12 scale. Favorite events here include the annual Christmas tree-lighting ceremony. Tours are available. Children who are about 8 or older would probably enjoy the museum the most. Three picnic tables are outside. Hours are Wednesday-Friday, 10-2; Sunday, 1:30-4:30. It may be open on Saturday during the summer. Admission is adults, $3; students and seniors, $1.50. The museum is located at Abram and Fielder.

The **M.T. Johnson Plantation Cemetery and Historic Park**, which has four Texas state historical markers, is located at 621 Arkansas Lane in Arlington. Visitors, by appointment, may tour the 1910 North Side School, which is furnished with school desks; the Joplin-Melear cabin; the P. A. Watson cabin, which is a dog trot house with a furnished kitchen on one side and bedroom on the other; the Bardin barn; and two Interurban way stations. Picnic tables are placed under a shade tree. Reading the cemetery stones is interesting as they date from about 1831. From the Fielder Museum, take Fielder south to Arkansas and turn east. It is located on the northeast corner of Arkansas and Matlock by the Mr. M Store. Further south on Matlock is Vandergriff Park, which has picnic tables, playground, pool, and Arlington Community Center.

While in Arlington, visitors may want to drive by the **Stallions at Lincoln Square** sculpture located at Highway 157 and I-30 in north Arlington.

HISTORIC CARROLLTON

A.W. PERRY HOMESTEAD MUSEUM AND BARN
1509 North Perry
Carrollton, Texas 75006 • 972/446-0442

Traveling in a covered wagon from Illinois to Texas in 1844, the Perrys were some of Carrollton's earliest settlers. This ten-room home built in 1909 is furnished with antiques and interesting memorabilia to remind us of "the way we were" and to share this history with children. They will like the old farm tools in the barn. The Homestead is open Tuesday, 9-4, Thursday and Sunday from 1 to 4. Tours are available. Admission is free, but donations are accepted.

OLD DOWNTOWN CARROLLTON SQUARE

The Old Downtown Square in Carrollton is bordered by Broadway and Main Streets and centered around a gazebo which serves as a focal point for festivities during special events and on holidays, such as the Carrollton Christmas Parade and the October Country Fair. On the square, visitors shop for antiques, for dolls in Dolls of Yesterday & Today, and for children's clothing. They usually stop for breakfast or lunch at Cafe on the Square or for ice cream at Rainbow Fountain & Ice Cream Parlor. Just a little north of the square at Main and Carroll is a historical marker.

———— HISTORIC DALLAS ————

In addition to Old City Park, the Hall of State, Samuell Farm, Age of Steam Railroad Museum, African-American Museum, Dallas Firefighter's Museum, Dallas Museum for Holocaust Studies, American Museum of the Miniature Arts, Frontiers of Flight Museum, the Sixth Floor, Telephone Pioneer Museum of Texas, and West End Historical District mentioned in "Places to Go," Dallas has many other landmarks worth visiting which are still very active.

DALLAS CITY HALL
1500 Marilla (Ervay and Young)
Dallas, Texas 75201 • 670-3011

The four-acre plaza surrounding City Hall with its imaginative sculpture by Henry Moore will first catch the interest of youngsters. The plaza is the setting of festivals, such as the Dallas International Bazaar in April, during the year and the site of the city Christmas tree and its annual lighting ceremony. Architect I.M. Pei designed the ten-level cantilevered building which opened in 1978. Inside, a view of the levels is good from the seventh floor, and there are usually art exhibits. Tours may be arranged by calling your local councilman or 939-2701. The Dallas Police and Fire Communication Center is located here. While you are in the neighborhood, visit the historic **Pioneer Park Cemetery** about a block west at Griffin and Young where many early Dallasites are buried. Dallas Convention Center is also nearby on Griffin. See "Tours of the Working World" for more details about City Hall.

Outdoors, between the cemetery and Convention Center, are the 70 bronze longhorn steers and watchful bronze cowboys erected to commemorate the cattle drives of the Old West.

DALLAS COUNTY HISTORICAL PLAZA

The Dallas County Historical Plaza is a memorial to Dallas history. Located in the center of Elm, Houston, Commerce, and Market Streets, the plaza is home for a representation of the **John Neely Bryan** log cabin built before 1850. A historical marker explains the contribution of the "Log Cabin Pioneers of Dallas County." On the southwest side, **the Old Red Courthouse**, a sandstone Romanesque Revival structure completed in 1891, allows a tour of the lobby area. The **John F. Kennedy Memorial**, a white cenotaph, is in front of Dallas' current courthouse. **Dealey Plaza**, located one block west, was the actual site of the assassination.

DEALEY PLAZA

Bordered by Houston, Elm, and Commerce, Dealey Plaza is dedicated to George B. Dealey, who founded the *Dallas Morning News*, but its location near the Texas School Book Depository, now the Dallas County Administration Building, has also made it the site of a memorial plaque to John F. Kennedy. The **Sixth Floor Museum** is located in the DCAB.

DAUGHTERS OF THE AMERICAN REVOLUTION HOUSE

Open to the public during the State Fair of Texas, the Daughters of the American Revolution **Continental DAR House** is a colonial white house located at the north end of Fair Park. The Jane Douglas Chapter houses a library of 3,500 genealogical books and bulletins as well as nineteenth-century memorabilia such as furniture, dishes, campaign buttons, and tools used in everyday life. The displays change each year. It is free to the public and handicapped accessible by the side door. Call 428-6964 for more information.

INTERNATIONAL MUSEUM OF CULTURES
7500 W. Camp Wisdom Road
Dallas, Texas 75236 • 972/709-2406

Opened in 1981 on the International Linguistics Center campus in southwest Dallas, the International Museum of Cultures is affiliated with the Summer Institute of Linguistics and Wycliffe Bible Translators. The museum features both life-size and miniature exhibits of people from other cultures based on the work members have done in languages around the world.

The exhibits display life in places like the village of Sarayacu, Ecuador, where a mother makes pottery as her small daughter learns to make rolls of clay for a new pot. In the miniature display, children can see little girls gathering clay at the river and a boy who is hunting with his blowgun.

There are some hands-on exhibits and a gift shop, and tours are available. It is handicapped accessible, and there are picnic tables outside the dining hall.

From I-20, take the Cedar Ridge Road exit and go 1/2 mile south to Camp Wisdom Rd. Turn right and go 1 mile west to the ILC entrance, and then turn west to the museum parking area. It is near Joe Pool Lake and the Dallas Nature Center. Admission is free, but a $2 donation for adults and $1 for children is suggested. Hours are Tuesday-Friday, 10-5; Saturday-Sunday, 1:30-5; and closed Monday.

PEGASUS PLAZA

The theme of this beautiful plaza, located at Akard and Main, is based on the Greek myth of the flying horse Pegasus. This symbol is particularly meaningful to Dallasites because of an oil company's "flying red horse" that has resided on top of downtown's Magnolia Building for more than 60 years.

The fountain, fed by a natural underground well, as well as boulders carved with symbols of the nine Muses, trees, and walkways provide a pleasant refuge from city traffic.

SCARBOROUGH FAIRE

For over a decade, Scarborough Faire has taken families back in time to an English Renaissance village where knights joust, jesters joke, and smoked turkey legs are fit for a king. Royal processions, fair maidens, a dragon swing, giant puppets, and crafters entertain throughout the day. Beginning at the end of April and going through mid-June on weekends, Scarborough Faire is located near Waxahachie, 30 minutes south of Dallas off I-35E (Exit 399A). Watch newspapers on weekends near the end of March for advance ticket discount information and specific dates and times.

SWISS AVENUE AND WILSON HISTORIC DISTRICTS

"Butcher Pen Road" was the original name of Swiss Avenue, which connected Jacob Nussbaumer's farm to the city of Dallas. He changed the street's name to Swiss Avenue to honor his Swiss relatives and friends who settled nearby.

In their glory days, the mansions along Swiss Avenue were owned by wealthy Dallas merchants and physicians, but now they are mainly used as offices for Dallas organizations. The neoclassical house at 5303 Swiss, built in 1905, is the oldest along that area between Fitzhugh and LaVista, which has been designated as a historic district. Children can see the differences in architecture from their own homes to those of the early 1900s. Some of these homes are usually on tour at Christmas or Mother's Day. At **Central Square** on Swiss Avenue just west of Hall near Baylor Hospital is a unique preschool playground with swings, slide, and little structures to climb in and on. Azaleas bloom here in the spring, and there are picnic tables and a Victorian gazebo.

The Swiss Avenue Historic District voice mail number is 220-9630. While on Swiss Avenue, you may also want to visit the Dallas Visual Arts Center at 2917 Swiss (821-2522).

Frederick Wilson married a niece of the Nussbaumers and built Queen Anne-style houses on the block to rent or sell. His family home, built in 1899, was at the corner of Swiss and Oak, and it was kept in the Wilson family until 1977. The Meadows Foundation renovated a block of these historic homes and offers rent-free office space to nonprofit community agencies. Free 45-minute tours of the district are offered for individuals and for groups with a reservation. The tours begin at the Wilson House at 2922 Swiss Ave. Inside the Wilson House is Preservation Dallas' In-Town Living Center, which offers a storehouse of information about older neighborhoods in Dallas. The interactive kiosks feature sites within Loop 12 and include pictures, historical background, and special information about what makes that neighborhood particularly worthwhile. Center hours are 10-4 Tuesday through Friday and 10-2 on Saturday. Call 220-9505 or 821-3290.

THANKS-GIVING SQUARE
P.O. Box 1777
Dallas, Texas 75221 • 969-1977

Located downtown at the intersections of Akard, Pacific, Bryan, and Ervay Streets, Thanks-Giving Square is "A symbol and a home for America's most beloved tradition...." according to President George Bush. In 1961 Dallas civic leaders decided to design a place of daily spiritual significance within the busy downtown area, a place of tranquility where citizens could reflect, pray, and count their blessings as Americans have been doing since before the Revolutionary War period.

Entering from Pacific, the three **Bells of Thanksgiving** ring out at noon on weekdays and every half hour on the weekends. Children will be drawn to the courtyard with the rushing waters in the fountains. A good view of the fountains is from the ramp above. In the exhibit room is a series of photographs taken by students at East Texas State University, which illustrate the three truths: We love God, God loves us, and We serve God singing. In the Hall of World Thanksgiving is the history of the American tradition of Thanksgiving, beginning with Samuel Adams' original proclamation of 1777 and continuing with presidents since then. Visitors will see a life-sized figure of George Washington kneeling in prayer next to the circular "river of life."

The Chapel of Thanksgiving is a place for prayer and reflection. The spiraled ceiling with its ring of bright lights and stained glass causes visitors to look upward in praise. Upon leaving, visitors are reminded to "Love your neighbor." Sam Houston, president and later governor of Texas, recommended Texans celebrate two Thanksgiving Days, one in the spring on March 2 for political independence and another in the fall for expressing thankfulness to God as Americans have been doing since the 1600s.

In 1997 a 15-ton monolith was dedicated to the Texas tradition of Thanksgiving. Four hundred years of celebration in Texas are out-lined on the stone slab, the last of three monoliths that have been placed at the perimeter of the square. The first words of thanks came from Coronado's exploration of Texas in 1541. It states, "It is right to give him thanks and praise."

Thanks-Giving Square is free and open Monday-Friday, 9-5 P.M. and on Saturday, Sunday, and holidays from 1-5. Donations are appreciated. You may want to combine a visit here with a tour of the underground walkway, which may be entered from Thanks-giving Tower on the Pacific Avenue side. See "Tours of the Working World."

UNION STATION
400 S. Houston Street
Dallas, Texas 75202 • 712-7270 or 651-1234

Built around 1914, Union Station was a center of rail activity in the area but now handles only the Amtrak passenger trains. See "Transportation" for short trips from Dallas. To reach visitor information, call 571-1300 between 9 and 5. A tunnel connects

Union Station to the Hyatt Regency Hotel and the 50-story Reunion Tower.

———— HISTORIC FARMERS BRANCH ————

FARMERS BRANCH HISTORICAL PARK
2540 Farmers Branch Lane
Farmers Branch, Texas 75234 • 972/406-0184

Farmers Branch Historical Park is the site of the oldest rock structure on its original foundation in Dallas County. This home once belonged to one of Dallas County's first doctors, Samuel Gilbert, and is furnished and open for tours. Within this 22-acre park are a church, original FB train depot, the home of William Dodson who was the first mayor of Farmers Branch, an 1856 "dog trot" stone house, a single and a double crib barn, and an 1847 log house. The single crib barn has a blacksmith shop.

The park is located near the intersection of I-35 and I-635 on Farmers Branch Lane at Denton Drive. Christmas is a special event here with "Dickens in the Park," which includes bell choirs, carolers, and horse and buggy rides as well as the "Christmas Light Drive Through" on weekends and scheduled evenings. The buildings are handicapped accessible, and picnic tables are available. Winter hours are 9:30-6, Monday-Thursday; Saturday-Sunday, noon-6. During Daylight Savings time in summer the park is open until 8 P.M. It is closed Fridays and major holidays. Groups may take guided tours by appointment on Tuesdays and Thursdays. Admission is free to the grounds, but the buildings are locked except at tour times. Adults, $1; children and seniors, 50 cents.

Mustang Trail is a 9.37-mile historic sightseeing trail following city streets and beginning and ending at Farmers Branch Historical Park. For details, call 972/406-0184.

———— HISTORIC GARLAND ————

LANDMARK MUSEUM
4th Street and State
Garland, Texas 75040 • 972/205-2749

Located behind Garland City Hall in Heritage Park, the Landmark Museum is in a three-room Santa Fe railroad depot which houses many interesting artifacts dating from the late 1800s. Visitors may also look over a 1910 Santa Fe Pullman car and two homes (unfurnished) built at the turn of the century. Admission is free, and the depot is open from 8:30-12 and 1-4:30, Monday-Friday. Please call first for group tours.

———— HISTORIC GRAND PRAIRIE ————

A tour of historic Grand Prairie, which was named after the wide area of grasslands bordered on two sides by lines of timber, should include a look inside three historic homes. The **Goodwin Cabin** is an 1846 log cabin that was moved to its present location by being rolled on logs for a distance of two and one-half miles. The community contributed to the rail fence. The cabin is located at Cottonwood Park, which is at South Carrier Parkway and SW Third Street, and may be peeked into but is not open except for special events.

Another historic home, the **Copeland Home**, is the recently renovated 1904 home of a former physician that houses antiques of old Grand Prairie families and tools of a physician's office of that period. The **Bowles Home**, 700 Northeast 28th Street, is a dogtrot log cabin from 1845 that was covered with boarding and then siding. The siding has been removed and the boarding recently repainted. Funds are needed to remove the boarding and restore it as a log cabin. Another small building nearby is called the Scout Hut because it may be rented for meetings.

The Copeland and Bowles homes may be seen by calling the Grand Prairie Parks and Recreation Department at 972/237-8100. If you would like a docent to lead a tour, call the Grand Prairie

Historical Commission or the Grand Prairie Historical Organization. Also, you might drive by City Hall Plaza for a look at the replica of the Liberty Bell, which was hung there during the Bicentennial. For further information about Grand Prairie, contact Visitor Information at 972/263-9588.

Grand Prairie Western Days celebrate the Old West with a parade, rodeo, county fair, and more family fun.

—————— **HISTORIC GRAPEVINE** ——————

The earliest settlers came to Grapevine by wagon train in 1844. Its name comes from the wild mustang grapes that once grew on the Grape Vine Prairie which is now the location of D/FW Airport. Grapevine has seventy-five historic homes and buildings dating from 1865, and the Visitor's Bureau can provide visitors with a list of homes and addresses. **Liberty Park Plaza** includes the Visitor's Bureau and Torian Log Cabin. Another place of historical interest is **Heritage Center**, which has the Historical Museum in a depot, a railroad section farmer's home, and a tenant farmer's home. The museum is open from 9-5, Monday-Saturday, and 12-5 on Sunday. The Grapevine Opry is also nearby for a Saturday evening of family entertainment. Grapevine Heritage Festival is a celebration of Grapevine's heritage and is held the third weekend in May; Grapefest is held in September, and Whistlestop Christmas is the first two weekends in December.

The *Tarantula* train leaves from Heritage Center at 707 S. Main on its way to the Stockyards in Fort Worth. Call for hours.

Grapevine is in the midst of a continuing preservation effort downtown. Architexas is re-creating the 1891 **Wallis Hotel**, a drummers lodging on the south side of Liberty Plaza across Main from the Opry. Look on South Main by the funeral home for the glass-enclosed hearse which was horse-drawn around 1900. Check with the Visitor's Bureau for more information (1280 S. Main, Suite 103, Metro 817/481-0454).

─────── HISTORIC IRVING ───────

Designated a historical landmark, the restored and furnished **Heritage House Pioneer Home** located at 303 S. O'Connor is open on the first Sunday of each month from 3-5 or by appointment. One of their special events is a Valentine Tea on the Sunday closest to Valentine's Day. Admission is adults $1; children free. Tours are available by appointment, and the fee is adults $1; children 50 cents. The house is not accessible by wheelchair. Call 972/438-5775.

Details about historic trails in Irving are in the book *Irving: A Texas Odyssey*, and the trails map is the model for the mosaic tile map in the **DART Station** in the Downtown Heritage District on Rock Island at Main.

MCDONALD'S FRIENDLY RED CABOOSE
301 W. Irving Blvd.
Irving, Texas 75060 • 972/259-7881

Within three blocks of Heritage Park is an unusual McDonald's restaurant. On the walls and on the table tops inside is memorabilia about trains and Irving's early days. In addition to a playground that includes two "trees" with tables underneath, a small carousel, a burger tunnel, see-saws, slide, and burger tree house is the Mo.-Pacific Friendly Red Caboose which is used for birthday parties. The restored caboose has booths on both sides of a center aisle.

NATIONAL MUSEUM OF COMMUNICATION
6301 N. O'Connor, Building One
Irving, Texas 75039 • 972/869-FILM

Housed within the Dallas Communications Complex in Las Colinas, the National Museum of Communication is part of the tour of the Studios at Las Colinas.

The museum fascinates visitors with its collection of memorabilia such as the TV camera that filmed the shooting of Lee Harvey

Oswald, the movie camera of Charlie Chaplain, the Merganthaler Linotype machine, the first TV set in Texas, and Thomas Edison's microscope and phonographs. See "The Studios at Las Colinas" in Chapter One.

─────── HISTORIC LANCASTER ───────

Located about twelve miles south of Dallas, Lancaster's town square was platted in 1852, modeled by a settler named Bledsoe after his hometown of Lancaster, Kentucky. The visitors bureau can give you a brief walking tour map pointing out historical buildings as well as a driving tour map of historic Lancaster. The driving tour includes an MKT Railroad depot, the site of a Confederate gun factory, and the Lancaster Airport, which was home of the Ghost Squadron of the **DFW wing of the Confederate Air Force** from 1939-1945. World War II artifacts and airplanes include the Coursair, which was used in WW II in the Pacific and the L-5/OY1, which is painted in Marine livery and was used in Okinawa. The museum is open on Saturday from 8-5. Call 972/227-9119 for information. Admission is $1.00.

Favorite events include the Second Saturday ArtFair, Air Show, town square's Halloween Pumpkin Festival, and the Christmas parade and lighting of the square. For more information, contact the Lancaster Chamber of Commerce at 972/227-2579.

─────── HISTORIC MCKINNEY ───────

Both the county and town were named after a member of the Committee of Five who drafted the Texas Declaration of Independence, Collin McKinney. The town square, framed by Virginia, Tennessee, Louisiana, and Kentucky Streets, is dominated by the Old Collin County Courthouse (1876). After browsing at the antique stores along the square, a favorite place to eat is the **Pantry** on Louisiana, well known for its home cooking and fabulous pies. Just northeast of the square is the renovated **Old Post Office Museum** on East Virginia at Chestnut which houses memorabilia of Collin County and the world wars, such as an 1891 typewriter and a mill wheel. As you enter the museum, look up to the right at the 1934 triptych mural done by Frank Klepper of an 1862 Civil War scene in McKinney Town Square. The museum is open on Tuesday from 11 A.M.-5 P.M. and the first Saturday of each month from 10 A.M.-3 P.M. No admission fee is charged.

Favorite festivals include Mayfair, October's Collin County Fall Festival, Dickens of a Christmas, and Tour of Homes. The chamber of commerce has a walk/ride tour map available which points out historic sites, such as the Old Collin County Jail and the Heard Opera House. Contact the Chamber of Commerce at 972/542-0163.

West of McKinney is the **Collin County Youth Park and Farm Museum** located on 83 acres. This developing museum houses agricultural artifacts such as early tractors and other farm machinery. Acquisitions include a Boll Weevil machine, a windmill, and a 1936 International truck. In addition to the museum, the park has a show and a horse barn, home economics building, and **Myer's Woods,** which is 35 wooded acres with hiking trails. It's a favorite campsite for Scouts. The Collin County 4H hosts an annual chili cookoff here in February. The museum is open Monday-Friday 8-5 and on weekends by appointment. For directions, call 972/424-1460 Ext. 4792 or 972/548-4792.

While in McKinney, you may also want to visit the **Heard Museum** mentioned in "Places to Go" and the **Bolin Wildlife Museum** discussed earlier in this chapter. To reach McKinney, go north on Central Expressway (US 75). Exit 40 (Louisiana) will take you to the square.

─────── HISTORIC MESQUITE ───────

In Mesquite, the **Florence Ranch Homestead** operates as a home museum and community park. Donated by the Florence family, the homestead was built in 1891 and was surrounded by 160 acres. Today, it is located on five acres at 1424 Barnes Bridge Rd. Most of the furniture is circa 1891 or earlier. The grounds are the site of community meetings and festivals, and tours may be arranged by calling Historic Mesquite at 972/216-6468. The house is open on the second Saturday of each month from 10 A.M. to 1 P.M. Admission is free. The Lawrence House near downtown is being renovated and will be open for tours upon completion.

You may wish to stay in Mesquite for a performance at the **Mesquite Arts Center** located at 1527 N. Galloway. The facility includes a concert hall, art gallery, black box theatre, puppet theater, and courtyard.

——— HISTORIC PLANO ———

Traveling north on Central Expressway just past Richardson takes visitors to Plano. An exit east on 544, 15th Street, leads from pavement to a red brick road taking you back in time to historic Plano. **Historic downtown Plano** offers shops, tearooms, services, a theater, skate park, and restaurants. The Queen of Hearts Costume Shop at 15th and Avenue K is a favorite of all ages. The antique/craft mall on the north side of 15th houses interesting shops and a tearoom. Cobwebs Antique Mall and Tearoom is located just off 15th at Avenue J and 14th Street. On the first Friday evening in December, the downtown streets are closed, and downtown is transformed into a Dickens-style English village that includes costumed characters and entertainment.

Settled by farmers from Kentucky and Tennessee in the 1840s, Plano survived two fires that devastated the downtown area, the last one in 1897. Since 1979, thirteen structures have acquired recognition as historic landmarks, and the Chamber of Commerce can provide visitors with background and maps of both the downtown area and other points of historic interest. A favorite stop is Haggard Park on 15th at Avenue H, which has a gazebo, fountain, and the **Interurban Railway Station Museum** as well as picnic facilities.

The Texas Electric Railway Car once ran from Denison through Plano on its way to Waco, and it has been restored. The Railway Station Museum, which opened in February 1992, contains artifacts of the railroad and early Plano and pictures of area settlers.

Operated by Plano Parks and Recreation, it is free and open for the public on Saturday from 1-5. For more information or to arrange a tour, call 972/516-2117.

While in Plano, remember the **Heritage Farmstead** mentioned in "Places to Go." For more information, contact the Plano Chamber of Commerce at 972/424-7547.

——— HISTORIC RICHARDSON ———

In pre-Civil War days, this community was called Breckenridge, but this changed when a farmer gave free right-of-way to entice the railroad to come up from Dallas. The railroad accepted his offer, and the town was named after the railroad contractor, E.H. Richardson, in the 1870s.

The enjoyment of history in Richardson could begin with the **History of Aviation Collection** at the University of Texas at Dallas. Located on the third floor of the Eugene McDermott Library, its collection of more than 20,000 reference volumes and 250,000 aviation periodicals makes it comparable to the Smithsonian's National Air and Space Museum Library. These are primarily for research, but the collection also contains more than 800 model aircraft and other artifacts. A glider is also on display. UTD is located at 2601 North Floyd Rd. at Campbell, and the hours are Monday-Friday, 9-5. Call 972/883-2570.

Also housed in the McDermott Library is the **Wineburgh Philatelic Research Library** which offers more than 18,000 books and journals for stamp enthusiasts to peruse as well as changing stamp exhibits.

While in Richardson, remember the **Owens Spring Creek Farm**'s museum with its collection of artifacts from the turn of the century introduced in "Places to Go." Two favorite annual events are the Wildflower Festival and the Cottonwood Art Festival. Call the Richardson Chamber of Commerce with questions about historic Richardson and other area attractions at 972/234-4141.

——— HISTORIC ROCKWALL ———

Rockwall was named for an ancient stone wall running under the town. Some scientists believe it to be part of the Balcones Fault, but some of its characteristics lead others to speculate that it may have been built by a prehistoric civilization. A small replica of the wall is outside the courthouse in the middle of the downtown square.

While in Rockwall, relax at Lake Ray Hubbard on the *Texas Queen* paddle wheeler or shop at **Goliad Place**, a cluster of quaint cottages that houses Krackerjacks children's clothing store and The Cottage Bookstore which has a wide variety of children's books. Eloise's Gifts and Antiques has collectible gnomes, PenniBears, and more. The Goliad House Restaurant is open for hungry shoppers. The address is 722 South Goliad (FM 740), 2¼ miles north of I-30. Call 972/771-6371 for more information.

——— HISTORIC TERRELL ———

Located 35 miles east of Dallas on US 80, Terrell is another Texas town that grew up along the railroad. The attraction for the railroad was a large underground lake which would provide water for the trains. The town was established in 1873.

The history of the town is preserved in the artifacts housed in the **Terrell Heritage Museum** in the Carnegie Building at 207 North Francis Street. In addition to historical items, such as a 1912 Estey pipe organ and Texas-Midland Railroad memorabilia, there is also a No. 1 British Flying Training School Association display of newspaper and magazine clippings, WW II uniforms, navigation equipment, and a plaque given in gratitude for the kindness shown to trainees in the flight school. Terrell was home base for about 2,000 British cadets in flying training school from 1941-1945. Call the Chamber of Commerce for museum hours. Go east on US 80, take the Business US 80 exit, and turn north on North Francis Street to the museum.

Also in Terrell is another memorial to airborne personnel of WW II called the **Silent Wings Museum**. Located at the Terrell

Municipal Airport, Silent Wings honors the military glider pilots who flew aircraft, such as the restored Waco CG-4A combat glider which is the focal point of the museum. In the Video Theater are shown combat and training films, one of which is *Eight Missions of the World War II Glider Pilot: What They Did and How They Did It!* Explaining the roles of glider pilots, paratroopers, mechanics, and tow pilots are displays and dioramas using newspapers, magazines, and other original documents as well as memorabilia such as medals and weapons. This free exhibit is open from 10 A.M.-5 P.M. on Tuesday-Saturday and 12-5 P.M. on Sunday. From I-20, exit north on Texas 34. Turn right on Airport Rd. and go right onto Silent Wings Blvd. It is located at 909 Silent Wings Blvd. From Business 80 in Terrell, go south on Texas 34 (S. Virginia) and east on Airport Rd. Call 972/563-0402 or write Box 775, Terrell 75160. Memberships are available.

While in Terrell, visitors may also want to stop by the **Tanger Factory Outlet** located on I-20. A favorite festival is the April Heritage Jubilee. Call the Terrell Chamber of Commerce at 972/563-5703 for more information about Heritage Tours of Terrell, Texas, and a copy of the historic trail map.

TOURS OF THE WORKING WORLD

Just as children love to go to their dad's and mom's offices to see what kind of work they do, family or group tours of the working world outside of their immediate family expand their horizons and begin the process in their minds of selecting careers for themselves. Many of these tours satisfy natural curiosity about how products are made or how services are performed. Most of the businesses that conduct tours ask that families and groups call ahead for appointments and remember to cancel the appointments if they cannot come, and the very popular ones often require reservations months in advance. If there is a minimum number for a tour, a family can sometimes join in a larger group. One other delightful aspect of taking tours is that most of them are free! Tours listed in other locations in this guide are **The**

Ballpark in Arlington and **Legends of the Game Museum** and **The Studios at Las Colinas**.

Some businesses are reluctant to advertise tours to the public because they do not have staff to guide tours on a regular basis, but if they were approached individually, they might consider it. Many of the tours listed below are for children who are at least school age because they have longer attention spans and would understand more of what they see than would preschoolers. Suggestions for younger folks include local spots, such as a restaurant, post office, bank, veterinarian's office, hospital, police substation, fire department, grocery store, bakery, donut shop, pet store, dog groomer, pharmacy, and nurseries or florist shops.

MRS. BAIRD'S BAKERY
5230 E. Mockingbird at Central
Dallas, Texas 75205 • 526-7201

Motorists along Mockingbird can tell long before they see the familiar building that they are approaching Mrs. Baird's Bakery by the mouth-watering aroma of bread baking. Many area parents will tell you that this was a favorite tour when they were children. The tour includes the entire bread making process: mixing ingredients, baking, wrapping, and distributing. The tasty finale is a buttered slice of Mrs. Baird's bread.

Because of construction on Central Expressway, tours have been postponed. When tours resume, call a month or two in advance or even earlier for a summer tour. Groups should number between eight and twenty-five people, and children should be in the first grade or above. Families may join a group. Call for days and times. Mrs. Baird's in Fort Worth also gives tours. FREE.

CARTER BLOOD CARE CENTER
9000 Harry Hines
Dallas, Texas 75235 • 1-800-DONATE-4

Groups who tour the Carter Blood Care Center come to understand how vital it is for the public to donate blood because just one donor can help four patients. They see the donation process: giving blood; referencing and transfusing; separating it into red cells, platelets, and plasma; and shipping it. There is time for questions and discussion about career opportunities.

Usually tours are given by request for groups of ten to fifteen who are in the seventh grade or older. Larger groups may be divided into two groups. The tour takes about an hour, and reservations must be made in advance. FREE.

CHANNEL 8/WFAA-TV
606 Young Street
Dallas, Texas 75202 • 748-9631

Although it does not include live broadcasts, a tour of Channel 8 does take visitors through the familiar newsroom as the guide explains how assignments are made, through their three broadcasting studios, and into the control room.

The 30-minute tours scheduled during weekdays require two weeks notice. Groups should range from seven to fifteen people who are 10 years old or older. A family could not join in these tours. FREE.

CHILDREN'S MEDICAL CENTER
1935 Motor Street
Dallas, Texas 75235 • 640-6280

The two-story layout of tracks for the miniature trains that wind through tunnels and around mountains is always a favorite stop on a tour of Children's Medical Center. Children can watch the trains run from the first or second floor. Preschoolers on the tour go to Admitting where they get a visitor's pass and see medical instruments, such as a stethoscope. Then they go on to Radiology where they may see an X-ray and learn about the process of taking X-rays. Older children also visit a treatment room and surgery if available. No one under 16 is allowed on patient floors. A special discussion may be scheduled for students in the fourth grade or older about health care careers.

Call Glenda Burford at least two weeks in advance to schedule a tour. One tour is scheduled each weekday around 10 A.M. Tours are arranged through Children's Medical Center's Pathways Program, which is comprised of both child life specialists and volunteers. Group size may range from six to fifteen children, and the length of the tour is 30 minutes to one hour, depending on the ages of the visitors. FREE.

DALLAS CITY HALL
1500 Marilla
Dallas, Texas 75201 • 939-2701

Tours of the impressive Dallas City Hall begin on the first floor and continue up to the sixth floor in City Council chambers. They include a peek in the mayor's office if it is not occupied. Tours usually last about 45 minutes. Your local councilman could take you on a tour. There are tables on the outside Plaza, and a cafeteria on the seventh floor. See the section on "History and Politics" for more about City Hall. FREE.

DALLAS/FT. WORTH
INTERNATIONAL AIRPORT
P.O. Drawer DFW
D/FW Airport, Texas 75261 • 972/574-8083, 972/574-8888

A tour of the second most active airport in the world allows guests to see the inside operations, ride on the air trans system, and tour the facilities. Make reservations at least four to six weeks in advance for groups no larger than thirty-five people. The tours, which last from 1½ to 2 hours, are conducted Monday-Friday at 9:30 A.M. and 1 P.M. for ages 5 and older. Families may join a group. Admission is FREE, but there is a $3 parking fee. D/FW is located between Dallas and Ft. Worth, north of Hwy. 183 on the western edge of Irving. When making a tour appointment, the guide will help with directions.

THE DALLAS MORNING NEWS
Communications Center
P.O. Box 655237
Dallas, Texas 75265 • 977-7069

The *Dallas Morning News* offers tours of the Downtown and North Plants for children 10 years old (5th grade) and older. The Downtown Plant tour is for groups of twenty or less and the Plano North Plant tour for groups numbering up to twenty-five. It may be possible to split and stagger larger groups into a double tour. The free tour needs to be reserved at least three weeks in advance, and hours are between 9 and 3 on Monday-Friday.

DALLAS PUBLIC LIBRARY
1515 Young Street
Dallas, Texas 75201

The best place for information about the programs of the Dallas Public Library is in the monthly *Almanac* published by the library. The downtown J. Erik Jonsson Central Library and all branches are listed, and announcements about special tours, exhibits, and educational classes are made.

Tours of the downtown Children's Center for groups of children in kindergarten through sixth grade may be arranged by calling 670-1671, and tours of the Central Library for adults and students may be arranged by calling 670-1789.

User Education Classes for students in grades seven through twelve and classes for adult and children's special interest groups may be scheduled by calling the User Education Librarian at 670-1712. Adult classes, such as "Learn to Use Your Library" and "A Guide to Business and Technology," will be listed in the *Almanac*. FREE.

DALLAS THEATER CENTER
3636 Turtle Creek Boulevard
Dallas, Texas 75219 • 526-8210

The behind-the-scenes tour of the Dallas Theater Center (Kalita Humphreys Theater) is led by volunteers of the Guild. They explain the history of the theater and its famous architect, Frank Lloyd Wright. Very casual clothes and flat shoes are recommended for this tour that takes visitors into the theater if there is no play or rehearsal, behind the stage, and into the Lay and Wynne Studios, which are now used for evening and weekend classes for the Teen/Children's Theater. On weekdays they go into the new Heldt Building and see the rehearsal hall, if it is not being used, and the costume shop. Here, there are pictures of the theater being built. Because of the stairs and narrow aisles backstage, much of the tour is not wheelchair accessible.

The theater is located on beautiful Turtle Creek, and there are two picnic tables on the grounds if the group wants to have a picnic, or they could bring blankets and have a picnic down by the creek.

Tours: A family or group (usually not more than twenty-four) may call in advance for a tour appointment with a volunteer guide any day. If a volunteer is available, a tour may be scheduled on the weekend, but the Heldt Building will probably not be open. FREE.

DALLAS WATER UTILITIES
1500 Marilla, Rm. 5AS
Dallas, Texas 75201

Dallas Water Utilities offers fascinating tours of its three water purification and two wastewater treatment plants. Water purification plant tours show how water is made clean and safe before it reaches the tap. Wastewater treatment plant tours show the complex process used to protect the environment by cleaning wastewater before it is released. A limited tour for fourth to sixth grade students includes a slide or video presentation about the process and a glimpse at part of the process. A full tour for seventh grade and older walks through the entire process. The ages are restricted for safety reasons.

Tours: The one- to two-hour tour should be scheduled at least two weeks in advance, and the tours are limited to under thirty people. There must be at least one adult for every ten children, and children must be in at least the fourth grade. Tours begin between 9-9:30 A.M. and between 1-1:30 P.M. FREE. Below are the plant names, locations, and phone numbers:

**East Side Water
Purification Plant**
Larkin and Long Creek Roads
(Sunnyvale) Mapsco 50A-N
670-0917 or 670-0900

**Elm Fork Water
Purification Plant**
1500 Whitlock Lane
(Carrollton) Mapsco 2-T
972/389-6012 or 972/389-6002

**Bachman Water
Purification Plant**
2605 Shorecrest
(Dallas) Mapsco 33-G
670-6587 or 670-6593

**Southside Wastewater
Treatment Plant**
10011 Log Cabin Road
(Dallas) Mapsco 79-H
670-0445 or 670-0400

**Central Wastewater
Treatment Plant**
1020 Sargent Road
(Dallas) Mapsco 55-H
670-7433 or 670-7411

Two popular annual events sponsored by Dallas Water Utilities are the May Pumphouse 5K run celebrating Drinking Water Week and a June tour of exceptional xeriscape gardens in the area. Both originate at the White Rock Lake Pump Station, 2900 White Rock Road, which has a xeriscape demonstration garden. The Pumphouse 5K includes mini-seminars and free children's activities.

DR PEPPER BOTTLING COMPANY
2304 Century Center Blvd.
Irving, Texas 75062 • 972/579-1024

Dr Pepper originated in Texas, and Waco even has a Dr Pepper museum. The tour of the plant near Texas Stadium begins in the lobby and goes throughout the plant, so visitors can see how the drink is made and put into bottles and cans. A video that explains operations is shown in the tour room, and each guest receives a free Dr Pepper and a pencil.

Tours: This 45-minute tour is best for ages 6 and older, and reservations should be made about six months in advance if planning a summer tour. Tours begin at 10 A.M. on Wednesday mornings and are limited to under forty. A family may join a tour if there is space available. FREE.

GENERAL MOTORS ASSEMBLY PLANT
2525 E. Abram
Arlington, Texas 76010 • 817/652-2200

Visitors to the General Motors Assembly Plant see how an automobile is mass produced from assembly in the body shop to the final product. Tours enter at the road test area and proceed on to see stacks of fenders, trunk carpet, and hundreds of other parts being attached to painted and unpainted frames moving on conveyers. The only thing visitors don't see is painting. The GM plant at Arlington can produce about 35 cars per hour and 400 in one day. Those living in the metroplex area hope that this plant making American cars continues to operate, but it is a good idea to call ahead to see if the plant is currently in production. The **Antique Sewing Machine Museum** and the **Fielder Museum** are also on Abram St.

Public tours are held Monday-Friday at 11:30 A.M., and reservations should be made for groups of ten or more. Groups should be no larger than fifty people, and children should be in at least the first grade to get the most benefit from the tour, which lasts one hour and fifteen minutes and involves lots of walking. From

Abram (at Highway 360), go to the southeast corner of the building through Gate 6 and parking is on the right. FREE.

KLIF/KPLX RADIO STATION
3500 Maple Street, Suite 1600
Dallas, Texas 75219 • 526-2400

The walk through the station for a behind-the-scenes look at the production of radio shows is limited to sixth grade and older or college students who have an interest in communications. However, each Christmas the station participates in a toy drive for children, and families who bring donations are allowed to look around.

The 30-minute tours are given Monday-Friday between 9 and 5 with an appointment made at least one week in advance. FREE.

MCKINNEY AVENUE TROLLEY
3153 Oak Grove Avenue
Dallas, Texas 75204 • 855-0006

The historic McKinney Avenue Trolley Barn tour is given by volunteers who explain the history of electric transit and basically what makes the trolley run. Visitors usually then take a round trip run along McKinney Avenue through the Arts District to the Dallas Museum of Art and back to the barn. Sometimes this is included in a birthday party tour in which a trolley is rented and decorated for the birthday person and from six to thirty-two of his friends. There is a shop at the barn that has souvenir T-shirts, visors, caps, and bumper stickers.

Anyone who comes in is welcome to a tour. Group tours should be scheduled in advance, and the barn is open from 10 A.M.-10 P.M. weekdays, and Friday and Saturday until midnight. Call for hours and days of trolley operation. The trolleys are heated in winter, and a round trip takes about 30 minutes.

Barn tours are FREE, but there is a small fee for the trolley ride: adults, $1.50; children under 12, $1; seniors, 50 cents.

MORTON H. MEYERSON SYMPHONY CENTER
2301 Flora Suite 100
Dallas, Texas 75201 • 670-3600

Tours of the majestic symphony center, located near the Dallas Museum of Art and the Arts District Theater, include a close look at the concert hall, Betty B. Marcus Park with its water wall fountain, and the Wall of Honor.

Public tours are held at 1 P.M. on selected Mondays, Wednesdays, Fridays, and Saturdays, and they last about one hour. Reservations are not required. Both families and school groups are welcome. Public demonstrations of the Lay Family Concert are given once a month. Private tours should be scheduled at least six weeks in advance for groups of fifteen or more who are in the sixth grade or older. Call 670-3600. FREE.

TEXAS STADIUM
2401 E. Airport Freeway
Irving, Texas 75062 • 972/554-1804

Best known as the football field for the Dallas Cowboys, Texas Stadium is also the site of concerts and other exciting events. It has 63,855 covered seats and 296 sky boxes. Tours usually begin at the Pro Shop at Gate 8 below Jerry Jones' suite for some information about the stadium and then go out onto the field if it is not being used for an event. A guest may bring a football to throw around and a camera to record his day on the turf. Visitors then go up the ramp into the locker room and take the coaches' elevator to the second floor to see a suite and the press box. Then the glass elevator takes them back to Gate 8 and the Pro Shop. "Walk-up tours" are given for the public on Monday-Saturday every hour from 10 to 3, Sunday each hour from 11 to 3, and they take about an hour. Call for the schedule of private tours. One-hour birthday party tours of the field and locker room may be arranged for children.

Admission for the public tours is adults, $5; children 6-12 and seniors, $3; ages 5 and under, free. Private tours are $75 for the first twenty-five people and $3 for each additional person.

TEXAS UTILITIES ELECTRIC COMPANY
Power Plant Tours/TU Services
2001 Bryan Tower, Room 1680
Dallas, Texas 75201 • 812-5709

Texas Utilities Electric Company offers tours of the gas plants in the Dallas area and the lignite plants in Mt. Pleasant, Henderson, and Fairfield. The tours are generally given for civic groups and education groups from fifth grade on. Groups who tour the gas plants see a video about operations, visit the control room, and look around the plant. The itinerary of the tour of the lignite plants depends on the age of the visitors. They see mining operations, ranging from pre-mining to reclamation efforts, drive around the plant, and might go inside for a closer look.

Appointments are made on weekdays at least two weeks in advance. Tours of the gas plants last about an hour, and those of the lignite plants may last two to three hours. Call to arrange a tour at the site closest to you. FREE.

UNDERGROUND DALLAS/DOWNTOWN

Although children will not find any Ninja Turtles in these underground tunnel networks, they will still enjoy the adventure of seeing how the buildings downtown are connected and eating at one of the many restaurants provided for the working world. The Dallas Convention and Visitors Bureau (571-1000) may be able to help with the three main areas of connected buildings.

One good place to start would be Thanksgiving Tower, which is right by Thanks-Giving Square on Pacific, and park underground (fee). Take the elevators to the underground. Various shops and restaurants are open during business hours. Children might enjoy lunch at one of the restaurants and a cookie from Mrs. Field's. Visitors could travel on to the NationsBank building and to One Dallas Center. Enter the tunnel system again at Lincoln Plaza at 500 N. Akard where the steps down are by cascading water wall fountains. This tunnel passes Dakota's restaurant and the Ross Garage before turning right to the Fairmont Hotel where your group might go up for a look around. Back into the tunnel again will take you to Fountain Place. Children will love this, especially on a warm day. Tiered fountains surround shaded tables, and trees rise from the middle of the pools. A favorite fountain is the one with dancing waters that shoot one- to six-foot sprays up from the ground. Watch out because the temptation to run through it may be too great to resist.

Families could combine a weekday trip to see a play at El Centro with a trek through the tunnels that begin at NationsBank Plaza on Lamar at Elm and go on to One Main Place, Elm Place, Renaissance Tower, and the Holiday Inn Building at Griffin and Elm. You will also be near the Kennedy Memorial Plaza and the West End. FREE.

TRANSPORTATION

The primary means of transportation in Dallas for many years has been the family car. However, with rising costs, overcrowded freeways, fitness awareness, and conservation efforts, other forms of transportation, ranging from bicycles to rail lines, are gaining in popularity. Some are here as pleasant reminders of bygone days, such as trolleys, paddle wheelers, steam engine driven trains, and surrey rides. Children love vehicles, beginning with the ones that they power with their feet moving along the sidewalk. They like to ring the bells on the boats and honk the horns on the motorcycles at the amusement parks. A wide variety of transportation is available around Dallas, from a short bus ride to a hot air balloon ride. Some conversation about what causes the vehicle to "go" makes any trip as educational as it is entertaining.

Several museums in the area are dedicated to preserving and informing the public about various types of transportation. These museums are listed in this guide as the **Age of Steam Museum** at Fair Park, **Cavanaugh Museum**, **Ennis Railway Museum**, **Confederate Air Force Museum**, **Silent Wings Museum**, **C.R. Smith Museum**, and **Pate Museum of Transportation**.

——— AIRPLANES, SHUTTLES, ——— HELICOPTERS, AND HOT AIR BALLOONS

Even though most of today's parents have grown up accepting airplanes as part of daily life, most of us will still pause to watch an airplane take off and ascend to unknown destinations. Children love to spot airplanes and helicopters and are intrigued by all the contraptions at an airport, from the revolving luggage conveyors to moving sidewalks. A leisurely trip to the airport when no one is in a hurry to check luggage and catch a flight is an inexpensive and entertaining way to introduce a child to aviation.

Most commercial flights in Dallas leave from D/FW or Love Field, but some of the smaller airports will allow tours. Shuttle services are available for families who do not wish to drive in airport traffic or leave cars at the airport. Those who would like a simulation of flying a jet fighter should look under "More Amusements" in this chapter for Arlington's **Air Combat School**.

Helicopters are often kept at the smaller airports, and some owners offer rides to the public for a bird's-eye view of landmarks and homes. Expensive, but fantastic, **hot air balloon rides** are also available. Two favorite annual events are the hot air balloon festivals in Mesquite and Plano. Museums devoted to the history of aviation are located at the University of Texas at Dallas, Love Field, D/FW, Addison Airport, Terrell Airport, and Lancaster Airport. See "History and Politics" for more details.

The first two discussed below are the major airports in Dallas, but the ones listed after also contribute a great deal to the community and would be worth a visit.

DALLAS/FT. WORTH INTERNATIONAL AIRPORT
P.O. Drawer DFW
D/FW Airport, Texas 75261 • 972/574-8888

Dallas/Ft. Worth International Airport, aptly named for its location between the two cities, offers 2,000 flights daily to almost 200 destinations. It has numerous stores and restaurants and lots of activity for children to watch. At Founder's Plaza, 30th and Carbon, is an observation deck with picnic benches and control tower conversation. See "Tours of the Working World" in this chapter for more information.

The **C.R. Smith Museum**, which has a restored DC-3 at its entrance, is located adjacent to the AA Flight Academy at the intersection of Highway 360 and FAA Road, southwest of D/FW Airport in Fort Worth. The American Airlines museum shows visitors what is needed to conduct a worldwide aviation system through interactive displays, hands-on exhibits, and video presentations on a thirty-foot tall screen. Summer day camps are available for children entering the fourth through seventh grades. Call metro 817/967-0997. Group tours are available, and admission is FREE. Hours are Tuesday-Saturday, 10-6, and Sunday, noon-5. Call metro 817/967-1560.

DALLAS LOVE FIELD AIRPORT
Cedar Springs at Mockingbird Lane
Dallas, Texas 75235 • 670-6080

Designated as a World War I training base in 1917, Love Field began its first passenger service in 1927 and has been an integral part of aviation in Dallas ever since. Until D/FW was built, it was the major airport in Dallas. It still serves airlines such as Southwest and has food service and **Frontiers of Flight Museum**. Look under "Places to Go" for more information about the museum.

ADDISON AIRPORT
4505 Claire Chennault Drive
Addison, Texas 75248 • 972/380-8800

Addison Airport is now the home for the **Cavanaugh Flight Museum**. Aviation history from World Wars I and II and Korea is brought to life through refurbished aircraft such as the Fokker D VII, P-51 Mustang, and MIG 15. Housed in airplane hangers, these planes are polished, kept in flyable condition, and used in air shows. An aviation art gallery and gift shop are at the entrance. Museum hours are 9-5 Monday-Saturday, and 11-5 Sunday. Admission is $5.50, adults; $2.75, children ages 6-12.

Alliance Airport
2250 Alliance Blvd.
Ft. Worth, Texas 76177 • Metro 817/890-1000

Arlington Municipal Airport
5000 S. Collins
Arlington, Texas • 817/465-2615

Lancaster Airport
730 Ferris Road/P.O. Box 551
Lancaster, Texas 75146 • 972/227-9119

Mesquite Airport
1130 Hudson Airport Boulevard
Mesquite, Texas 75149 • 972/222-8536

Red Bird Airport
5303 Challenger
Dallas, Texas 75237 • 670-7612

A shuttle service that serves both D/FW and Love Field is SuperShuttle Dallas/Ft. Worth (Metro 817/329-2000). The following are businesses that offer helicopter and hot air balloon rides. Children who ride hot air balloons should be at least 10 years old.

Airventure Balloonport
1791 Millard, Suite D
Plano, Texas 75074 • 972/422-0212

Zebra Air Helicopters
Dallas Love Field
7515 Lemmon, Bldg. J
Dallas, Texas 75235 • 358-7200

——— BUSES, TRAINS, AND TROLLEYS ———

While DART buses are taking families downtown and McKinney Avenue trolleys are taking them uptown, AMTRAK trains and Greyhound buses are taking them out of town. Any of these modes of transportation are going to delight and entertain children. Why not leave the car at home and hop on a bus downtown to see a Dallas Children's Theater play at El Centro's theater? You might discover the Underground and Fountain Place while downtown. You could park the family car at the trolley barn on Oak Grove and ride the trolley to the Dallas Museum of Art or Meyerson Symphony Center for a performance or tour and then eat at one of the fantastic restaurants on McKinney Avenue before riding back to the trolley barn. You could catch the DART rail line and ride to the West End or Reunion Arena.

Both native Dallasites and out-of-towners would enjoy sightseeing excursions around Dallas on commercial tour buses because often we never take the time to see the sights closest to home and know little of the history of our own hometown. For families who would like to vacation and leave the driving to someone else, Greyhound would be happy to escort you to a number of exciting cities in and out of Texas.

If your family has been to the Age of Steam Museum at Fair Park and the children really want to experience travel by rail, plan to catch AMTRAK at Union Station going either east or west daily or drive down to Palestine to ride the Texas State Railroad round trip. Look under "Day Trips" for passenger trains in Ft. Worth and Palestine. Six Flags Over Texas has a passenger train that takes visitors around the perimeter of the park. Visitors to Ft. Worth enjoy rides on the *Tarantula* train that boards at the Stockyards.

AMTRAK
Union Station - 400 S. Houston
Dallas, Texas 75202 • 653-1101, 800/872-7245

ALL ABOARD! Amtrak's passenger train service departs from historic Union Station to Ft. Worth and Cleburne going west and to Longview going east in the afternoon daily. The only drawback is that passengers cannot go round trip in one day. The earliest return trip is the next afternoon. The price is $9 one way to Ft. Worth and $28 to Longview, and two children per adult may pay half fare each if between the ages of 2 and 15. Call the 800 number for information about other destinations and a copy of their magazine, *Amtrak's America*.

DALLAS AREA RAPID TRANSIT

The wheels on the DART buses go all over Big D and around thirteen other communities providing inexpensive transportation and saving an estimated 24 million pounds of carbon monoxide from polluting our blue skies. Students, RideShare commuters, senior citizens, and mobility-impaired passengers take advantage of DART's special programs. Cash fares are adults, $1; students, disabled, and children (ages 5-11), 50 cents; and seniors (65 or over), 50 cents. Transfers are free. Call 979-1111 for information about routes, schedules, and fares. Weekend service is limited.

The DART rail Red line makes stops from Park Lane near Northpark and passes the West End, Union Station, Reunion Arena, and the Zoo on its way to the end of the line at Westmoreland in Oak Cliff. The Blue line goes from Illinois through downtown to Pearl. Coming from South Irving, the commuter train called the Trinity Railway Express stops at Medical/Market Center and again at Union Station where riders can transfer to one of the other rail lines if they wish. Note the art at many of the stations. For more information, call DART at 979-1111.

DART offers Handiride buses, which have wheelchair lifts (828-6800), and special *DART Flyers*, which are buses to sporting events such as Dallas Cowboys games.

Presently, DART is carrying out its twenty-year plan to include both a light rail system and commuter rail service. DART also plans to expand the High Occupancy Vehicle (HOV) lanes and begin special transit "circulator" systems connecting heavily occupied centers.

DART offers guest speakers, audiovisual presentations, and special exhibits for groups and school classrooms. Call 749-2668 for information.

GRAY LINE TOURS
3615 Ross Avenue
Dallas, Texas 75204 • 630-1000

Gray Line buses are a familiar sight in most major cities as they take passengers to see a wide variety of attractions. The "Downtown Dallas" tour which includes the Kennedy Memorial, Old City Park, SMU, Highland Park, and Farmers Market is popular. Fees run from about $20 for adults and $10 for children.

GREYHOUND
205 S. Lamar
Dallas, Texas 75202 • 655-7082

There are some suburban stations with bus service, but most Greyhound buses leave from Lamar to destinations such as Austin, San Antonio, Ft. Worth, Houston, Corpus Christi, Shreveport, Wichita Falls, and Amarillo. It is recommended that passengers arrive at least 30 minutes early. Call for fares and schedule information.

McKINNEY AVENUE TROLLEY
3153 Oak Grove Avenue
Dallas, Texas 75204 • 855-5267

Clang! Clang! The bells of the McKinney Avenue trolleys ring as passengers stop at exciting sites and tempting restaurants, such as the Hard Rock Cafe, all along the 2.8-mile route, which begins near the Oak Grove trolley barn by McKinney Avenue and goes on by the Crescent and the Dallas Museum of Art. The trolleys, operated by volunteers, are beautifully restored and are heated in winter. Ninety-year-old "Rosie" is the oldest operating streetcar in North America. They may be rented for birthday parties. See "Tours of the Working World" for more information. Tickets are $1.50 for adults; 50 cents for seniors; and $1 for children. Call for the current schedule of operation.

YELLOW ROSE TOURING COMPANY
1331 Regal Row
Dallas, Texas 75247 • 637-0046

Even native Dallasites might like to lean back in a comfortable coach seat and let the Yellow Rose company do the driving to sites such as Ft. Worth Stockyards, Waxahachie Gingerbread Trails, and Granbury, especially Dad who misses a lot because he is keeping his eyes on the road so much or Mom because she would like to leave the planning and navigation to someone else.

———————— BOATS ————————

Texas is well known for its large lakes and water sports. Read under "Sports and Recreation" for areas to ski, fish, and sail and for boat and water bike rentals. One very tranquil boat ride is aboard the *Texas Queen* riverboat on Lake Ray Hubbard in Rockwall. The paddle wheeler usually casts off from the landing at Elgin B. Robertson Park just off I-30 at the Dalrock Road exit. Call 972/771-0039 for information about excursions and dinner cruises. The Mandalay Canal's **water taxis** in Las Colinas were mentioned in "Places to Go." Look under "Day Trips" for riverboat trips in Granbury and Ft. Worth.

A popular event in early January is the **Dallas Boat Show** held at the Dallas Convention Center at 650 S. Griffin for ten days. More than 200 colorful fishing boats, water-ski boats, and yachts drop anchor here for all to admire whether interested in buying or not. Children enjoy workshops on topics such as necessities for tackle boxes, and some giveaway items to the first 500 children in the door. Dropping a line into the trout tank is another favorite of young, hopeful anglers. Watch the newspapers for announcements. The summer boat show is also a favorite.

—— CARS, CAMPERS, AND CARRIAGES ——

For a child living in Dallas, getting a driver's license is the number one rite of passage. Most Texans are accustomed to driving their own cars and transporting large groups of children as evidenced by the soaring numbers of mini-vans and suburbans in the carpool lines, beside soccer fields, and on Scout field trips. Dallas does have several taxi and limousine services for visitors. Three taxi services are **Taxi Dallas** (823-3950), **Cowboy Cab** (428-0202), and **Yellow Cab Company** (Metro 817/318-8088). Limousines and mini-vans may be rented from **Carey Limousine** (638-4742) and **Valet Limousines, Inc.** (690-1040). A wide variety of cars may be rented from **Alamo Rent a Car** (1-800/327-9633), **Avis Rent a Car** (574-4130), and the **Hertz Corporation** (1-800/564-3131). Campers can be rented from **Capps Van and Car Rental** (630-6555 or 328-VANS). See the *Yellow Pages* for additional listings of all these vehicles.

Children who are fascinated with driving at an early age would enjoy cars designed with them in mind at amusement parks, such as the **antique cars** at **Six Flags**, the mini-virage race cars at **Malibu Speedzone**, and go-karts at **Go-Karts Plus** and **Celebration Station.**

Families can step back in time with a surrey ride through the West End. **Dallas Surrey Services** offers carriage rides during good weather. They also offer ponies for parties. Call 946-9911 for schedules and fares. Usually during Christmas, Highland Park Village (559-2740) and Old City Park (421-5141) offer tours of lights in carriages.

Each April, the Dallas Convention Center is filled with all kinds of new cars, ranging from sports cars and luxury sedans to cars of the future, in the **Dallas Auto Show.** Families enjoy radio personalities and exhibits that include car care products, car phones, and automobile memorabilia. Elementary school students participate in the exhibit of the Car of the Future in a display of their ideas of what cars will look like. The Auto Show lasts five days, and children 12 and under are free. Discount coupons are at car dealerships. For more information, call the New Car Dealers Association at 637-0531. Another very popular annual car show is held at the Automobile Building at the State Fair in October.

The **Dallas Grand Prix** is an exciting race usually held in spring or summer around Addison Airport, but the event may be moved to downtown Dallas. Watch the newspapers or call the visitor centers in Dallas and Addison for information.

STORYTELLING, LIBRARIES, AND BOOKSTORES

STORYTELLERS

Some people express fear that the magic of storytelling is disappearing with the onset of video games and a bumper crop of TV tater tots, but the art really is alive and well in many homes where parents still read to their children nightly, recite ageless nursery rhymes, and relate favorite tales heard in childhood from their parents and grandparents. Children love this tradition and the cozy, undivided attention of their parents.

Stories are woven weekly in area libraries as children's librarians sit before a semicircle of preschoolers and guide them through exciting tales. The rapt audiences cry for more.

Those who love folk humor and recounting stories have formed at least three guilds in the North Texas area. The **Dallas Storytelling Guild** meets each third Wednesday at 7:30 P.M. to share stories. In the fall, they sponsor "Tellabration," an evening concert of storytellers in which four or five members tell favorite stories. Occasionally, members present workshops, and they have a list of storytellers and the types of stories they like to tell if an individual or group would like to contact them. Storytelling is becoming popular at children's birthday parties. One storyteller weaves the children's names and words they have chosen into her story. Call Janice Giles, who works at a Dallas library, at 670-6445 or 972/720-9430, or Shelly Kneupper at 817/481-0924.

One very active storyteller is Elizabeth Ellis who tells stories for both adults and children at a wide variety of occasions. To reach Elizabeth Ellis, call 381-4676 or 800/989-4441/Box 2001205 and leave a message.

A storyteller who encourages natural toys and games, such as string games, is Gene Richardson. His personas include Jacob the Farmer and characters from the 1800s. He can be reached by calling 271-TELL. Monthly meetings of Dallas Storytellers are held at the Sequoia Bookstore, which specializes in Texas and Native American West literature (Preston and Royal).

A popular event for the last nine years is the **Texas Storytelling Festival** in March in which storytellers gather at Texas Women's University in Denton for a weekend of "folktales, fantasy, and music." Workshops for the storytellers are combined with storytelling sessions that the public may attend. At Friday evening's "Olio," participants tell stories to introduce themselves, and on Saturday afternoon a "Family Olio" and "Traditional Texas" tales are also open to the public. Some performances are interpreted for the deaf. For details, write the Tejas Storytelling Association, Box 2806, Denton, Texas 76202, or call 940/387-8336.

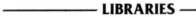

LIBRARIES

DALLAS PUBLIC LIBRARY

Twenty-one branches stem from the J. Erik Jonsson Central Library to form the Dallas Public Library system. Daily, children discover a love of reading from the story times, educational user classes (including free computer classes), reading clubs, and special events designed to inspire and encourage them. Patrons who live in Dallas may apply for a free library card, but those who live outside the city limits must purchase a fee card: $15 for 5 items checked out, $40 for 15 items, and $150 for unlimited check-out for one year. A fee of 25 cents per day is charged for overdue books. Most books and magazines may be checked out for three weeks and may be renewed. Videos, books and music on cassette tapes, large print books, ESL tapes, and paintings may be borrowed, also. To renew by phone, call 670-1735 on weekdays. To renew through dial-in access, call 670-1069. Free Internet access is available at all locations. The Dallas Public Library's home page is at http://central4lib.ci.dallas.tx.us/.

J. ERIK JONSSON CENTRAL LIBRARY
1515 Young Street at Ervay
Dallas, Texas 75201 • 670-1400

Families who make regular trips to the downtown library like the exhibits, usually displayed on the lobby level, in the 4th floor gallery, and in the 7th floor O'Hara exhibit hall, as well as the multitude of books from which they may choose their favorites. The best guide to special exhibits, programs, tours, and events is to pick up a copy of the *Almanac* published by the library each month. It is free at the downtown library or any of the branches. Families who are puzzled by a subject at home should call Information and Reference at 670-1700. An annual program greeted with enthusiasm each year is the **Summer Reading Club**. Certificates and rewards are given for the number of hours a child reads or is read to, and it is climaxed with a recognition party. Upper elementary students could combine this program with reading the year's new Bluebonnet book selections so he can vote for his favorite during the school year if his school library participates.

The imagination of children is stimulated by the 2nd floor Children's Center which opened in 1989 with its storytelling forest, a "village" to read in, and the Kahn Pavilion used for plays, puppet shows, films, and story times. The microcomputer area contains educational software, and the "Writing to Read" computer program has been implemented to help fight illiteracy in children. Microcomputer orientation classes are scheduled regularly to familiarize children with the computers. They cannot use the computers until they take the course, and preregistration is required. Preschool stories in both English and Spanish are offered regularly. Call 670-1671 for information about children's activities. See "Tours of the Working World" for information about special tours and user education classes for both children and adults.

Consider a family ride on a DART bus to the library for an outing. Be sure to browse in BookEnds, the Used Bookstore, for great bargains on books and magazines. The downtown library is open daily: Sunday 1-5; Monday-Thursday, 9-9; and Friday-Saturday, 9-5.

The following are the branches of the Dallas Public Library. Regularly there is discussion at City Hall about cutting back branch library services as a way to save money. If you enjoy the service of your branch library, please let your local representative know how vital its services are to you and your neighborhood. All branch libraries are closed on Sunday and on either Thursday or Friday. Contact each library for days and hours of operation.

Audelia Road	10045 Audelia Rd.	670-1350
Dallas West	2332 Singleton Blvd.	670-6445
Hampton-Illinois	2210 W. Illinois Ave.	670-7646
Highland Hills	3624 Simpson Stuart Rd.	670-0987
Lakewood	6121 Worth Street	670-1376
MLK Library	2922 Martin L. King Blvd.	670-0344
Park Forest	3421 Forest Lane	670-6333
Renner-Frankford	6400 Frankford Road	670-6100
Skyline	6006 Everglade Road	670-0938
Walnut Hill	9495 Marsh Lane	670-6376
Casa View	10355 Ferguson Road	670-8403
Forest Green	9015 Forest Lane	670-1335
Fretz Park	6990 Belt Line Road	670-6421
Lancaster-Kiest	3039 S. Lancaster Rd.	670-1952
North Oak Cliff	302 West Tenth Street	670-7555

Oak Lawn	4100 Cedar Springs Rd.	670-1359
Pleasant Grove	1125 South Buckner Blvd.	670-0965
Polk-Wisdom	7151 Library Lane	670-1947
Preston Royal	5626 Royal Lane	670-7128
Mountain Creek	6102 Mountain Crk. Pkwy.	670-6704
Skillman/Southwestern		670-6078

——— BOOKSTORES ———

Children love to read their favorite books over and over. Being able to write your own name and the date that you acquired the book is a special pleasure. Some of the most unique collections of books for children are not housed in a bookstore but in a museum gift shop specializing in science or nature.

Many of the retail chain bookstores house a wonderful collection of fiction and nonfiction books and tapes for children of all ages. These include **Taylors, B. Dalton, Bookstop, Waldenbooks, Barnes and Noble,** and **Half Price Books.** Bookstores with a Christian family emphasis are Deeper Life Bookstore, Tree of Life Bookstore, Family Bookstores, The Christian Bookstore: English and Spanish, and Joshua Christian Stores. Black Images Book Bazaar and Pan-African Connection bookstores carry books of cultural interest, and Imported Books offers books in Spanish and other foreign languages. Large discount warehouses like Sam's, or department and grocery stores such as Target, Wal-Mart, K-Mart, and Tom Thumb, often carry entertaining children's books and tapes at reasonable prices. The addresses and phone numbers for these bookstores are listed under "Book Dealers—Retail" in the *Yellow Pages*. On a visit to a neighboring junior college or university, stop by the college bookstore for a look at its children's books. For announcements about local literary events, look each Sunday in the *Dallas Morning News* "Books" section for the literary calendar. Many area colleges have literary festivals and special library exhibits.

Summer reading clubs are a traditional form of summer entertainment. These clubs often offer prizes for a designated number of books read or hours spent in reading or being read to. Look for these clubs at bookstores, public libraries, church libraries, and movie theaters.

Earful of Books is an audio book retailer that carries children's books on tape for rental. This is a real nerve saver on long car trips. They have two locations, 11810 Preston Rd. #150 (972/239-4028) and in Plano at 4909 W. Park Blvd. #107 next to Kroger (972/985-6447).

THE ENCHANTED FOREST BOOKS FOR CHILDREN
6333 E. Mockingbird at Abrams, Suite 231
Dallas, Texas 75214 • 827-2234, 800/BOOKS-56

Cheerful trees painted on the windows of this bookstore invite children into an enchanting 2,700 square foot "forest" of colorful books, toys, and projects. Visitors are directed to subject areas by clouds hanging from the sky-blue ceiling. A six-foot Paddington Bear presides over a stage area on which children are encouraged to play, and the walls behind the stage serve as a chalkboard for them to create artwork. Special guests and programs in addition to Camp Forest in the summer make this a very kid-friendly place to visit. They have a large middle grade section and a reference section. Regular hours are Monday-Friday 10-6, except Thursday when it stays open until 7:30 to allow working parents time to shop, and 10-5 on Saturday.

A LIKELY STORY
Preston at Park Blvd.
Plano, Texas 75093 • 972/964-8838

A Likely Story is a very "kid friendly" bookstore. A Brio Train area is available to give children something to do while parents browse. Children also like to have their favorite editions autographed by guest authors. In addition to a wide variety of books, there are educational toys, crafts, games, science and art projects, puppets and much more for infants through age 14. This bookstore also has free gift wrapping. A Likely Story is open Monday-Saturday 9:30-6, and Sunday noon-5.

ROOTABAGA BOOKERY
6717 Snider Plaza
Dallas, Texas 75205 • 361-8581, 800/888-1895

Just as children open the door of the Rootabaga Bookery, they will recognize that this is the bookstore just for them. Stuffed animals and puppets rest comfortably above shelves of colorful books, games, puzzles, toys, stamps, stationery, kites, flashcards, and paper dolls. Nonfiction books help children with ways to save the earth and ideas for science fair projects. The "New Baby" section has chubby baby books and parenting books. Another section specializes in Bible stories and another in foreign language books, such as *Jorge E Curioso*.

Several times each year a well-known author of children's books comes to the bookstore for a signing party. Rootabaga's newsletter brings news of exciting new books and signing parties to those on the mailing list. The bookstore is open Monday-Friday 10-5:30 and Saturday 10-5.

Afterwards, visit the fountain at Milton and Snider Plaza or get a treat from TCBY. Combine a visit to the bookstore with more shopping at Foot Loose Shoes for Kids and Kidswap, a resale shop. Balls, a hamburger place with a sports theme, might be just the place for lunch. Just across Hillcrest is SMU, and the Meadows Museum invites you to stop by for a look at new art exhibits.

SMALL ART MUSEUMS, GALLERIES, AND ART CENTERS

Artists agree that the earlier children are exposed to art, the more they will appreciate it throughout their lives. They are attracted to the colors and designs at a very early age, and a home with easy access to crayons and watercolors and art paper encourages creativity in budding artists.

Art is all around you in Dallas. It's hanging in the halls in school buildings, in the sculptures in the parks, in the center aisles at the malls, and in the gallery at City Hall. Sometimes a small art center or gallery is just the right speed for younger children who do not have long attention spans or like to walk long distances. All of the area community colleges and universities have small galleries that feature local artists, and personnel will be happy to mail information about the exhibits scheduled. Many city halls, libraries, community cultural centers, and museums display changing exhibits regularly, and local art groups regularly sponsor art exhibits and offer classes for both children and adults. Many art museums and community colleges hold summer art classes and day camps.

The Friday "Guide" of the *Dallas Morning News* lists museums and galleries and their current exhibits, and many of these also have mailing lists. See "Festivals and Special Events" for Artfest and Imagination Celebration, two popular family art festivals. Richardson's Cottonwood Art Festival is another favorite event.

ARLINGTON MUSEUM OF ART
201 West Main at Pecan
Arlington, Texas 76010 • 817/275-4600

Throughout the year, exciting permanent and changing exhibits focusing on contemporary, regional art are on display. On selected Saturday afternoons there are family art days and activities that are coordinated with the Arlington Public Library. Call about special events, summer day camps, gallery tours, and children's classes. Parking is available at nearby City Hall. *Hours:* Wednesday-Saturday, 10-5.

BATH HOUSE CULTURAL CENTER
521 E. Lawther Drive
Dallas, Texas 75218-0032 • 670-8749

Located on the east shore of White Rock Lake in northeast Dallas, the Bath House beach was a popular swimming area in the 1930s. Today, no swimming is allowed in the lake, and the Bath House has been converted into a cultural center which fosters the "growth, development, and quality of multicultural arts within the city of Dallas."

Part of the City of Dallas Office of Cultural Affairs, the Bath House includes a 105-seat theater, the Main and Hall Galleries, and several workshops. Plays, concerts, art exhibits, and workshops for both children and adults are regularly scheduled. Classes for children include printmaking and weaving, and student art exhibits are often displayed in the galleries. Write or call the center to be on their mailing list for advance notice of activities.

You might like to bring a picnic lunch and plan to spend some time on playground equipment at White Rock Lake while there. To reach the Bath House from North Buckner Blvd., turn west on Northcliff. Signs are there to guide you.

Hours: Office hours are Tuesday-Saturday, 10-6.

BIBLICAL ARTS CENTER
7500 Park Lane / P.O. Box 12727
Dallas, Texas 75225 • 691-4661

A feeling of stepping into Biblical times is evoked at the limestone entrance modeled after Paul's Gate in Damascus at the nondenominational Biblical Arts Center. Its focus is to help all people better understand the places, events, and people of the Bible through artwork and historical artifacts, theater, music, and film.

The "**Miracle at Pentecost**" mural, measuring 124 feet by 20 feet and featuring more than 200 characters from the Bible, is unveiled once each hour on the half hour, and a 30-minute light and sound show is presented based on Acts 2.

A life-sized replica of Christ's Garden Tomb at Calvary is featured in the atrium. Galleries display both permanent and changing exhibits. A gift shop carries religious books and artwork. Call or write to be added to the mailing list.

Admission is free to the galleries. Admission to "Miracle at Pentecost" is adults, $4; children ages 6-12, $2.50, 13-18, $3; and seniors ages 65 and older, $3.50. Group rates are available. The museum is located west of Northpark Center. Hours are Tuesday-Saturday, 10-5 except Thursday when they are open until 9, and Sunday, 1-5. Closed major holidays.

THE BLACK ACADEMY OF ARTS AND LETTERS, INC.
Dallas Convention Center Theater Complex
650 S. Griffin (at Canton and Akard)
Dallas, Texas 75202 • 743-2440

Dedicated to promoting and preserving the works of Black Americans, the Academy presents workshops, exhibitions, and seminars. It is located near City Hall. Call for a brochure of events and concerts. Hours: Monday-Friday, 9-5:30, and during events, the gallery stays open on weekends.

CRAFT GUILD OF DALLAS
14325 Proton
Dallas Texas 75244 • 972/490-0303

Classes for children and adults in fiber arts, book binding, and paper art, jewelry, ceramics, surface design, and other mediums are offered by the Craft Guild of Dallas. Fees vary with discounts available to members. A holiday craft fair is offered in December and children's camps in the summer.

CREATIVE ARTS CENTER/SCHOOL OF SCULPTURE
2360 Laughlin Drive
Dallas, Texas 75228 • 320-1275

The Creative Arts Center offers classes in mixed media for children ages 7-12. They participate in weaving, painting, stenciling, collage, pottery, and more. A wide variety of adult classes are scheduled, and discounts are given to members. The center is off Ferguson Rd. near I-30.

DALLAS VISUAL ARTS CENTER
2917 Swiss Avenue
Dallas, Texas 75204 • 821-2522

Dallas Visual Arts Center is a nonprofit agency that exists to provide community access to and education about the art and artists of Texas. Located in a 24,000-square-foot renovated warehouse in the historic Wilson Historic District, the Center provides year-round exhibitions, art classes, and a Resource Room of art-related periodicals and art organization materials. Information concerning the Center's latest exhibition may be found in the Center's newsletter, *Visual Exchange*, and the "Galleries and Art Shows" listing in the newspaper each Friday.

The Center offers several exhibition opportunities throughout the year. The Annual Membership Exhibition is open to all members of the Center. The Collectors Exhibition features the works of an artist selected by the Collectors and the Medici levels of the Center's membership. The Mosaics Exhibition Series focuses on Texas artists whose ethnicity is an essential element of their work. An annual juried competition, Critics Choice, is open to all Texas artists and in all media. Following a visit to the Center, you and your children might enjoy a picnic in the scenic Central Park Square and a stroll down Swiss Avenue along the row of Victorian and Queen Anne-influenced houses in the Wilson Historic District. Hours are Monday-Friday, 9:30-5 and Saturday, noon-4.

JESUIT DALLAS MUSEUM
12345 Inwood
Dallas, Texas 75244 • 972/387-8700

Housed in Jesuit College Preparatory School, the museum's collection includes 375 pieces by artists such as Henry Moore, Joan Miro, and Eduardo Chillida. Call for information about viewing the exhibit, and the school office will give you the name of a docent who can lead a tour. It is not open to just drop in.

J'S ART STUDIO
17618 Davenport, Suite 3
Dallas, Texas 75252 • 972/931-1933

Art classes for ages 4 through adults are offered at J's Art Studio. They use multimedia projects, which include painting, drawing, sculpture, pottery, and printmaking, as well as alternative approaches to art, such as collage and assemblage. Classes meet once each week beginning in mid-August, and summer camps are also offered. The studio is located between Campbell and Frankfort, east of Preston.

KID ART
3407 Milton Ave.
Dallas, Texas 75225 • 750-7118

Located in Snider Plaza, Kid Art offers art classes and summer camps for children.

LAKEWOOD ARTS ACADEMY
1911 Abrams Parkway
Dallas, Texas 75214 • 827-1222

Classes for ages 4 through adults are planned according to the age and needs of each student in a studio environment. Creative opportunities are offered in two- and three-dimensional art by founder Tammy Gore. They have added music education, the expressive arts, yoga, and a variety of art-related short courses for adults. Summer camps, some of which include field trips to locations such as the Arboretum, are also offered.

MEADOWS MUSEUM
Southern Methodist University
Bishop at Binkley Street
Dallas, Texas 75275 • 768-2516

Located in the Meadows School of the Arts, the Meadows Museum houses the most comprehensive collection of Spanish art in the United States, including sculpture, drawings, paintings, and prints dating from the 15th century. Free tours are scheduled by calling Anju Gill. School tours are given for groups of ten to forty-five on Monday, Tuesday, Thursday, and Friday, and advance notice of two weeks should be given. Call Partnership Booking Service at 823-7644 to schedule the school tour. Tours in Spanish are given upon request, and the artworks are identified in English and Spanish. A family could join a tour. Children also enjoy the sculpture garden outside the Meadows Building. A summer art program is offered for ages 5 to 14. Admission is free, but donations are appreciated. Memberships are available.

Hours: Monday, Tuesday, Friday, and Saturday, 10-5; Thursday, 10-8; Sunday 1-5; closed Wednesday.

Directions: From Mockingbird Lane, go north on Bishop into SMU. Signs for visitor parking instruct you to turn right on Binkley by Boaz Hall and left on Ownby to the lot. The museum is on the west side of Bishop.

YOUNG ARTIST
David Cantrell and Kristin Shauck, Directors
972/935-9712

For the past twenty years, Dorothy Pierce, Ph.D., has directed the Young Artist Program, the first of its kind in the region. Since its inception in the late '70s at SMU, the program has evolved and grown to become an independent nonprofit organization whose goal is to provide the best available visual arts instruction for the children of the Park Cities and the surrounding areas. Year-round classes provide age-appropriate instruction in the foundations and techniques of drawing, painting, printmaking, and sculpture.

Through exposure to the great masterpieces of art history in addition to personal art-making experience, children from ages 4-18 learn about different cultures and history as well as develop confidence of self-expression. Call for location of classes.

OUTDOOR SCULPTURE AND MURALS IN DALLAS

Visitors to downtown might want a copy of the Dallas Convention Center's guide to the thirty-two sculptures located there. They include some lifelike pieces, such as the elderly lady who is knitting while sitting on a park bench at Olive and Ross. Many other pieces located throughout the Dallas area are also catalogued. Call 746-6677 for details.

Other sections of the guide list metroplex outdoor sculpture, such as the garden at the Dallas Museum of Art, Connemara Conservancy, Dallas City Hall, the Pump House at White Rock Lake, the Dallas Zoo (tallest in Texas), the Natural History Museum, and Meadows Museum.

Northpark Center developer Raymond Nasher has promised to construct a two-acre sculpture garden on land across Harwood from the Dallas Museum of Art. The free public garden will be the setting for 30-40 sculptures at a time from his collection, which consists of more than 250 masterworks. Included in the selection for the garden will be Jean Dubuffet's *The Gossiper* and Rodin's *Eve*.

In the Quorum Business Center in Addison is a sculpture that is an **equinox marker**, which marks the equinox twice yearly when fall and spring begin. The sun shines through the metal arch and aligns with marks on a metal ball below it. John V. House's sculpture is located west of the tollway and south of Belt Line Road in a traffic circle at the Quorum.

Huge murals are being painted in downtown Dallas by artists from Eyecon Inc. Some are painted on the sides of parking garages and may take up a city block. Three locations and titles are *Mass Transit* at Griffin and Pacific, *Resources* at St. Paul and San Jacinto, and *The Storm* (12 stories high) at San Jacinto and Leonard.

TRUETT HOSPITAL/BAYLOR

On permanent display at Baylor's Truett Hospital are more than 86 casts of hands that are the work of orthopedic surgeon Dr. Adrian Flatt. Famous hands in the display are those of U.S. presidents, actors, athletes, writers, and more. The hands of Nolan Ryan hold a baseball.

DALLAS CONVENTION CENTER
650 S. Griffin
Dallas, Texas • 658-7000

The $9 million Pioneer Plaza includes a nineteenth-century "cattle drive" with a herd of 40 bronze longhorns and attending cowboys on horseback heading downhill to water. The historic Shawnee Trail ran through the area near today's Reunion Arena, and the sculptures celebrate it as well as the introduction of longhorn cattle to our land more than 500 years ago. This is a definite photo opportunity.

TRAMMEL CROW CENTER
2001 Ross Avenue at Olive
Dallas, Texas 75201 • 863-3000

Located near the Dallas Museum of Art downtown, the Trammel Crow Center includes two pavilions which house changing art exhibitions. Children especially like the sculptures that surround the building. Call for information about current exhibits or read the gallery listing in the Friday newspaper.

SHOPPING AND HOBBIES

SHOPPING

Shopping is such a favorite pastime in Dallas that the city is able to claim that there are more shopping centers per shopper than any other city in the United States. "Shop til ya drop" is more than a motto. However, this is accurate only for teenage mall dwellers on up. Most 5-year-olds would not place a trip to the mall as a top 10 activity, but there are usually some shops at the malls or centers that focus on the younger set and some fast food restaurants that are just their speed. Many shopping centers have fountains and displays with flags that catch the eye of little ones, especially during holiday seasons.

Check with the malls near you for a calendar of special events. Health fairs, children's art exhibits, puppet shows, petting zoos, Santa, and the Easter Bunny are often part of mall activities. The mall or a particular restaurant may offer breakfast and photos with the latter two.

Hobby shops are great places to spend time with your young shopper. Starting a collection at an early age makes a real adventure out of shopping as he tries to find a certain baseball card or she adds to her dollhouse.

One of the most entertaining family shopping days can be found at local flea markets and trade days, such as the one at Canton.

Listed below are only some of the metroplex area's malls and their shops and fast food restaurants that would appeal to children. Look under "Hobby" and "Toys" in the *Yellow Pages* for additional shops. Many unique stores for collectors are found in historic downtown areas, such as those in Dallas at the West End Marketplace. Near to most of the wonderful shops is sure to be a place to make the necessary stop for ice cream or other rejuvenating snack.

SHOPPING MALLS

COLLIN CREEK MALL
811 Central Expressway
Plano, Texas • 972/422-1070

The Disney Store
KayBee Toys
Tilt Arcade
Family Bookstore
Natural Wonders
Kinderfoto
Gallery of History
Gymboree
Gap Kids
Waldenbooks

NORTHPARK CENTER
Park Lane and Central
Dallas, Texas • 363-7441

The Disney Store
Gymboree
McDonald's
Mrs. Field's Cookies
The Nature Company
Gap Kids
Noah's Ark
B. Dalton Bookseller
Candy HQtrs.
Champs
FAO Schwartz Toys
General Cinema
Johnny Rockets Diner
Le Theatre de Marionette
The Museum Company

GALLERIA
I-635 at Dallas Parkway
Dallas, Texas • 972/702-7100

B. Dalton Bookseller
Ice Skating Center
McDonald's
Noah's Ark
TCBY Yogurt
Discovery!

RICHARDSON SQUARE MALL
501 S. Plano Road
Richardson • 972/783-0117

Barnes and Noble
Dillard's
Fun-N-Games Arcade
Oshmans

PRESTONWOOD TOWN CENTER
5301 Belt Line
Dallas, Texas • 972/980-4275

B. Dalton Bookseller
Burger King
Ice Skating Rink
Jerry's Perfect Pets
Kay-Bee Toys
Mrs. Field's Cookies
Oshmans

NORTHPARK CENTER

Outdoor Ice Skating-winter
Playhouse Parade in May
Rand McNally Map & Travel
Texas Kids Shoes
Visitor Center
Warner Bros. Studio Store

TANGER OUTLET MALL

I-20 and Highway 34, Exit 501 301 Tanger Dr.
Terrell, Texas • 972/524-6255

Levi's
Bass Company Store
OshKosh B'Gosh
Publisher's Warehouse
Reebok

TOWN EAST MALL

Town East Blvd. at LBJ Frwy.
Mesquite, Texas • 972/270-2363

B. Dalton Bookseller
Gymboree
Jerry's Perfect Pets
KayBee Toys
Disney Store
Glamour Shots for Kids
Wendy's Hamburgers
Aladdin's Castle Arcade
Tilt Arcade
Kinderfoto
Sanrio Surprise (Girls)
Waldenbooks
Family Bookstore
The Disney Store
Kid's Club Program

PRESTONWOOD (cont.)

Stride Rite Bootery
Waldenbooks

Farah
Planet Heroes Food Service
Big Dog Sportswear
Liz Claiborne
Leggs/Hanes/Bali
Nine West

VALLEY VIEW MALL

Preston Rd. at LBJ Frwy.
Dallas, Texas • 972/661-2424

Dallas Puppet Theater
B. Dalton Bookseller
Family Bookstore
Funny Pages
Waldenbooks
Joysticks Arcade
KayBee Toys
Disney Store
Jerry's Perfect Pets
McDonald's
Mrs. Field's Cookies
Cinnabon
Taco Bell
Sbarro
Champs

GRAPEVINE MILLS OUTLET CENTER
121 North and Grapevine Mills Pkwy.
972/724-4900
(150 outlet strores)

Rainforest Café ($$)	Gap
GameWorks Arcade	KayBee Toys
Penney's	Maternity Works
Baby Guess	Cinnabon
The Sports Authority	Dickey's Barbecue
Warner Brother's Studio Store	Books-A-Million

—— HOBBIES AND COLLECTIONS ——

In addition to the hobby and collection shops in the malls, some very interesting and helpful shops are located all around the city. A business that specializes in craft and hobby items but that also carries toys, party supplies, and a variety of other items is MJ Designs, which has several locations around town. Below are some more popular shops that have personnel who are very interested in your hobby or collection and have some genuine expertise to offer.

ART-A-RAMA
1531 Ave. K
Plano, Texas • 972/423-4554

CRAFTY KIDS
3115 W. Parker, Suite 545
Plano, Texas • 867-5818
(Plaster, paint, parties)

THE DOLL COLLECTION
6959 W. Arapaho at Hillcrest
Dallas, Texas • 972/458-7823
(Dolls, furniture, accessories)

BP'ERS CERAMICS
731 S. Sherman
Richardson • 972/705-9754

**COLLECTIBLE TRAINS
AND TOYS**
109 Medallion Center
Northwest Hwy. at Skillman
Dallas, Texas • 373-9469
(Trains and related items)

**HOBBY LOBBY
CREATIVE CENTERS**
Mesquite, Irving, Lewisville

FRIENDZE
Coit and Arapaho
Richardson, Texas
972/866-6770
(jewelry making)

HOBBY TOWN USA
11255 Garland Rd. at Jupiter
Dallas, Texas • 327-2372

MAC'S CERAMICS
2239 Gus Thomasson
Dallas, Texas • 324-5584
(Greenware, paint, firing)

NOT JUST DOLLS
Casa View Center
2447 Gus Thomasson
Dallas, Texas • 321-0412
(Dolls, bears, clothing)

PAINT YER POTTERY
17194 Preston and Campbell,
NE corner
Dallas, Texas • 972/248-0001

TANDY LEATHER CO.
127 Medallion Center
Dallas, Texas • 361-2718
2548 N. Belt Line
Irving, Texas • 972/258-6121

TEXAS R/C MODELERS
230 W. Parker Rd.
Plano, Texas • 972/422-5386

HOBBY HOUSE
4822 Bryan at Fitzhugh
Dallas, Texas • 821-2550
(Trains, planes, cars)

LET'S PLAY DOLLS!
Plano Rd. at Belt Line
Richardson, Texas
972/671-4119

THE MILITARIA
601 Business Pkwy.
Richardson, Texas
972/690-6666
(Model military figures)

PAINT 'N PARTY
7130 Campbell at Hillcrest
Dallas, Texas • 972/713-0086
(Plastercrafts, parties)

THE STAMP STORE
Main Post Office
I-30 and Sylvan
Dallas, Texas • 760-4490

THE ROCK BARRELL
13650 Floyd Rd.
Dallas, Texas • 231-4809
(beads, jewelry supplies)

TOY STORES AND LEARNING STORES

Most children are willing to take time out from whatever they are doing for a trip to the toy store. The aisles of **Toys R Us** are almost overwhelming with their array of games, dolls, skates, books, bicycles, school and party supplies, and other toys as well as many items for babies and preschoolers. Toys R Us and the companion clothing store **Kids R Us** have several locations around Dallas. Some of the other toy stores listed below are also not located in the malls and often carry popular toys as well as some challenging and educational toys, collectible items, and nature-related projects. Nature stores, museum gift shops, and bookstores listed earlier in this chapter often have some fascinating toys to help children learn more about the world around them.

CONSTRUCTIVE PLAYTHINGS
1927 E. Belt Line at Josey
Carrollton, Texas • 972/418-1860
(Toys, teacher supplies, catlg.)

KAYBEE TOYS
Arlington
Collin Creek Mall
Grapevine Mills
Town East Mall
Valley View Mall

LEARNING EXPRESS
6818 Snider Plaza
Dallas, Texas
696-4876

LAKESHORE LEARNING STORE
13846 Dallas Pkwy.
Dallas, Texas • 972/934-8866

TOYS UNIQUE
5600 W. Lovers Lane
Dallas, Texas • 956-8697

Second location:
3100 Independence
Plano, Texas • 985-0711

Third location:
11929 Preston at Forest
Dallas, Texas • 972/8697

FAO SCHWARTZ
Northpark Center
Dallas, Texas • 750-0300

FUNCOLAND
Multiple locations
(Previously played video games/equipmnt. at discount)

PARTY SUPPLIES

Sometimes nothing else will do for your child's birthday but the face of his or her favorite character on invitations and party plates. A wide assortment of paper goods, decorations, party favors, and invitations may be found at the area's stores devoted solely to helping you organize a fun and hassle-free party. **Discount Party Warehouse**, **Party City**, and **Paper Paper** have multiple locations around the city. Paper Paper also carries supplies for teachers. Two other favorite party suppliers are listed below.

PARTY BAZAAR
4435 W. Lovers Lane
Dallas, Texas • 528-4795

PARTY PLACE
Preston Center
Dallas, Texas • 696-4550

—— FLEA MARKETS AND TRADE DAYS ——

FIRST MONDAY TRADE DAYS
P.O. Box 245 Highway 19
Canton, Texas 75103 • 903/567-6556, 903/567-2991

The tradition of trading and swapping goods and animals began at the turn of the century in Canton around the courthouse in the square. Farmers and vendors would come on the first Monday when the court was in session. The popularity of the trade day outgrew its surroundings, so in 1965 it was moved to a location a little north of town that could accommodate the crowds and provide 100 acres for vendors. Be prepared for a great deal of walking. A new area is The Mountain with 32 acres in a theme park setting (903/567-5445).

Hours: Canton Trade Days are Thursday-Sunday before the first Monday of every month, 7 A.M. until dark, rain or shine. Some of the vendors are covered.

Directions: Take I-20E about 60 miles. Exit on Hwy. 19 or FM 859 and go one mile south.

TRADERS VILLAGE AND RV PARK
2602 Mayfield Road
Grand Prairie, Texas 75051 • 972/647-2331

More than 1,600 dealers set up shop in the 106-acre flea market every Saturday and Sunday. Traders Village also has great festival foods, kiddie rides, and arcade games. Special events include the Prairie Dog Chili Cookoff in April and the National Championship Indian Pow Wow on the weekend after Labor Day, as well as other family activities. *Hours:* 8 A.M. until dark. Admission is free, $2 parking fee. *Directions:* Traders Village is located just off Hwy. 360 on Mayfield, one mile north of I-20 or five miles south of I-30.

HOTEL HIATUS

If your family enjoys staying in hotels, letting someone else cook and make beds, lounging by the pool (or splashing wildly in it) but hates the long rides in the car that it often takes to reach vacation spots, try a weekend at one of our local hotels. Sometimes discount rates are available because the business folks have flown home and the rooms are empty and waiting. If it is winter, pick one with an indoor pool, such as the Embassy Suites Hotel-MarketCenter or the one by Dallas Love Field, both of which also have rooms with refrigerators, ranges, and two televisions. Others with indoor pools include the Colony Parke Hotel, the Grand Kempinski, Holiday Inn North Dallas, Sheraton Suites Market Center, and Crown Sterling Suites. Some even offer complimentary breakfast.

Some are within walking distance of major attractions, and others, like the Westin by the Galleria, are attached to shopping centers. The Galleria has an ice rink, movie theater, and wonderful shops, and the Crescent is on the trolley line to the Arts District. In Las Colinas, the Mandalay is on the canal that winds through a shopping area and by the famous Mustangs sculpture. Several times each year family festivals are held here. Not far away is the Las Colinas Equestrian Center and The Studios at Las Colinas.

Sunday brunch at the hotels is a real family treat. What appears to be acres of beautifully displayed breakfast/lunch dishes are bound to encourage even your pickiest eaters. Hotels with scrumptious Sunday brunch include Loew's Anatole, the Conservatory at Crescent Court, Doubletree Hotel at Campbell Center and at Lincoln Center, Ramada Renaissance Hotel, and Cafe Esplanade at Hyatt Regency Reunion. Watch the weekend newspapers around holidays for other special meals and surprise visits from characters like the Easter Bunny.

HYATT REGENCY AT REUNION
300 Reunion Boulevard
Dallas, Texas 75207-4498 • 651-1234

One of the favorite landmarks of the downtown skyline that children love to spot, especially at night, is the sight of the ball atop **Reunion Tower.** The multifaceted glass facade of the hotel reflects the growing downtown area and fantastic Texas sunsets. Children enjoy riding the glass-fronted elevator up fifty stories whether or not they are treated to lunch at **Antares**, the revolving restaurant with a panoramic view of the city. At night the dome "dances" in a computer-operated light show. Inside the hotel is an eighteen-story atrium, an interesting "mineral ball," and more glass elevators. Just outside the hotel are fountains cascading into a serene pool. Those staying at the Hyatt have access to the outdoor swimming pool, three tennis courts, jogging track, health club, and four restaurants.

Reunion Arena, which is also part of the complex, is home to the Dallas Mavericks, ice skating performances, concerts, circuses, and a variety of other entertainment. Reunion is so named because of its location as the site of an early settlement, so it is part of a historic district that includes **Union Station** next door. Union Station, once a thriving railway station, now is the site of restaurants, a DART rail stop, and Amtrak.

RESTAURANTS WITH MORE

Dallas has so many restaurants that a family could easily eat out every night without dining in the same restaurant twice. The "staple" foods for children, such as pizza, hamburgers, and fried chicken fingers, are readily available as well as Dallas' famous Tex-Mex and many other delicious ethnic foods. But some of the area restaurants don't just satisfy hunger; they also entertain with the addition of small rides, music, arcades, play areas, and costumed characters.

When you ask the very young where they would like to go for lunch, the first reaction is likely to be McDonald's, Braum's, or Burger King because of the soft-floored play areas with slides and other toys to play on, as well as little prizes to take home if you buy the child's meal. Some Burger Kings and McDonald's also have an indoor play park. However, as they grow older, they notice that in addition to these great restaurants, Dallas has many others designed with their entertainment in mind. They also are good places for birthday parties.

PIZZA AND MORE

CRYSTAL'S PIZZA
930 W. Airport Frwy.
Irving • 972/579-0441
(Arcade, video room)

MR. GATTI'S PIZZA
1305 Promenade Center
Coit at Belt Line
Richardson • 972/783-2222

CHUCK E. CHEESE'S PIZZA

Arlington	817/861-1561
Garland	972/681-1385
Irving	972/256-1600
Richardson	972/234-8778
Dallas	972/298-7973

HAMBURGERS, STEAKS, AND MORE

BALLS HAMBURGERS
4343 W. NW Hwy./Midway
Dallas • 352-2525

DAVE & BUSTER'S
10727 Composite
Dallas • 353-0620

3404 Rankin/Snider Plaza
Dallas • 373-1717
(Sports theme, TV,
six video games)

HARD ROCK CAFE
2601 McKinney Avenue
Dallas • 855-0007
(Rock memorabilia, loud
music, souvenir store)

TRAIL DUST STEAK HOUSE
10841 Composite
Dallas • 357-3862
21717 LBJ Fwy. at Military
Mesquite • 972/289-5457
(Casual family seating,
country music, long slide)

PLANET HOLLYWOOD
603 Munger Ave., Suite 105
West End Historical District
Dallas • 749-STAR
(movie memorabilia, large
dinosaur sculpture out front)

Walnut Hill at Central
Dallas • 361-5553
(Arcade)

MAGIC TIME MACHINE
5003 Belt Line
Addison • 972/980-1903
(Costumed waitpersons,
unique table settings)

WHITE ROCK YACHT CLUB
7530 East Grand at Gaston
Dallas • 328-FUNN
(Skeeball, basketball, three
video games, pool tables,
sand and water volleyball,
playground)

CLUBHOUSE GRILL
Corner of Preston and
Frankford
Plano • 972/267-1265
(soundproof game room for
kids, private room for parties)

COOK YOUR OWN

MELTING POT
4900 Belt Line
Addison • 972/960-7027

SIMPLY FONDUE
2108 Lower Greenville
Dallas • 827-8878
(older children cook chicken
dip fruit at table)

U.R. COOKS
Irving Market Centre
4023 W. Airport Fwy.
(Hwy. 183) at Cheyenne
Irving • 972/252-9700
(Select raw steak, chicken,
or fish; season and grill
it yourself; salad and
potato)

――――― **DINNER THEATER** ―――――

MEDIEVAL TIMES DINNER AND TOURNAMENT
2021 Stemmons at Market Center
Dallas • 761-1800

Return to the age of chivalry and knighthood at Medieval Times Dinner and Tournament. As you feast on a sumptuous four-course banquet, you will witness feats of skill and daring adventure. See the beautiful Andalusian stallions dance and the graceful falcon soar. Cheer as six brave knights compete in the Tournament Royale, a joust and combat to determine the true champion of the castle. Dinner in the 1,000-seat castle is $22-$34. Call for reservations or group discounts.

COMMUNITY COLLEGES

The Dallas County Community College District offers both credit and noncredit courses for adults, but it is also a place for children. Each college has a different program, but most offer a few classes during the school year and a wide variety of classes and day camps in the summer. The classes vary according to interest and availability of instructors. If the college has a drama department, there will probably be some plays for the family included, and some of them are free. Each campus also has literary and music festivals, art exhibits, guest lecturers, and sports events. Some campuses have mailing lists to which community members may be added by calling Student Programs or Continuing Education. If the college that you are interested in does not mail out, then stop by those offices and pick up their schedule of events periodically. Listed below are the colleges and an overview of some of their programs.

BROOKHAVEN
3939 Valley View Lane
Farmers Branch, Texas 75244 • 972/620-4600
Continuing Education: 972/620-4715, 972/620-4723
Student Programs: 972/620-4700

During the school year, Brookhaven offers three levels of Farsi and SAT preparation courses. Four weeks of "Free to Be" summer day camps are offered for ages 6-11, and activities include computer, ball sports, cooking, nature hikes, puppetry, mime, and water play. Each camp day is 8 A.M.-5 P.M. A Teen College is offered in the afternoon from 1-5, and a morning Computer Camp is provided for ages 11-15. Brookhaven also has a child development center.

CEDAR VALLEY
3030 N. Dallas Avenue
Lancaster, Texas 75134
Continuing Education: 972/372-8210
Student Activities: 972/372-8236

Cedar Valley has a wonderful variety of exciting and educational classes for children year round. Classes generally include cooking, reading, math, manners, gymnastics, piano, karate, off-campus horseback riding, ballet, and creative dance. Summer day camps are also offered, and they have a mailing list to keep the community aware of their activities.

EASTFIELD
3737 Motley
Mesquite, Texas 75150
Continuing Education: 972/324-7113
Student Programs: 972/324-7185

During the year Eastfield presents delightful plays that family members may attend, and children may come along with parents on some of the scheduled canoe trips. Courses offered during the year include reading and math improvement, drawing, guitar, piano, voice, modeling, swimming, and sign language. An exciting annual event promoting physical fitness is Kidsport Triathlon and Funfair held each September. Eastfield has a highly recommended child development center.

EL CENTRO
Main and Lamar
Dallas, Texas 75202 • 860-2037

Since El Centro is surrounded by busy downtown streets, it was too difficult for it to offer much in children's programming, but they do cosponsor the **Dallas Children's Theater** and provide one of their two theaters. To learn more about their classes and performances, call 978-0110. For information about El Centro's productions, call 860-2037.

MOUNTAIN VIEW
4849 W. Illinois Ave.
Dallas, Texas 75211
Continuing Education: 860-8612
Student Programs: 860-8680

A wonderful program of classes includes dance, piano, gymnastics, karate, fencing, and remedial math and reading as well as SAT preparation. The Theatre/Conservatory division presents a play for the children of the community during the fall. In the summer, classes are offered during the day and evening, and swimming lessons are offered for ages 6 months to adult. Week-long camps in aviation, creative writing, computer basics, soccer, and gymnastics add to summer fun.

NORTH LAKE
5001 N. MacArthur Blvd.
Irving, Texas 75038
Continuing Education: 972/273-3360

North Lake offers swimming lessons for adults and children throughout the year. Week-long summer camps and classes for ages 6-12 are also available.

RICHLAND COLLEGE
12800 Abrams Road
Dallas, Texas 75243
Continuing Education: 972/238-6144
Student Programs: 972/238-6130

Swimming and tennis lessons are part of summer fun. Richland has added an amphitheater on the campus, and the drama department usually shares production of a children's play with area theater programs each summer. The college also offers children's computer classes. Richland is sometimes the site of Richardson's annual Fourth of July celebration.

3. Performing Arts for Children

Although all of us are not blessed with a beautiful singing voice, an unfailing sense of rhythm, limber joints, and the ability to convincingly assume the personality of a character in a play, we are able to sit back at a performance and appreciate the talents of others and leave with the feeling that we are better for it whether the music is opera or opry and the play *Romeo and Juliet* or *Snow White*. Encouraging creative expression in children is an important part of parenting, and the arts in the Dallas area have numerous avenues to help parents introduce their children to many types of theater, music, and dance. Opportunities for children to attend stimulating classes and become performers themselves are available in all of the arts to help children develop skills and self-confidence. Performing arts festivals held throughout the year enable families to relax together and to be thoroughly entertained by live performances, far away from televisions and video games.

In the Friday "Guide" of the *Dallas Morning News*, notices are given of performances and festivals for families with children, and the Sunday issue includes a "Community Arts Calendar." Daily, performances are advertised in the "Arts and Entertainment" section. Their **ARTSLINE** number is **522-2659**. A recorded message gives the name, location, phone, price, and date of current productions.

If a parent is not sure if a performance is appropriate for his child, he should call the performing arts group and ask what ages would most enjoy the performance. Many arts organizations and performing arts centers have mailing lists that can keep you up-to-date on their schedules. Usually discounts are given for children and groups, and some performances are free. **Half-Price Tickets** offers unsold tickets at a discount for many performances (696-4253). It is located at Foley's in Preston Center and open from 12-3 Tuesday-Friday; for matinee performances, 10 A.M.-1 P.M. Saturday, and 11 A.M.-1 P.M. Sunday. The tickets are one-half of face price plus service charge.

A matinee is a good time to introduce younger children to classical music and dance because the atmosphere is more informal. Shorter performances are often presented at the Dallas Museum of Art on the weekends. Many of the performing arts groups have outreach programs that allow them to perform in schools, and some of the Dallas County Community Colleges and other area colleges include children's theater in their season. Listed below are some of the major performing arts centers in the area that include performances for families. Your chamber of commerce can give you the phone numbers of performing arts groups in your community.

Water Tower Theatre
15650 Addison at Mildred
Addison • 972/404-0228

ArtCentre Theatre
1028 E. 15th Street
Plano • 972/422-7460

The Crescent Theater
2215 Cedar Springs
Dallas • 978-0110

Dallas Theater Center
3636 Turtle Creek Blvd.
Dallas • 526-8210

Irving Arts Centre
3333 N. MacArthur
Irving • 972/252-ARTS,
972/258-0156

Meadows School of the Arts
SMU—Bishop and Binkley
Dallas • 768-2880

Arts District Theatre
2401 Flora
Dallas • 922-0427

Dallas Convention Center
650 S. Griffin
Dallas • 939-2700

**Garland Center for
the Performing Arts**
300 N. Fifth St.
Garland • 205-2780

Majestic Theatre
1925 Elm
Dallas • 880-0137

Meyerson Symphony Center
2301 Flora, Suite 300
Dallas • 871-4000

Reunion Arena
Sport Street
Dallas • 658-7068

Music Hall
Fair Park
Dallas • 565-1116

Park Cities Playhouse
6719 Snider Plaza
Dallas • 691-7469

Starplex Amphitheater
Fair Park
Dallas • 421-1111

Theatre Three
2800 Routh, Quadrangle
Dallas • 871-3300

Pocket Sandwich Theater
5400 E. Mockingbird
Dallas • 821-1860

Theatre Arlington
305 W. Main
Arlington • 817/275-7661

Mesquite Arts Center
1527 N. Galloway
Mesquite • 972/216-8122,
972/216-6444

DANCE

ANITA N. MARTINEZ BALLET FOLKLORICO DANCE STUDIO
4422 Live Oak
Dallas, Texas 75204 • 828-0181

The performance season for this professional Hispanic dance company runs from June through September and includes both public and private performances. The dancers are also teachers in the Anita M. Martinez Ballet Folklorico Academy of Ballet who train children 6 years of age and up to perform regional folk dances of Mexico.

DALLAS BLACK DANCE THEATRE
P.O. Box 1290
Dallas, Texas 75221 • 871-2376

The Dallas Black Dance Theatre, a modern contemporary dance company, has entertained local, national, and international audiences since 1976. During each performance season, they schedule three major concerts at the Majestic Theatre. They also perform in the September *Dallas Morning News* Dance Festival and the Imagination Celebration and for Young Audiences. As part of an outreach program, they present School Day Matinee Performances for area schools and other groups. In their Dallas Black Dance Academy, students ages 3 to adult study dance on site at the Arts District facility and off site for DISD, private schools, and other youth centers. Their repertory consists of jazz, modern, ethnic, and spiritual works by well-known choreographers.

They offer boys and girls ages 9-16 the opportunity to audition for their summer dance program, providing the dancers have had some experience.

FORT WORTH DALLAS BALLET
6845 Green Oaks Rd.
Fort Worth, Texas 76116 • 800/377-9988
Dallas 696-3932

This dance company is formed from the Fort Worth Ballet and the former Ballet Dallas. The Dallas season is presented in the Music Hall at Fair Park, First and Parry.

MUSIC AND CHORUS

CHAMBER SYMPHONY OF THE METROCREST
P.O. Box 111333
Carrollton, Texas 75011-1333 • 972/306-4164

The Chamber Symphony of the Metrocrest is a nonprofit chamber symphony with a core group of seventeen professional string musicians. They perform four subscription concerts in the cities of Carrollton, Farmers Branch, and Addison. In the city of Farmers Branch, they perform free concerts annually at the Christmas Tree Lighting Ceremony at City Hall and Dickens in the Park at the Historical Park. They also perform Kinder Concerts and

Backstage Visits at the Farmers Branch Manske Library and at the Frankford Village Branch Library in Carrollton. There is no charge for these family concerts or for the annual Outdoor Labor Day Concert at the Perry Homestead Museum, 1509 N. Perry in Carrollton. Call the above number or check the city calendars to learn the dates and times of these family concerts.

THE CHILDREN'S CHORUS
OF GREATER DALLAS
Cynthia Nott, Director • 503-6159

The Children's Chorus is an ethnically diverse group of children who are in the fourth through the eighth grade. The members come from all over the metroplex. Their goal is to bring diverse cultures together to experience unity through singing beautiful music. The chorus sings all kinds of music, classical as well as jazz. Auditions are in May; they are divided into a Training Choir and a Concert Choir, and they practice once a week at the Cathedral de Guadalupe downtown. It is a tuition-based ensemble, and a scholarship program is available.

DALLAS CHAMBER ORCHESTRA
Sammons Center for the Arts
3630 Harry Hines, Suite 302
Dallas, Texas 75219 • 520-3121

An award-winning orchestra of fifteen strings, the Dallas Chamber Orchestra presents a diverse repertoire and highlights local soloists and world class artists in a comfortable and less formal atmosphere. In their Family Matinee Series primarily held in Caruth Auditorium at SMU, children attend free with two paid adult subscriptions. This series consists of five matinee concerts on Sunday afternoons.

DALLAS CLASSIC GUITAR SOCIETY
P.O. Box 190823
Dallas, Texas 75214 • 528-3733

Concert presenters of classical guitar and related forms, the Dallas Classic Guitar Society offers a Tuesday evening series at Caruth Auditorium (tickets $15), but the most family-oriented performances are their Saturday afternoon concerts at the Dallas Museum of Art. About five or six of these 3 P.M. performances are held each year at $6 for adults, $3 for students. Their outreach program for schools, nursing homes, and churches, called Guitar in the Community, reaches more than 50,000 people yearly. They also perform at festivals, such as the Imagination Celebration, Montage, and Artfest. The International Series at the Meyerson and Majestic costs from $15 to $60. A list of guitar teachers will be provided upon request.

DALLAS JAZZ ORCHESTRA
P.O. Box 743875
Dallas, Texas 75374 • 972/644-8833

The Dallas Jazz Orchestra, a twenty-piece big band, plays original and traditional big band jazz music. They perform regularly at The Village, 8310 Southwestern, and high school age and older really enjoy attending. Once each July they perform with DISD's Dallas Area Youth Orchestra and college groups at the Village. Families are more familiar with their free summer Sunday afternoon performances at Lee, Samuell, and Kidd Springs parks. They have made ten recordings.

THE DALLAS SCHOOL OF MUSIC
2650 Midway Road, Suite 204
Carrollton, Texas 75006 • 972/380-8050

The Dallas School of Music provides enjoyable programs in all styles of music, including classical, jazz, rock, and country. Preschoolers through senior citizens take lessons in keyboard, brass, woodwind, percussion, voice, and string instruments.

Children's courses include Musical Beginnings for ages 2-3 years and their parents and Musical Explorations for ages 4-7.

DALLAS SYMPHONY ASSOCIATION, INC.

Morton H. Meyerson Symphony Center
2301 Flora Street, Suite 300
Dallas, Texas 75201 • 871-4000

Celebrating its 100th anniversary in the year 2000, the Dallas Symphony performs year round in the internationally acclaimed Meyerson Symphony Center. In addition to a Classical, Pops, and Summer Festival Series, the DSO presents numerous concerts throughout the year for children and their families. The Ida M. Green Youth Concert Series features the DSO performing educational programs approximately 45 minutes in length. Sixteen daytime concerts are offered for children grades 3-6. Eight concerts each year are presented for children grades pre-K-2. The DSO also presents an annual High School Concert featuring a side-by-side performance with the Greater Dallas Youth Orchestra.

In addition to the Youth Concert Series, the Dallas Symphony offers numerous free concerts throughout the year. The "Sites and Sounds of Summer" concert series each April through June features free concerts in Dallas parks. Other free concerts in the Meyerson include the annual SundayFest concerts as well as the annual Hispanic Festival Concert and the African-American Festival Concert. For ticket information, please call 692-0203.

FINE ARTS CHAMBER PLAYERS

Sammons Center for the Arts
3630 Harry Hines Boulevard
Dallas, Texas 75219 • 520-2219

The Fine Arts Chamber Players include musicians from the Dallas Symphony, Dallas Opera, and music teachers who perform many free concerts annually. Several of these are in DISD elementary schools. Every Sunday afternoon in July, they perform classical music designed for family entertainment at Fair Park's Garden Center. These free performances begin at 3 P.M. and end at 5 P.M. with one intermission.

A good format for children to be exposed to classical music in a more informal setting is their "**Fourth Saturday at the Museum**" free series held at the air-conditioned Dallas Horticulture Center at Fair Park. These six concerts begin at 3 P.M. and last for one hour.

School children especially like the Dream Collectors, which is a performing group consisting of musicians and actors who feature classical music, mime, masks, and storytelling in 45-minute presentations for school groups.

GREATER DALLAS YOUTH ORCHESTRA ASSOCIATION, INC.
Morton H. Meyerson Symphony Center
2301 Flora
Dallas, Texas 75201 • 528-7747

During the last twenty years, the Greater Dallas Youth Orchestra Association has grown from 30 to more than 300 musicians, ages 5 to 18. The young players are divided into four ensembles: the **Young Performers Orchestra**, the **Dallas String Ensemble**, the **Philharmonic Orchestra**, and the **Greater Dallas Youth Orchestra**, a group of about 100 members. Call for a brochure listing performances.

MEADOWS SCHOOL OF THE ARTS
Southern Methodist University
Dallas, Texas • SMU-ARTS

Performances in music, dance, and theater are held at the Meadows School of the Arts. The *Dallas Morning News* "Community Arts Calendar" on Sunday lists performances, and SMU has an artsline to call. Student presentations of classic, modern, and musical productions are held in the Greer Garson and Bob Hope theaters.

MUSIC MILL AMPHITHEATER
2201 Road to Six Flags
Arlington, Texas 76010 • Metro 817/640-8900

Pop, country, gospel, and many other types of superstar concerts are enjoyed during Six Flags summer season as well as throughout the year. Concert ticket prices are usually in addition to the park entrance fee.

RICHARDSON SYMPHONY ORCHESTRA
1131 Rockingham Lane, Suite 110
Richardson, Texas 75080 • 972/234-4195

The Richardson Symphony Orchestra usually holds six evening performances in the Performance Hall at Richardson High School. They also help to sponsor the RSO/Lennox Young Artists Competition in January. Young musicians from all over the country come to compete in three categories, and the winners of the top honors perform with the RSO in the March concert. The Sounds of Freedom patriotic program is held annually in the spring in conjunction with the Richardson Wildflower Festival, and they also present Symphony Days for the RISD third graders. In late September they present a free concert on the UTD campus called "Sounds of Class." Families may bring a picnic and sit on the grounds. A small children's carnival entertains small children.

STARPLEX AMPHITHEATER
3839 S. Fitzhugh at Fair Park
Dallas, Texas 75210 • 421-1111

Starplex Amphitheater presents concerts by popular musicians and singers year round, but the summer season is a favorite. This outdoor theater can seat 20,000 people, and concessions are available. Tickets are available at Ticketmaster outlets or by calling 373-8000 or 972/647-5700.

SOUTH DALLAS CULTURAL CENTER
3400 S. Fitzhugh at Second Ave.
Dallas, Texas 75210 • 670-0314

The South Dallas Cultural Center has a wide variety of activities for all ages and income groups. Music resounds on the fourth Sunday of most months in the Sunday Music program, which features different artists each month. Admission varies. Plays are presented by the SDCC Community Theater. Also, free art exhibits are held monthly, and classes for ages 5 or 7 to adult are held in dance, voice, sculpture, painting, and drawing with fees somewhat based on ability to pay so that low income families may participate. A summer program is included in the activities. The center is open Tuesday-Friday, 12-8, and Saturday, 10-8 during the summer and 10-6 the rest of the year.

SUNSHINE GENERATION, INC.
Ella Romney 5003 Victor
Dallas, Texas 75214 • 827-7088

Part of a national company, the Sunshine Generation is a children's performing group designed for ages 3 through teens. Divided into groups by age, the children take part in weekly one-hour classes in which they learn music theory and appreciation, songs, and dance steps. About 85 children are enrolled in the program, and they perform once each month in places like the State Fair, Six Flags, the Dallas Zoo, and festivals. Sunshine Generation is nonauditioned and nonreligious. A camp is offered each summer. Classes are generally held at Ridgewood and Huffines Recreation Centers.

TEXAS BOYS CHOIR
2925 Riverglen
Ft. Worth, Texas 76109 • Metro 817/429-0066

Founded in 1946 in Denton, the Texas Boys Choir moved to Ft. Worth in 1957 and have since opened a satellite campus in

Dallas. Choir members as young as 8 meet at St. Thomas Aquinas on Monday and Wednesday after school for training as well as in Ft. Worth. Open auditions for Tour Boys are held year round for boys 10 and up. If selected for tours, the boys attend school on the Ft. Worth campus and continue their studies as they tour for four to six weeks. The choir usually performs "The Littlest Wise Man" at the Scott Theater at Christmas. Sometimes they perform with the Dallas Symphony.

TEXAS GIRLS CHOIR
4449 Camp Bowie
Ft. Worth, Texas 76107 • 817/732-8161

The 200-voice Texas Girls Choir has been an active performance group for more than thirty years. The talented girls, ages 8-14, audition to become members of the choir who perform locally and also take two tours each year, one primarily in the South and the other abroad. The concert choir includes approximately forty of the girls, and the remainder are in a preparatory choir. Choir members are drawn primarily from Tarrant, Dallas, Johnson, and Parker Counties. All rehearsals are held on the Fort Worth campus, and the semester fee is about $195. Concerts are usually held in October, December, February, and May, and tickets are from $5 to $30. Call for locations.

OPERA

THE DALLAS OPERA
The Centrum
3102 Oak Lawn Avenue, Suite 450
Dallas, Texas 75219 • 443-1043

The Dallas Opera season, November through March, consists of approximately six operas and usually an additional holiday presentation held at Fair Park's Music Hall. The Sunday matinee would be a good time for a family with older children to attend.

One hour before the 1 and 6 P.M. performances on Saturday is Opera Overtures in which background information about the opera is given. Call 443-1000 for tickets.

The **Puppet Opera Theater** visits more than sixty schools to present short puppet shows for K-3 students. Other school programs are offered to older students, such as the four student matinees each season. The **Dallas Opera Young Artists** bring performances of selected arias and duets, sung in English and original languages, to the community each spring in shopping areas, schools, and other institutions for a suggested donation of $50.

When working with school groups, the Opera provides teaching materials, in-service teacher training, and backstage tours.

OPRY

The oprys in Texas should be on each country music lover's list of family entertainment. They are smaller but similar to Nashville's Grand Ole Opry in that they provide great singers and bands and a wholesome, lively atmosphere, free from the smoke and liquor of honky-tonks. Concessions are provided, and some offer group rates and dinner and show combinations. Some recommend reservations. Dress casually and get ready for a toe-tappin' good time.

GARLAND OPRY
605 W. State Street
Garland, Texas • 972/494-3835

The Garland Opry has been operating for more than twenty years. Eight bands rotate to provide country music entertainment on Saturdays at 8 P.M. Occasionally, they perform at the Garland Performing Arts Center.

GRAPEVINE OPRY
308 S. Main St.
Grapevine, Texas • Metro 817/481-8733

Grapevine Opry, which has a lower floor and a balcony, is usually packed at its 7:30 P.M. Saturday performances. Sometimes, talented youngsters appear to sing, clog, and fiddle. The second half of the program is often arranged around themes, such as "Waltz Across Texas," gospel songs, and patriotic songs. Dinner and show combinations for groups are offered. Occasionally, the singers and musicians in Grapevine will rotate with performers from other oprys. Gospel music is presented on the fourth Friday of each month. A concession stand is available.

PUPPETRY

The antics of puppets have entertained all ages for hundreds of years. In the Dallas area, the public libraries often present free puppet shows for children, and the Dallas Opera's Puppet Opera Theater performs for elementary school children at their schools. Shopping malls, such as Northpark, sometimes offer December puppet shows, and groups who offer series for children, such as the Jewish Community Center's FamiliArts, often include puppet shows. One of the most entertaining puppet shows is held downtown each Christmas at First Baptist Church's "Singing Christmas Tree" in which the children move the puppets to music and song before the adult choir's performance. KIDSarts, the summer program of the Irving Arts Center, sometimes offers classes in puppetry.

DALLAS PUPPET THEATRE
Valley View Center, Upper Level
Dallas, Texas • 972/716-0004

The Dallas Puppet Theatre presents a storybook-type puppet show at its theater by the Disney Store on the upper level at

Valley View Mall and others at schools during the week. A new puppet show is presented each month. The puppeteers offer birthday parties as well as workshops and classes year round for ages 6 and up. They also appear at festivals, such as the Imagination Celebration at the DMA and McKinney's Spring Fling.

LE THEATER DE MARIONETTE
462 Northpark Center
Dallas, Texas • 369-6614

Le Theatre de Marionette performs at Northpark Center near Neiman Marcus on the upper level. Ages 3 and above are recommended. Tickets are adults $8 and children $7. School discounts and birthday parties are offered.

THEATER

ACT II CHILDREN'S THEATRE OF ADDISON
15650 Addison Road
Addison, TX 75248 • 972/450-6229

Classes at ACT II are designed to encourage artistic self-expression, and the young actors create an original production through experiences which include story building, acting, design, and even stunt fighting. Choices abound in mime, improvisation, Shakespeare, theatre dance, and music. Classes are approximately $150 per class, and they are held after school and on Saturday for ages 3 to teen. A summer camp program is also available for ages 5-13.

They offer field trip performances on weekdays and after-school drama clubs at schools.

CAPERS FOR KIDS
12306 Park Central Drive
Dallas, Texas 75251 • 972/661-2787

Capers for Kids, located just north of Medical City, is an educational creative arts school that offers a faculty of degreed teachers who teach classes in drama and visual arts Monday through Saturday for nine months. They also work in twelve private schools in the area with mainstream students and also those with learning differences. The half-day Summer Arts Camps are held in the morning and afternoon for ages 3-14 on Monday-Friday for two-week sessions.

CREATIVE ARTS THEATRE AND SCHOOL
1100 West Randol Mill Road
Arlington, Texas 76012 • Metro 817/265-8512

The Creative Arts Theatre is a youth theater that includes classes for ages 4 to adult in dance, acting, creative dramatics, technical theater, and more. On the first two weekends each month, they present the "Spotlight" shows for a total of six in the main season. Three shows are presented in the summer at 10 A.M. for one week in June, July, and August. A special two-week summer program is offered for out-of-town gifted students. Regular summer classes are in two-week sessions.

DALLAS CHILDREN'S THEATER, INC.
2215 Cedar Springs
Dallas, Texas 75201 • 978-0110

The Dallas Children's Theater presents exciting professional theater performances by actors with advanced degrees and extensive experience. Their Storybook Season of plays is presented at the El Centro Theater at Market and Main and the Crescent Theater at 2215 Cedar Springs just west of the Crescent. Most of the plays have an intermission, and drinks and snacks may be purchased. Season tickets are available. Also, on the second Friday night performance of each show, signing is offered for the hearing impaired. School matinees are available to area schools, and year-round classes are open to ages 3 and up. There are three summer sessions that last for one week each and feature a performance on Saturday. Group discounts for ten or more are offered on weekends.

DALLAS SUMMER MUSICALS
The Box Office 6013 Berkshire Lane
Dallas, Texas 75225 • 691-7200 (no phone sales)
Ticketmaster charge-by-phone 373-8000
Administrative offices
P.O. Box 710336, Dallas, Texas 75371 • 421-5678

The Dallas Summer Musicals is a nonprofit organization dedicated to bringing the very best of American musical theater and Broadway shows to the Dallas area. They have produced a summer season of entertainment since 1940 in the Music Hall at Fair Park and are also presenting the Broadway Contemporary Series in the winter at both the Music Hall and the Majestic Theater.

DALLAS THEATER CENTER
3636 Turtle Creek
Dallas, Texas 75219-5598 • 526-8210

The Dallas Theater Center opened its doors in 1959, and it continues to hold performances in the **Kalita Humphreys Theater**, designed by Frank Lloyd Wright, and in the Arts District Theater at 2401 Flora. A family favorite during their regular season, which runs from September through April, is their annual performance of *A Christmas Carol*. See "Tours of the Working World" for information about touring the theater, rehearsal halls, and costume shop. The Dallas Theater Center also offers classes in theater for children, ages 3½ to 18, which are taught by professional actors and teachers with extensive theater experience. These students have the opportunity to audition for children's parts in the professional productions, such as *A Christmas Carol*. The teen company does a summer production.

GARLAND CIVIC THEATRE'S CHILDREN ON STAGE
1721 Reserve / P.O. Box 461252
Garland, Texas 75046 • 349-1331

Young people perform in the plays produced by Children On Stage. Two shows, such as *Dorothy Meets Alice* and *Joseph and the Amazing Technicolor Dreamcoat*, are presented in the summer, one in the fall, and another in the spring. These performances are at the Performing Arts Center in downtown Garland at 300 North 5th. Theater classes are offered for ages 8-18 in the fall and spring with two-week camps held during the summer. A COS On Tour production is conducted in June.

JUNIOR PLAYERS
3630 Harry Hines Blvd.
Dallas, Texas 75219 • 526-4076

The Junior Players is the oldest children's theater group in Dallas. Their goal is to introduce children to theater arts and to help them develop self-confidence and self-esteem. To achieve this, they hold thirty free summer camps at recreation centers and other locations in the area. During the summer they work with high school actors and the Shakespeare Festival of Dallas to present a Shakespearean play in late July or early August at Samuell-Grand's amphitheater. Call their office for specific dates and times.

KD STUDIO ACTORS CONSERVATORY
2600 N. Stemmons
Dallas, Texas 75207 • 638-0484

KD Studio Actors Conservatory offers classes for teens and children who want to learn the fundamentals of acting for film, TV commercials, and theater.

METRO PLAYERS
Irving Arts Center
3333 N. MacArthur Blvd.
Irving, Texas • 972/252-ARTS

For more than fifteen years, the Metro Players have been performing in community theater for the Irving area. "Come Home to Family Fun" is their motto. They perform in about three plays each year, two musicals and a drama, at the Dupree Theater. Call the Irving Arts Centre's artsline at 252-ARTS or read in their newsletter for notices of performances.

THE INTERNATIONAL THEATRICAL ARTS SOCIETY (TITAS)
3101 N. Fitzhugh
Dallas, Texas • 528-5576 or 528-6112

TITAS is a nonprofit organization that brings national and international performing companies to the Dallas area. Groups in the past have included the Kodo Drummers of Japan, the Imperial Bells of China, and the Festival of Indonesia. It is a unique experience, especially to help some children understand the cultural heritage of their parents' homeland. They have a mailing list, and announcements are given to the newspapers.

MEADOWS SCHOOL OF THE ARTS
Community Education P.O. Box 750356
Dallas, Texas 75275-0356 • 768-3343
24-hour on-line registration (www.smu.edu/~meadows)

Community Education offers noncredit classes for children and adults in the arts. Workshops and classes for children ages 7-17 are offered in musical theater and creative dramatics and more.

PLANO CHILDREN'S THEATRE
1301 Custer Road, Suite 832
Plano, Texas 75075 • 972/422-2575

The Plano Children's Theatre is an active nonprofit educational theater that offers skill classes for grades K-12 in acting, creative drama, art, voice, and musical theater. The PCT also has production classes in which every child in the class gets a part in a play that is produced as a finale. In addition, PCT has a touring performance series for children that is performed by adults, as well as workshops and special holiday shows that are performed by adults and children together.

POCKET SANDWICH THEATRE
5400 E. Mockingbird
Dallas, Texas 75206 • 821-1860

Many of the performances by the Pocket Sandwich Theatre are suitable for families, but if you have a question, just call the theatre and someone who is familiar with the play can discuss it with you. Melodramas, in which the audience can hiss, boo, and throw popcorn, are favorites of families. Performances are held Thursday, Friday, and Saturday nights at 8 with food service open at 6:30, and on Sunday at 7 with food service open at 5:30. There is table seating, and the optional menu consists of sandwiches, soup, quiche, nachos, and individual pizzas. Prices for the plays are $6-12 depending on the evening you attend, and a $2 discount is offered for seniors and children. It is located in the corner of the L-shaped shopping village.

RICHARDSON CHILDREN'S THEATRE
525 W. Arapaho #20 at Custer
Richardson, Texas 75080 • 972/690-5029

A nonprofit organization dedicated to providing an excellent experience in theatre for children, the Richardson Children's Theatre offers both classes and workshops for children to develop their self-esteem and understanding of the theatre. A company of professional adult actors present plays, such as The *Princess and the Pea* and *The Trial of the Big Bad Wolf,* for family audiences. Auditions for the company are held in January of each year for actors, ages 11 to adult. Summer workshops are held in June and July, and the Children's Summer Art Series is held at the UTD Theater at Campbell and Floyd.

THEATRE THREE
2800 Routh St./The Quadrangle
Dallas, Texas 75201 • 871-3300

Theatre Three has some performances each season that are suitable for families with older children. They occasionally present a play for younger children, particularly during the summer. They have an outreach program with DISD called "Tumbleweed Theatricals" which is a cultural field trip for elementary students at 10 and 11:30 A.M. during one month.

YOUNG ACTORS STUDIO
AND PERFORMANCE CENTER
11496 Luna Road #G
Dallas, Texas 75234 • 401-2090

For more than eleven years, the Young Actors Studio has been encouraging young actors and actresses through classes and performances. They take pride in creating a positive learning environment to bring out the talent in each child. Approximately eight shows are scheduled each year, and a newsletter keeps students and parents informed of activities.

———— VARIETY SERIES FOR CHILDREN ————

FAMILIARTS
The Jewish Community Center of Dallas
7900 Northaven Road
Dallas, Texas 75230 • 739-2737, Ext. 215

FamiliARTS premiered in 1991-92 to the delight of children and their families. The series, geared to children ages 3 to 9 or 10, allows families to enjoy nationally and internationally renowned children's artists performing educational, entertaining, interactive programs that enchant audiences of all ages. Most public performances are Sunday matinees. Monday performances provide a field trip opportunity for schools throughout the metroplex. Performances are held in the 450-seat Zale auditorium at the JCC. Membership in the Magical Kids Club as well as season subscriptions are available. Theater birthday parties can be arranged. It is best to arrive early on performance days if you have a small child.

ANNUAL CONCERTS AND PERFORMANCE AND FILM FESTIVALS

JANUARY

KidFilm, AMC Glen Lakes Theatre (821-NEWS, 821-6300). Kid-Film is a film and video festival for kids sponsored by the USA Film Festival. It includes features, shorts, and animation, and offers tributes to greats in children's arts. Selections are viewed on Saturday and on Sunday afternoon. Admission fee.

MARCH

McKinney Avenue Shamrock Music Festival, South McKinney Avenue (855-0006). This outdoor street festival features bands, foods, exhibits, and some children's activities. A trolley ride during this event is a good way to see the various activities, and you might include a stop at the Dallas Museum of Art.

APRIL

Country Fair, Texas Stadium, Irving. A Thursday evening concert kicks off Country Fair, which continues through Sunday and includes country music concerts, concessions, exhibits, and a carnival. Admission is free, but a ticket is needed to enter.

Fan Jam, West End Downtown. In this three-day festival of country music, both national and local artists perform and sign autographs. Arts and crafts, food, and a carnival add to the fun.

Lee Park Annual Easter Concert, Corner of Lemmon Ave. and Turtle Creek Blvd. (692-0203). A Dallas Symphony Association "Sites and Sounds of Easter" free performance is held annually at Lee Park. As part of the NationsBank Community Concert Series, families are invited to the park on Sunday afternoon for a picnic and music.

Richardson Community Band Spring Concert, Berkner High School, Richardson. This lively Sunday afternoon concert sponsored by RISD is free. The band sometimes offers a free Sunday Family Night in June as part of their summer season.

MAY

Gospel Festival, Morton H. Meyerson Symphony Center (953-1985, 953-1977). Choirs and bands feature the music and heritage of black Americans through gospel music on a Sunday evening. Free.

Mesquite Music Festival: Civic Expressions, City Lake Park and Mesquite Arts Complex, Mesquite (972/216-6444). Music and theater performances are scheduled on Friday and Saturday nights and an art fair and children's festival on Saturday. Groups participating usually include the Mesquite Community Theatre, Mesquite Civic Chorus, Mesquite Symphony Orchestra, and Mesquite Community Band.

Memorial Day Pops Concert, Carrollton Amphitheatre, 2201 East Jackson, Carrollton (972/466-3080). The Chamber Symphony of the Metroplex performs and encourages families to "Bring your own basket."

Sites and Sounds of Summer, Dallas City Parks (692-0203). The Dallas Symphony Orchestra performs free outdoor concerts at area parks and other sites such as the West End, Flag Pole Hill, and the Arboretum in April and May. Families bring blankets and picnics and enjoy the concerts held usually at 3 or 8 P.M. The Symphony also offers **SundayFest**, which is a series of five free concerts held at the Meyerson and spread throughout the year. Doors usually open at 1:30 and the performance begins at 2:30.

Playfest, Dallas Children's Theater (978-0110). Held at the Crescent Theater, 2215 Cedar Springs, Playfest is a fundraising festival that includes skits, games, workshops, readings, and food on Saturday. Admission is free, and tickets may be purchased for activities.

SUMMER

Basically Beethoven, Dallas Horticulture Center at Fair Park (520-2219). The Fine Arts Chamber Players perform every Sunday in July from 3-5 P.M. selections from Beethoven and other composers.

Dallas Jazz Orchestra, City Parks (972/644-8833). These free concerts are held on Sunday afternoons at 3 P.M. at various city parks.

Dallas Summer Musicals, Music Hall at Fair Park (691-7200). The Dallas Summer Musicals presents spectacular dramas, comedies, Las Vegas-type shows, and many others in both matinee and evening performances. There are usually five plays in the summer, one during the State Fair, and one in March. A buffet is offered at the Crystal Terrace (565-0591) and lighter fare at the Bistro (565-1116).

Jazz Under the Stars, Dallas Museum of Art (922-1200). For more than ten years, the museum has provided entertainment for visitors with concerts each Thursday evening at 8:00 at the Ross Avenue Plaza.

Patriotic Pops Concert, Las Colinas, Irving (972/257-1210). The Irving Symphony Orchestra presents this free evening concert in Williams Square, site of the famous Mustangs sculpture.

Lawn chairs, blankets, and picnics are encouraged, and fireworks follow the concert held on July 4.

Shakespeare Festival of Dallas, Samuell-Grand Park Amphitheater (559-2778). Two or three free Shakespeare plays are performed each June and July. Families may bring picnics and have dinner before the performance. Those with blankets sit closer to the front while those with lawn chairs are nearer the back, but the sound system is excellent and you will be able to hear and see no matter where you sit. Children will enjoy the play more if they are familiar with the characters and plot before they attend. The gates open at 7 P.M., and the play begins at 8:15. There is an intermission, and the play ends around 11:15. Concessions are available as well as T-shirts and other souvenirs. The park is located at 5808 East Grand. Portable restrooms are provided, and bringing insect repellent is recommended. The amphitheater is located across from Samuell-Grand's Municipal Rose Garden. A $3 donation is appreciated.

The Sounds of Freedom, Richardson Symphony Orchestra (972/234-4195). Usually held on the grounds of MCI, 2400 N. Glenville in Richardson, The Sounds of Freedom celebration is an evening of music and fireworks in mid-June. The gates open at 5:30 for those with lawn chairs and picnic dinners. Activities are planned for children, and the free concert begins at 8 P.M. Concessions are available.

Festival of Drums and Bugles, Lake Highlands High School Stadium, 9449 Church Road. This lively performance festival by high school players is sponsored by the Lake Highlands High School Band Club annually on an evening in latter July. Around seven groups from throughout the U.S. compete, and a clinic is held earlier in the afternoon. All seats are reserved, and tickets are about $11.

SEPTEMBER

The *Dallas Morning News* Dance Festival, Artists Square Downtown (953-1977). Dance groups such as the Dallas Black Dance Theatre, Ballet Dallas, and many others perform during this free Friday-Sunday fete held at 1800 Leonard between the Meyerson and the Arts District Theatre.

Montage, Arts District Downtown (361-2011). This fund-raiser/arts festival is held on a weekend and includes dance, drama, music, and arts and crafts. Tickets are around $4.50, and children under 5 are admitted free.

OCTOBER

Grass Roots Multi-Arts Festival, Lee Park. This free annual festival offers children's activities and music performed by the winners of the Dallas Songwriter's Association Showcase as well as arts and crafts. Visitors may bring picnics, and a concession is available.

DECEMBER

A Christmas Carol, Dallas Puppet Theatre (716-0004). This puppet show includes five different styles of puppetry and a live actor as Scrooge.

A Christmas Carol, Dallas Theater Center (526-8210). This family favorite is presented each year at the Kalita Humphreys Theater or the Arts District Theater.

A Christmas Celebration, Meyerson Symphony Center (871-4000). The Dallas Symphony Orchestra presents "**Deck the Halls**," a magical afternoon of family fun focused on ages 3-12. They also present five family-oriented Christmas concerts of a pops nature.

Christmas in the Branch, City Hall Plaza, Farmers Branch. Farmer's Branch Chamber of Commerce holds a free concert for families followed by Santa's arrival on Friday evening at City Hall Plaza on William Dodson Pkwy. at Valley View Lane.

Dallas Children's Theater, El Centro College Auditorium (978-0110). Each Christmas the Dallas Children's Theater presents a wonderful holiday program, such as *The Best Christmas Pageant Ever.*

The Littlest Wise Man, Texas Boys Choir (Metro 817/429-0066).

The Night Before Christmas, McFarlin Auditorium at SMU (361-0278). This fanciful, full-length ballet is performed by adults and children of the Dallas Metropolitan Ballet during two December weekends.

The Nutcracker. Various groups perform this traditional favorite. One of the best ways to enhance its enjoyment by young children is to read them the story first so they are familiar with the story line and anticipate the entrance of the characters. Some of the performing companies are the Tuzer Ballet, Dallas Ballet Center, and Ft. Worth Dallas Ballet.

The Singing Christmas Tree, First Baptist Church, Downtown (969-2494). The faces of the First Baptist Choir illuminate a 33-foot tall "Christmas tree." Admission is free, but a ticket is needed. A musical puppet show is held 30 minutes prior to the performances. The concert is usually broadcast later on Channel 11.

4. Sports and Recreation

Observing a generation of children often referred to as "couch potatoes" or "tater tots" because of their sedentary lifestyle in which they are parked endlessly in front of TV sitcoms, rented movies, and video games, more and more parents are recognizing the need to get these children outdoors and moving. The Dallas area has abundant opportunities for physical exercise and fun for individuals, teams, and families. Finding activities such as hiking, bicycling, or fishing that the family can enjoy will not only aid in physical fitness and an appreciation of the world outdoors, but create some wonderful memories as well.

SPECTATOR SPORTS

MAJOR LEAGUE SPORTS

Dallas Cowboys (National Football League). Preseason and regular season games for the silver and blue team begin in August and end in December. The Cowboys play home games in Texas Stadium, 2401 E. Airport Freeway, Irving. The *Dallas Cowboys Official Weekly* may be subscribed to by calling 972/556-9972. DART provides shuttles to the home games. For more information about the Cowboys, call 972/556-9900. Season and group sales, 972/579-5100. The Fan Club number is 972/556-9978.

Dallas Mavericks (National Basketball Association). The Dallas Mavericks basketball team plays more than 50 games each season, which extends from January through April. Home games are played at Reunion Arena, 777 Sports Street. For schedule and ticket information call 748-1808. Summer basketball camps for ages 8-18 are offered. The Maverick Info Hotline is 972/988-3865.

Dallas Sidekicks. The Dallas Sidekicks play exciting indoor soccer games at Reunion Arena when in town. Their season begins in late October and goes through April. For other information call 653-0200, or for tickets call Dillard's Box Office or go by the Reunion Arena box office. Young soccer players may want to ask about the **Junior Sidekicks Club.** The Sidekicks hold youth soccer camps during spring break and the summer.

Texas Rangers (American League). This baseball team plays at The Ballpark in Arlington. See "Places to Go" for more information about the stadium and the season which runs from April through October. Special promotion nights allow all children ages 13 and under with a paid admission to receive items such as baseball gloves, backpacks, and jerseys. The Rangers usually hold an open house for fans during the winter. While at the park, visitors may want to see baseball memorabilia in the Legends of the Game Museum (817/273-5600) or have dinner at Friday's located inside the stadium.

Half-price tickets for Tuesday and Thursday home games are available at Tom Thumb locations. For information about schedules, tickets, or membership in the **Junior Rangers Club**, call Metro 817/273-5100.

Dallas Burn (Major League Soccer). The Dallas Burn soccer team begins its season in April. Home games are at the Cotton Bowl. For tickets call Ticketmaster or call 979-0303 for their office.

ARENA SPORTS

Dallas Dragoons (National Polo League). The Dragoons play arena polo at the Coliseum at Fair Park in April, July, and October during the State Fair. They also play and give lessons at Bear Creek Polo Ranch, 550 Bent Trail, Red Oak, Texas 75154. Call 979-0849 for more information.

Dallas Stars (National Hockey League). The Dallas Stars ice hockey team play home games at Reunion Arena in a season that runs from October through April. Ask at Tom Thumb about the **Junior Stars Club.** Fans may watch the Stars practice at the Dr Pepper Star Center in Valley Ranch (214-GO-SKATE). Summer camps are offered there. Call 972/868-2890 for information and 467-8277 for tickets.

Willow Bend Polo Club. Willow Bend offers arena polo and private lessons at 2310 FM 720 in Little Elm, Texas. Call 972/248-6298 for season information.

COLLEGIATE SPORTS

Cotton Bowl, Fair Park. Annually the Cotton Bowl is the site for at least three exciting collegiate football games, the Cotton Bowl Classic on New Year's Day and the State Fair matches between the University of Texas and the University of Oklahoma and between Grambling University and their opponent. State high school playoffs are also scheduled here.

Southern Methodist University (Southwest Conference). SMU football is played at the Cotton Bowl Stadium. Other popular sports include men's and women's basketball played at Moody Coliseum, swimming, baseball, track, and soccer. Call 768-2902 for schedules. Summer sports camps for youth are held on campus as well as cheerleading camps and camps for talented and gifted students. Moody Coliseum is the site for the annual SWC Women's Post Season Basketball Classic and the SWC Post Season Men's Basketball Classic usually held in March. The SMU Swim Center is the site for the *Dallas Morning News* Swimming Classic held in late January. SMU invites the top five finishers in the NCAA Swimming Championship to compete with the SMU team. SMU sponsors the **Big Shots Kids Club** for young fans 3-18. Call 768-4051.

Other College Sports. Many other colleges in the metroplex have sporting events open to the public. Here are some phone numbers if the family is interested in going to cheer them on.

Dallas Baptist University, 333-5324
Dallas County Community College District, call each campus.
University of Dallas, 972/721-5009
University of North Texas, Denton, Metro 817/267-3731
University of Texas at Arlington, Metro 817/273-2261

AUTO RACING

Devil's Bowl (972/222-2421). This raceway is located at 1711 Lawson, off Hwy. 80 in Mesquite. Races are usually on Friday night from March through October.

Outlaw Speedway (972/264-5800). Races are on Saturday at this track in Grand Prairie.

Pontiac Grand Prix of Dallas in Addison (701-9091). Racing dates and location are determined yearly.

Texas Motor Speedway (817/215-8500). NASCAR racing is held here on a 1.5-mile track. The 150,000-seat facility is located on SH 114 and I-35W in Roanoke. The cars average more than 180 mph. Track officials advise sunscreen, earplugs, comfortable shoes, and plenty of liquids. Fans may bring a 14-inch cooler. The park also hosts concerts and other events. Concessions and souvenirs are available.

GOLF

GTE Byron Nelson Classic (972/717-0700). Held at the Four Seasons Resort and Club at Las Colinas, Irving, the activities in this May golf tournament usually extend for one week. A free youth clinic is usually scheduled on one afternoon, and there are door prizes and giveaways and a free golf club after the exhibition is over. Look for the statue of Byron Nelson.

Colonial National Invitational. The PGA tournament is held at Colonial Country Club in Ft. Worth on a 7,010-yard, par-70 course in May.

RODEOS, HORSE RACING, AND HORSE SHOWS

Rodeo events and horse shows, such as the **Texas Black Invitational Rodeo** and the **Big D Charity Horse Show** in May, are scheduled periodically throughout the metroplex. The **Mesquite Rodeo** and **Rodeo Parade** are covered in "Places to Go." Year-round indoor rodeo is held each weekend at **Kowbell Indoor Rodeo**, Mansfield, FM 157 and Business 287 (Metro

817/477-3092). See Ft. Worth in "Day Trips" for more rodeo events. The **Collin County Youth Park and Farm Museum** northwest of McKinney has a show barn with a complete rodeo arena, and various rodeos, horse and livestock shows, and team roping, cutting, and penning are scheduled here (Metro 214/231-7170, ext. 4793). Horse shows and competitive exhibitions, such as the annual Mercedes Grand Prix series and the AGA Grand Prix, are held at **Las Colinas Equestrian Center**, 600 W. Royal, Irving (972/869-0600).

Lone Star Park (800/795-RACE). 1000 Lone Star Parkway, Grand Prairie, Texas 75050. The 315-acre Lone Star Park's thoroughbred horses race on Wednesday-Sunday from mid-April through July and again on Sunday-Thursday in October and November. Simulcasting is used the rest of the year. Up to 8,000 fans may sit in the Grandstand and 1,500 in the Post Time Pavilion. A playground, picnic tables, petting zoo, and pony rides are offered in a family area. Dining is in the Pavilion and outdoor patio. LSP is located one-half mile north of I-30 just off Belt Line Road in Grand Prairie. Parking is $2-4, and general admission is $2. Special seating is $3-10, and valet parking is $5.

HOT AIR BALLOONING

Two spectacular hot air balloon festivals are held in the area each year. In Mesquite's Paschall Park in July (972/285-0211) and in Plano's Bob Woodruff Park in late September (972/422-0296), colorful hot air balloons fill the skies over a weekend. In addition to the races, there are usually arts and crafts, exhibits, food, and carnivals. On the opening Friday evening of the Mesquite festival, there is a beautiful "Balloon Glow" at dusk on the east side of Town East Mall if it is not too windy. See the "Transportation" section of Chapter Two for information about taking private balloon rides.

TENNIS

Texas Open. National Hardcourt Tournament at Canyon Creek Country Club, Richardson. July or August. 972/231-2881.

Irving Tennis Classic. Top-ranked male players on international circuit. Irving. September. 972/252-7476.

Dr Pepper Open. Ages 10-80. July. Sites change. 342-9597.

ZATS zone qualifiers. January-June. Dallas usually hosts two, Plano hosts one; ages 14-18, boys and girls; call Dallas Tennis Association for schedule, 342-9597.

MCB Indoor Tennis Classic Superchampionship Major Zone. May. Girls and boys: 14, 16, 18, and adults. Various sites. 342-9597.

Boys National 18 Indoor Tournament. Top players from US nationally ranked juniors. Brookhaven Country Club and other locations. Thanksgiving.

INDIVIDUAL, FAMILY, AND TEAM SPORTS

ARCHERY

The National Field Archery Association sponsors archery for youth. There are Cubs (ages 4-10), Youth, and Young Adult levels in lessons and competition. In the *Yellow Pages*, look up "Archery Equipment and Supplies" for the location of outdoor and indoor ranges, and the proprietor can give you information about clubs near you.

BASEBALL, SOFTBALL, AND T-BALL

Youngsters all over the metroplex begin warming up in April for baseball season, which lasts into July. Recreation centers, churches, YMCA, and athletic associations field hundreds of recreational teams with players ages 4 and up. Baseball camps are offered in the summer. Very popular with boys who are serious about the game is **Boys Baseball Inc.** (320-1771). Baseball card collecting is a popular hobby for some fans. For a list of stores that sell cards, look in the *Yellow Pages* for "Baseball-Sports Cards and Memorabilia." All across town are batting cages so players can practice their swings, but some may have height requirements. Adair Baseball World is an indoor facility with batting cages, radar gun, instructors, pitchers mounds, and hitting leagues.

Adair Baseball World, 3222 Skylane, Carrollton, 972/732-7247
Carter Softball Complex, 440 Oates, Garland, 613-7729
Mesquite Go-Carts and Batting Cages, 1630 E. Hwy. 80, 288-4888
Eaglequest Golf Park, 8787 Park Lane, 341-9600
Twin Rivers Amusements, 1200 E. Belt Line, Richardson, 972/234-2291

BASKETBALL

Basketball is usually offered for third grade and up at recreation centers, YMCA, athletic associations, and churches. Practice usually begins in December and play in January-early March. Basketball clinics are often advertised through the newspaper or athletic clubs, and summer camps are abundant.

The **Hoop-It-Up** is a three-on-three street basketball tournament held for children and adults at the West End on a weekend in late June. Wheelchair teams are included. The team entry fee is $108, and each team should play at least three games (972/392-5700). The Hoop-It-Up Winter Warmup takes place in March at Fair Park. Both are free for spectators.

BICYCLING

Bicyclists of all ages and skill levels enjoy Dallas area bike trails. Covering more than 500 miles of city streets, the bike routes are marked by "Pegasus on wheels" signs. **Bike trail maps** may be obtained from the Dept. of Transportation. Maps are also available at bike shops. The east-west routes are the three-digit even numbers, and north-south routes are two-digit odd numbers. A helpful bicycling book is *Bicycling in the Dallas/Ft. Worth Area* by Bill

Pellerin and Ralph Neidherdt. Call your parks and recreation department for bike routes in your area. Remember your helmet!

The **Greater Dallas Bicyclists** is an active club that sponsors more than 60 rides/month (946-BIKE). Monthly, they publish the *Spokesman* with information about rides, rallies, festivals, clinics, bike care, and trails. A family membership is $25.

May is National Bicycle Month, and one celebration is **Cycle Dallas**, a free cycling festival at White Rock Lake sponsored by the Transportation Department and the Greater Dallas Bicyclists. A Bicycle Rodeo is held for young children, and other clinics are scheduled for older cyclers. Every hour, small groups leave on 6-mile instructional trips. For information, call the Greater Dallas Bicyclists or P. M. Summer of the Transportation Department at 670-4039.

Dallas Bike Trails:

Bachman Lake (3.08 mi.)
2750 Bachman

Glendale Park (1.7 mi.)
1300 E. Ledbetter

Juanita J. Craft Park
4500 Spring (1.41 mi.)

Kiest Park (2.4 mi.)
3000 S. Hampton

L.B. Houston (5 mi./mtn. bike)
1600 California Crossing

Trinity Park (.66 mi.)
3700 Sylvan

Samuell/Elam/Crawford
8700 Elam (2.13 mi.)

White Rock Cr. Greenbelt
7000 Valley View (7.5 mi.)

White Rock Lake (11.1 mi.)
8300 Garland Road

BOWLING

Children have become so much a part of bowling that most bowling lanes have designated youth directors, and young bowlers take lessons and play in leagues and tournaments under the leadership of the Youth American Bowling Alliance. Youth leagues usually play two games on Saturday mornings in mixed leagues for ages 6-8 and three games for ages 9-11 and 12-14. Local winners play in a state tournament. Some centers have youth-adult leagues. Bowling is a great family sport, and children as young as 3 may play using six-pound balls. Bumpers may be added so very young bowlers don't get discouraged. Birthday parties at the bowling lanes are great fun, and some lanes will take party members behind the scenes so they can see how the pins are loaded and balls returned.

CHEERLEADING

Cheerleading is good fun and exercise for both girls and boys. Lessons and summer camps are offered through recreation centers, gymnastic centers, high school fundraisers, and private cheerleading schools. Some of the cheerleading schools also offer birthday parties. Area schools include **NCA Supercenter**, 2010 Merritt, Garland, 972/840-2282; **ASI Gymnastics**, Mesquite, 972/288-5510; **Dallas Gymnastics Center**, 351-0033; and **Metroplex Gymnastics**, 343-8652.

DANCING

Dance lessons are a part of many young girls' and boys' education. Ballet, tap, and jazz are all very popular with children. In the *Yellow Pages*, look under "Dancing" for schools near you. Some dance companies with classes for children are listed in Chapter Three. Dancing is also offered through recreation centers and some community colleges. An introduction to popular dances and the social graces for upper elementary and middle school-aged children is through **Dick Chaplin's Cotillion** (972/239-1269). A family place for country western dancing is **Trail Dust Steakhouse**.

DISC GOLF

A Frisbee, a pretty day, and a good arm are all that are needed to participate in one of Dallas park's disc golf courses. Call the parks and recreation dept. for the location of one near you. Tournaments are sometimes scheduled. The following are some courses in the area: B.B. Owen Park, Kingsley and Plano Road; Shawnee Park, near Ave. P and Parker Rd., Plano; Fritz Park, Britain Rd. one block south of Shady Grove, Irving; Victoria Park, Northgate at Pleasant Run, Irving; Greenbelt Area 2, Southern Oaks and Josey Lane, Carrollton.

FENCING

Fencing for youth usually begins at 6 years old in a local fencing club. Students at **Lone Star Fencing Club** meet at Lone Star Fencing Center, 2636 Walnut Hill Lane (352-3733). The director is a three-time Olympian, and instructors are certified. Classes are held for ages six through adult. Students may belong to the United States Fencing Association and compete on local, divisional, sectional, and then the National Junior Olympic Competition level. The LSFA has other area locations.

FISHING

Look under "Lakes" in this chapter for some great fishing in the metroplex and surrounding area, and see White Rock Lake in Chapter One for fishing in the city. Anyone 17 years old or older is required to have a fishing license, which costs about $13, or a temporary fourteen-day license, which is $7. Fishing supply stores usually have them. A *Texas Fishing Guide* may be obtained by calling 800/792-1112. Call the Athens, Texas, Chamber of Commerce about the super fish hatchery and educational center called the **Freshwater Fisheries Center**, 5550 Flat Creek Road in Athens, Texas 75751. Located on FM 2495 near Lake Athens, it is an innovative aquarium and hatchery complex with more than 300,000 gallons of aquaria and home of the ShareLunker Program (903/676-BASS). Fish are stocked in a two-acre casting pond, and here children can learn the fundamentals of fishing. KIDFISH is a popular program that gets kids involved in fishing and the out-of-doors. National Fishing Week is held during the first week of June. At this time and throughout the month, fishing activities for kids are planned at the Fisheries Center and on area lakes. An event is held on the lake at The Ballpark in Arlington. Call the KIDFISH Regional Director at 817/429-8793. A similar program is called "Get Hooked on Fishing, Not Drugs," which is sponsored by Texas Black Bass Unlimited. They sponsor a June Fishfest on White Rock Lake. Call 328-8228.

Samuell Farm (972/670-8262). Seven ponds are stocked for fishing at Samuell Farm in Mesquite. The only fee is the entrance fee. Bring your own gear, bait, insect repellent, and lawn chair.

Catfish Corner (972/222-2823). Catfish are raised here, and fishing is year round from about 8 A.M. until dark. Admission is adults, $2, children, $1, with $1.85/pound for fish caught. Bait is available. It is located east of Mesquite at 120 Lawson off I-30 East.

Gone Fishin' (Metro 972/427-6694). Channel catfish are caught year round. Bait, tackle shop, and take-out restaurant are available. There is little shade. Highway 175, Exit 741, at Crandall (nine miles from LBJ Frwy.).

FOOTBALL

Youth football is offered through private associations, such as **Spring Valley Athletic Association**, for fourth-, fifth-, and sixth-graders, and the teams play other teams on their grade level. Look under "Athletic Organizations" in the *Yellow Pages*. Football in school begins in the seventh grade, and many coaches feel that is soon enough. Some YMCAs offer flag football for elementary grades.

An annual four-on-four Air-It-Out flag football competition that includes some youth activities is held by Dallas Cowboys NFL usually in November.

GOLF and MINIATURE GOLF

The **Northern Texas PGA Junior Golf Foundation** (972/881-GOLF) sponsors the *Texas Golf Quarterly* junior tours, the Texas State Junior Championship, PGA Junior Qualifying, and the Junior Tournament of Champions and Cup Matches. Many area recreation centers and country clubs offer lessons, youth rates, summer golf programs, and tournaments. Some driving ranges also offer lessons. A junior golf clinic is offered at the Byron Nelson each year. The five public golf courses in Dallas that offer youth programs are listed below:

Cedar Crest   1800 Southerland   670-7615

Grover Keaton	2323 N. Jim Miller	670-8784
L.B. Houston	11223 Luna Road	670-6322
Stevens Park	1005 Montclair	670-7506
Tenison Park	3501 Samuell Blvd.	670-1402

The following are more family golf parks and miniature golf parks.

Green Oaks Golf Center, 1301 NE Green Oaks Blvd., Arlington (817/860-6917). This golf center has a 50-station golfing range and an area where you can practice getting out of a sand bunker or putt on a regulation green. Golfers can play on a 36-hole miniature golf course and take individual and group lessons.

Eaglequest Golf Park, 8787 Park Lane (341-9600). Eaglequest features a Cayman ball golf course, three outdoor miniature golf courses, one indoor miniature golf course, driving range and teaching facility, bent grass putting green and a chipping and bunker green, video arcade, remote-controlled boats, restaurant, and batting cages, all in a beautiful setting.

Fun Town, 1201 Red Oak Road, Red Oak (972/617-8696). Fun Town features Big Ball Golf in which golfers hit an orange over-sized golf ball over a nine-acre golf course. Two miniature golf courses, go-karts, and video rooms add to the fun. The season opens in mid-March.

Twin Rivers, 1200 E. Belt Line, Richardson (972/234-2291). Twin Rivers has three miniature golf courses, video games, and ten batting cages.

More Miniature Golf and Games
Belt Line Station, 1503 N. Belt Line, Irving, 972/313-1550
Celebration Station, 4040 Towne Crossing Blvd., Mesquite, 972/279-7888
CityGolf (indoor), West End Marketplace, 855-7888
Malibu Speedzone, 11130 Malibu Dr. I-35E & Walnut Hill, 972/247-RACE
Mountasia, Parker and US 75, Plano, 972/424-9940
Putt Putt, several locations

Sandy Lake Park, I-30E North at Sandy Lake Rd., Carrollton, 972/242-7449

Hit 'N Go, 210 W. Centerville, Garland, 972/864-4653

GYMNASTICS and TUMBLING

Gymnastics and tumbling help children with flexibility, control, and confidence. Young gymnasts in Dallas take lessons through recreation centers, the YMCA, summer camps, and private gyms. Many offer USGF competitive teams, and some Dallas youths have national ranking. Mom and tot classes are available through these centers and the nationally known **Gymboree**, 341-2FUN. Another gym for younger children is **The Little Gym** for ages 4 months to 12 years. It is located at Coit and Belt Line (972/644-7333). Some private gyms offer birthday parties and parents' night out. In the *Yellow Pages*, look under "Gymnastics Instruction." **Dallas Fun and Fitness Center** in Addison offers sleepovers for Scouts and other groups (972/960-1108).

HIKING and VOLKSMARCHING

Look under "Nature" in Chapter Two for beautiful, woodsy places to hike in the Dallas area. Groups such as the Sierra Club and the Audubon Society regularly publish calendars of hiking and back-packing adventures. A Texas Forestry Association brochure lists eleven East Texas trails maintained by timber companies (409/632-8733). Volksmarchers, who often trek through nature areas, belong to clubs that measure routes, set trail markers, bring water, sign walkers in and out, and give medals and stamps indicating completion of walks. One Dallas club is **Dallas Trekkers Inc.** (723-6536). Call 800/830-WALK for American Volkssport Association's list of Texas walks.

HUNTING AND SPORTING CLAYS

As a sideline of the Texas Wildlife Association, the **Texas Youth Hunting Association** serves ages 9-17 who pay a membership fee of $10. Other requirements include buying a hunting license, signing a medical release, and passing a hunter education course. The Association tries to find a place for each young hunter to hunt at least once a year. Sometimes this is before the official season begins. For more information, call 210/930-2177.

Designed to stimulate different types of wild bird hunting conditions, sporting clays is a shotgun clay target game. Target speeds, shooting positions, and angles change, unlike skeet and trap where clay targets are thrown from standardized speeds and positions. Sub-junior and junior competitions are held at various locations. Courses in the area include **Elm Fork Shooting Park, Inc.**, 10751 Luna Rd., 556-0164, and **Sporting Clays International of Dallas**, Rt. 1, Allen, 972/727-1998.

ICE HOCKEY

Sign-up time for ice hockey for ages 4-19 is in September, and ice skating lessons are not required for younger players but are recommended for older divisions. The season lasts from October-March. For information about ice hockey teams in the area, contact the **Dallas Junior Hockey Association** at 972/506-7825, or call the ice skating rinks.

ICE SKATING and BROOMBALL

Ice skating is fun any time of year, but in the heat of a Texas summer, it is the coolest spot in town. Ice skating rinks offer public skating, lessons and competition in the US Figure Skating Association, ice hockey, and broomball. Birthday party packages and group rates are available, and the rinks may be rented for broomball. The Galleria rink is particularly beautiful in December with a huge Christmas tree in the center.

Americas Ice Garden, Plaza of the Americas, 700 N. Pearl at San Jacinto, 922-9800

Northpark on Ice (outdoor rink), Northpark Center, November-March, 421-RINK

Iceoplex, 15100 Midway Rd. (at Belt Line), 972/991-PLEX

Galleria Ice Skating Center, 13350 Dallas Pky., 972/392-3363

Dr Pepper StarCenter, 211 Cowboys Pkwy., Irving, 75063, 972/467-5283

Prestonwood Ice Capades Chalet, Prestonwood Town Center, 5301 Belt Line Rd., 972/980-8988

KITE FLYING

Kiters in **Jewels of the Sky** kite flying club meet regularly to share information about kite construction and flying techniques and to fly their extraordinary kites. Children are welcome with parental supervision. Flag Pole Hill at Northwest Highway and N. Buckner is a favorite spot to fly kites.

LACROSSE

To locate a lacrosse team in the area, contact Ray Maitland at 972/964-2732. He can also tell you about summer camps and clinics in Texas. In lacrosse, ten players in protective gear are on the field at a time, and they are trying to move the ball toward the opponent's goal by running with the ball in the basket of the stick. They run, pass, and change directions in this full-contact sport.

MARTIAL ARTS

Those who love karate and other martial arts believe that they not only foster physical fitness, but also build a positive self-image, self-discipline, confidence, and respect for others. Classes are offered at recreation centers, YMCA, and some schools. It's a good idea to observe a class before enrolling. Look in the *Yellow Pages* under "Karate and other Martial Arts" for private instruction.

MOTOR SPORTS—CARS, CARTS, AND MODEL PLANES

Go-Karts and Mini-Virage Cars
Celebration Station, I-30 & I-635, Mesquite, 972/279-7888
Indoor Grand Prix, 11511 Emerald, 972/247-5278, and 10101 Royal, 503-7223
Malibu Speedzone, 11130 Malibu, 972/245-RACE
Mesquite Go Carts, 1630 E. Hwy. 80, Mesquite, 972/288-4888
Putt Putt, 17717 Coit Rd., 972/248-4653
Precision Karting, 2525 Southwell, 972/243-0714

Shake, Rattle, and Roll, 6606 S. Loop 12, 398-4826

Texas Indoor Cart Racing, 1210A Scyene, Mesquite,
  972/285-5515

Many hobbyists in the area enjoy the remote-controlled cars and planes, model rockets, and the slotcars. Supplies for all sorts of RC vehicles may be found at Texas RC Modelers, 230 W. Parker Rd. Plano, 972/422-5386. Call 972/821-2550 for activities of the **Dallas Model Aircraft Association** who are usually out at Samuell-Garland Park, which is located at Northwest Hwy. and Garland Rd., on Sundays from noon to 4. The **R/C Flyers Association** and the City of Irving sponsor the George W. Meyer Craftsmanship Fly-in which features radio-controlled planes from all over the nation at the model runway at North Lake Park in Irving (972/253-7476 or 817/430-3507, 262-1063).

ORIENTEERING

In orienteering, hikers use a compass and topographical map to go from one point to another. Many children learn this skill through Boy Scouts or Girl Scouts. Orienteering clubs with members of all skill levels sometimes have theme meets or canoe trips. In the **North Texas Orienteering Association**, a family membership is $18 (369-1823).

PADDLEBOATING

The new lightweight paddleboats are much improved over the ones some of us remember as children. Paddleboating in the area is available at the places listed below:

Bachman Lake (usually), 3500 W. Northwest Hwy.

Double D Ranch, Mesquite, 972/289-2341

Sandy Lake Amusement Park, I-35E North at Sandy Lake Road
  West, Carrollton, 972/242-7449

PAINTBALL

Probably best for families or youth groups with junior high school students, paintball is a team game in which team members eliminate other team players while they try to capture the other team's flag and protect their own. They carry air-powered guns that shoot colored paint pellets and wear masks, goggles, and long-sleeved shirts. **Action Indoor Paintball Games of Dallas** (972/554-1937) and **Survival Games of D/FW** (Metro 817/267-3048) are two local places to play.

RAFTING, CANOEING, TUBING, and KAYAKING

Although the area around New Braunfels, San Marcos, and Glen Rose has some great tubing and rafting, there are a few popular spots closer to home. Canoes may be rented from **High Trails Canoe**, 3610 Marquis Dr., Garland (972/2-PADDLE), and **North Texas Canoe Rentals**, 2316 Daybreak (972/245-7475), which also provides shuttles. One recommended Trinity River trip is on the Elm Fork from TX 121 near the dam at Lake Lewisville to I-35 bridge (5.5 mi.) or on to McInnish Park on Sandy Lake Rd. in Carrollton (9.4 mi.). For information about the river, call 434-1666. For information about paddling on the Brazos below Possum Kingdom Dam, call **Rochelle's Canoe Rental** (817/659-3341) and the **Brazos River Authority** (817/776-1441). Canoes and kayaks may be rented on area lakes. See "Day Trips" for information about Glen Rose and Tyler State Park. **Texas River Expeditions** plans family rafting weekends and one-day trips (800/950-RAFT).

Lessons are offered through the American Red Cross, May-September (681-6260), and some of the community colleges, such as Eastfield and Richland, offer canoeing trips.

ROCK CLIMBING

The only way is up at local rock climbing gyms. Kids can scale boulders using safety equipment and also take classes. They may require parents to sign an insurance liability release form.

Exposure, 2389 Midway #B, Carrollton, 972/732-0307
Stone Works Climbing Gym, 1003 Fourth Ave., Carrollton, 972/323-1047

ROCKETRY

The **Dallas Area Rocket Society** has a full calendar of events. Two sites for events are outside Justin, Texas, and Windom, Texas. For information about building rockets and launching them, call John Dyer 343-3080 or Chuck Gibke 817/429-0789.

ROLLER SKATING

In the Dallas area, there are more than twenty roller skating rinks listed in the *Yellow Pages* under "Skating Rinks." Skaters may bring their own skates, but that usually does not affect admission prices. Most rinks will let preschoolers wear their Fisher-Price skates if the skates are in good condition. On Sunday, some rinks let parents skate free with their children, and some have special preschool skating hours during the week. Lessons, group rates, and birthday parties are usually offered.

RUNNING

See Chapter Two about the hike/bike/jog trails in the nature areas of the metroplex. The "Sports Section" of the *Dallas Morning News* mentions upcoming runs in "Around the Area," and many of these have a children's division and a one-mile fun run/walk. These runs are often part of festivals or fundraisers, such as Artfest Run for the Arts, Thanksgiving Turkey Trot, the Symphony Fun Run, and the companion/pet SPCA Lakewood Love Run. Most area communities have jogging trails and parcourses. There are parcourses at Richland College, White Rock Lake, and Bachman Lake. Just contact the Parks and Recreation Department for locations.

SAILING and MOTOR BOATING

Many area lakes, including White Rock, have sailing clubs that feature regular sailing events and beautiful regattas. The **U.S. Coast Guard Auxiliary** offers lessons and certification in boating. Look under "Boat Rental" and "Charter" in the *Yellow Pages* and in the "Lakes" section in this chapter about renting boats of all kinds. Some of the marinas with rentals also offer lessons in boating and water skiing.

Remember, the Coast Guard Auxiliary requires that all children in a boat wear approved life jackets, and a jacket should be in the boat for all adults on board. For information about the nearest certified safety instructor for Texas Parks and Wildlife's boating safety course, call 1-800/253-4536.

SCUBA DIVING

For information about learning to scuba dive, look under "Divers Instruction" in the *Yellow Pages*. Some of the businesses that sell equipment also offer PADI lessons, and the first "Discover Scuba" lessons are free. Scuba lessons may also be offered through recreation centers, YMCAs, some of the community colleges continuing education, and the Tom Landry Sports Medicine and Research Center (820-7800). Scuba West, which has three locations, offers instruction, equipment, and trips as does Aqua Adventures at their two locations. Popular lakes for scuba diving are Possum Kingdom and Lake Travis.

SKATEBOARDING and ROLLERBLADING

A favorite place to try out skateboarding and rollerblading skills is at **Rapid Revolution Indoor Skateboard Park**, 2551 Lombardy Ln., #150 (350-6419), for ages 5 and up. There are monthly events and competitions. You must bring your own skateboards and rollerblades. Remember pads and helmets! The park opens daily at 9 A.M.; Monday-Wednesday they close at midnight; Thursday and Sunday at 9:30 P.M., and Saturday at 3 A.M. A new skatepark is **Eisenberg's**, which offers room for skateboarding, skating, and BMX biking. It is located at 930 E. 15th St. in Plano (972/509-7725). K2 rental skates are available at Sun & Ski Sports, 5500 Greenville at Lovers Lane, 696-2696.

SKIING, WATER

Waterskiing is usually great on area lakes from June-September. Listen to news reports for wind advisories. Marinas with boat rentals may offer skiing lessons, and some summer sports camps offer lessons. A ski school in the area is **DFW Water Ski School** (972/784-8115).

SOCCER

Millions of youngsters across the nation are enthusiastically playing a game that their parents knew little about as children. Soccer has become incredibly popular as a sport for both boys and girls and will probably become even more popular as a spectator sport as these young players become adults. Soccer teams are fielded by recreation centers, YMCAs, and private athletic associations. For the name of an association near you, call the **North Texas State Soccer Association** (972/323-1323), which is the regulating group for area soccer, or look in the *Yellow Pages* under "Soccer Clubs."

Soccer usually begins with an under-6 league and ends with under 19, and members play on a team determined by where they live or go to school. Avid players may try out for a "select" team at the under-11 age group and sign yearly contracts. Children also play indoor soccer almost year round. Soccer Spectrum, 1251 Digital, Richardson (972/644-8844) and Inwood Soccer Center, 14800 Inwood Rd. (972/239-1166) are indoor soccer centers.

An exciting annual tournament is the **Dallas Cup** held each April at Lake Highlands Stadium. Approximately 170 teams from twenty-five countries compete for championships in five boys' divisions and two girls' divisions.

SPECIAL OLYMPICS and DISABLED SPORTS ASSOCIATION

Each year, more than 3,700 athletes and 1,700 coaches participate in the **Special Olympics** for athletes who are both mentally and physically disabled. The Olympics begin with an opening ceremony on a Wednesday night and end with a closing ceremony on Friday afternoon in May. Cities bid on the right to host the games. For more information, call 943-9981 or 817/429-7724.

The **Disabled Sports Association of North Texas** (972/462-7089) provides lessons and competitions for those with physical disabilities and/or blindness in groups, ages 4-7, 8-18, and adult, in several sports. Also, the **Bachman Therapeutic Recreation Center** (670-6266) offers special programs year round and summer camps for children with disabilities. More activities are part of the fun at **Variety Wheelchair Arts and Sports Association**, which offers sports for children 6-18 (972/494-3160). See "Playgrounds" and "Horseback Riding" in this chapter for more activities for physically challenged youth.

SWIMMING

Swimming in the Texas summer heat is next to breathing. The Parks and Recreation Dept. offers pools at twenty-two of their recreation centers. Samuell-Grand pool and Lake Highlands North have a wading pool. American Red Cross swimming lessons are offered at many of the recreation centers for a low fee. A responsible person 16 years or older must accompany children ages 6 or under. Below is a list of Dallas' public pools:

Bachman, 2750 Bachman Blvd., 670-6266
Bonnieview, 2124 Huntington Ave., 670-1960
Churchill, 7025 Churchill Way, 670-6177
Everglade, 5100 N. Jim Miller, 670-0940
Exline, 2430 Eugene St., 670-0350
Fretz, 14739 Hillcrest, 670-6464
Glendale, 1534 Five Mile Dr., 670-1951
Grauwyler, 2157 Anson Rd., 670-6444
Harry Stone, 2403 Millmar, 670-0950
Hattie R. Moore, 3122 N. Winnetka, 670-1391
Highland Hills, 6901 Bonnie View, 670-0982
Jaycee, 3125 Tumalo Trail, 670-6465
Juanita Craft, 3125 Lyons St., 670-0343
Kidd Springs, 807 W. Canty, 670-6817
Lake Highlands North, 9940 White Rock Trail, 670-1346
Martin Weiss, 3440 W. Clarendon, 670-1906
McCree, 9016 Plano Rd., 670-0389
Pleasant Oaks, 8701 Greenmound, 670-0941
Redbird, 1808 Ariel, 670-1917
Samuell-Grand, 3201 Samuel Blvd., 670-1379
Tietze, 6115 Llano, 670-1380
Tipton, 3607 Magdaline, 670-6466
Walnut Hill, 4141 Walnut Hill Ln., 670-6433

Members of the YMCA and YWCA also enjoy swimming and lessons, and some of the community colleges schedule lessons for youth and adults and public swimming hours. Many public and private pools offer a summer swim team. Swimming for ages 6 and older and diving classes are taught at SMU (692-2200).

Wave pools are fun at Garland's **Surf 'N Swim** and **Hurricane Harbor** mentioned in Chapter One. Sandy Lake also has a very large public pool, and the White Rock Yacht Club restaurant has a volleyball pool and playground alongside their sand volleyball courts. **NRH2O** is a wave pool with water slides, endless river, and children's area that has opened in North Richland Hills on Grapevine Highway across from Tarrant County Jr. College NE Campus (817/656-6500). Burger's Lake is a favorite swimming hole near Ft. Worth.

The YMCA and Sportsridge Athletic Club indoor pools are available for rental for parties.

The City of Richardson (COR) Swim Team is a year-round program for RISD students, and Richardson's community pools offer lessons. The City of Plano Swim Team (COPS) is a private swim team that has tryouts, and classes are offered year round at the indoor pools at the Aquatics Center (972/964-4232) and Community Natatorium (972/578-7171) for ages 6 months to adult. Both have public swim hours. Call the Parks and Recreation Dept. in your community to see if they have this type of program.

Dallas' **Loos Natatorium**, 2839 Spring Valley (972/888-3191) is the site of some exciting swim meets. Their Dallas Aquatics Club is a swim team for children ages 6-18 who practice weekdays from 5:30 or 6 to 7:30 P.M. Call about tryouts, and there is a fee to join. A child may accompany an adult in lap swimming between 9 A.M. and 2 P.M. and 7:30-8 P.M. on Tuesday and Thursday for $2 per person.

The **Pirouettes of Texas**, a synchronized swim team that practices at North Lake Natatorium in Irving, accepts girls ages 8-18 (972/254-4010). Another similar program is offered by the City of

Richardson for ages 8-18 called the **Richardson Dolphinas** (972/234-8678).

See the sections about "Lakes and State Parks" and "Day Trips" for more great swimming holes. Other community pools and facilities include the following in case you would like to try new pools every week:

Carrollton. **Rosemeade Aquatic Center**, 1330 Rosemeade Parkway, 972/492-1791. Pools: wading with fountain, training, main pool, diving well with three platforms, water volleyball.

DeSoto. **Mosely Park Pool**, 600 E. Wintergreen Rd., 972/224-7370. Pools: baby, wading, main pool. Across from a Leathers-designed playground.

Duncanville. **Armstrong Swimming Pool**, 200 James Collin Blvd., 972/780-5083. Pools: wading pool, main pool. By Leathers-designed playground, Kidsville.

Farmers Branch. **Don Showman Pool**, 14302 Heartside, 972/243-9079. Pools: baby pool, main pool with water slides and high dive.

Mesquite. **Evans Pool**, 1200 Hillcrest, 972/289-9151. Pools: wading pool, main pool with water slide.

Plano. **Jack Carter Pool**, 2800 Maumelle, 972/578-7173. Pools: wading pool, main pool with diving board.

Richardson. **Cottonwood Park**, 1321 West Belt Line, 972/680-8209. Pools: wading, main, and diving pools.

TENNIS

Tennis is a favorite sport year round in Dallas, especially with some communities and clubs offering indoor courts. The City of Dallas operates five tennis centers that offer lessons, ball machines, tennis merchandise, racket repair, league play, and lighted courts. Court reservations can be made one day in advance. See "Spectator Sports" for popular tournaments.

Fair Oaks, 7501 Merriman Parkway, 670-1495

Fretz, 14700 Hillcrest, 670-6622
Kiest, 2324 West Kiest Blvd., 670-7618
Samuell-Grand, 6200 East Grand Ave., 670-1374
L.B. Houston, 11223 Luna Rd., 670-6367

Call 670-8745 for reservations at neighborhood courts. The Parks and Recreation Dept. works in cooperation with the **National Junior Tennis League** to provide year-round tennis programs for children of all ages, including lessons, clinics, and tournaments. Call the Dallas Tennis Association at 342-9597 for more information.

The National Junior Tennis League is an eight-week summer program in which the Park Department in conjunction with several sponsors provides instructors, courts, and equipment for clinics, lessons, and tournaments for youth in more than thirty recreation centers. Call your nearest recreation center for more information. Some of the community colleges and SMU (768-2200) offer summer lessons, and some country club tennis programs include nonmembers in lessons.

TRIATHLON

Eastfield Community College, 3737 Motley, Mesquite, sponsors **KIDSPORT Triathlon and Fun Fair** on a Sunday in mid-September. Participants run, swim, and ride bicycles.

Rainbo Bread IronKids Triathlon (443-9901 ext. 5450, 712/580-7110). Swimming, bicycling, and running are the events in this triathlon for kids ages 7-14 held in May or June. This is the only national series of triathlons for children, and five winners receive trips to the national championship.

SUMMER SPORTS CAMPS

With schoolwork out of the way, the summer is a great time to sharpen skills in favorite sports. A good place to check for camp listings is the February issue of *dallas child*. Recreation centers and the YMCA offer day camps in most of the popular sports for youth. Look under "Tennis" and "Golf" in this chapter for opportunities with the Dallas Parks and Recreation Dept. Some private schools, such as St. Marks, Greenhill, and Hockaday, offer sports camps with instruction in more than one sport in addition to other types of day camps. Trinity Christian Academy Camps (391-8325) include football, basketball, wrestling, baseball, and tennis for boys and volleyball, basketball, and tennis for girls. Listed below are some programs that provide instruction and fun.

BASEBALL

Adair Baseball World, 3222 Skylane, Carrollton (972/732-7247). Camps held at Trinity Christian Academy for ages 7 and up.

Eastfield College Baseball Camp, 3737 Motley, Mesquite (972/324-7140). Boys, 8-18.

Lutheran High School Summer Baseball School, 8494 Stults Road, Dallas (349-8912). Boys and girls, ages 9-14.

BASKETBALL

Dallas Mavericks NBA Basketball Camps (653-0241). Ages 8-18, boys and girls. Various locations.

Premier All-Star Football and Basketball Camps, P.O. Box 870515, Dallas (985-1067). Held at various locations and features Dallas Cowboys and NBA stars. Ages 7-14.

Bishop Lynch Friar Basketball Camp. Boys, grades 5-12. 9750 Ferguson Rd. (324-3607, Ext. 115).

Dr Pepper Co./Nancy Lieberman Cline Girls Basketball Camps (612-6090). Grades 4-12. Bishop Lynch H.S.

Little Caesar's/Coca-Cola Basketball Camps (972/985-1067). Boys and girls ages 7-14.

John Shumate Basketball Camp, Southern Methodist University, Moody Coliseum (692-3501). Camps for boys ages 8-18, day or overnight.

Lady Mustang Basketball Camp, SMU Box 216, Moody Coliseum, Dallas, Texas 75275 (768-3681). Ages 9-18. Day or overnight.

Lady Express Basketball Camp, Collin County Community College, Plano (972/881-5888). Girls 8-14.

FOOTBALL

Premier All-Star Football and Basketball Camps (see BASKETBALL entry above).

Jay Novacek Football Camp. East Texas State University, Commerce (800/555-0801). Boys ages 8-18.

Little Caesar's/Coca-Cola Football Camp (985-1067). Ages 7-14.

SMU Football Camp, Ownby Stadium (692-3667). Day or overnight camp for boys to age 18.

SOCCER

SMU Soccer Camps, 6024 Airline (768-2875). Overnight camp for ages 10-18 and day camp for ages 6-18.

Tatu's All Star Soccer Camp (248-TATU). Day and overnight camps for ages 6 and up at various locations.

Techniques Soccer Camps, P.O. Box 830086, Richardson 75083 (972/699-3653). Bobby Moffat's camps for ages 4-19. Half-day, full-day, and resident camps at various locations.

TENNIS

Nike Tennis Camps, University of North Texas, Denton (1-800/433-6060). Coed camps for ages 9-18. All levels.

National Junior Tennis League 670-7115. Ages 7-17.

Summer Tennis Camp, SMU, Box 216, Moody Coliseum, Dallas 75275 (768-2664). Coed tennis camps for ages 9-17.

RECREATION CENTERS
AND YOUTH ORGANIZATIONS

RECREATION CENTERS

The recreation centers in Dallas literally have something for everyone from tots to seniors. The Parks and Recreation Department operates more than forty centers, and half of them have swimming pools. Signing up for classes and teams is usually done quarterly, and those for youth include almost all popular sports, arts and crafts, cooking, music, and performing arts. Gymnastics "Mom and Me" classes begin as early as 2 years old, and Red Cross swim lessons are offered at many of the pools. Some of these classes are free or cost less than $30.

Summer day camps are annual favorites, with some conducted at the recreation center and some that include many field trips. **S.L.Y. (Slow Learner Youth) Camp** is held at some rec centers, such as Lake Highlands North. Performing arts groups such as the Junior Players, and sports facilities such as bowling lanes and skating rinks combine resources with the centers to provide excellent instruction. Programs for children and adults with disabilities are available at Bachman Recreation Center. For youth ages 6-22 with disabilities, an after-school program from 3-6 P.M. and once a month special activities are offered. Call 670-6266 for program information. Special events, such as Easter egg hunts and Fourth of July parades, are scheduled regularly at the recreation centers.

YOUTH ORGANIZATIONS

BOY SCOUTS OF AMERICA (902-6700). The Circle Ten Council and national headquarters are located in Irving. In addition to traditional favorite activities such as hiking and camping, the Boy Scouts have included atomic energy and computers into their merit badge activities. In the last ten years, the number of Scouts in the Dallas council has risen from 29,000 to more than 50,000, and more than 6,000 have physical disabilities. Boys may begin at age 6 as a Tiger cub and move up. The Boy Scouts sponsor both day camps and resident camps in the summer. *Family Camping* is a guide offered by the Scouts at their retail stores to encourage families to camp anywhere from the backyard to state parks.

BIG BROTHERS AND SISTERS OF METROPOLITAN DALLAS (871-0876). This organization pairs up disadvantaged youth with individuals or couples for two to four hours/week of one-on-one companionship for a period of at least one year. Often, the children come from single-parent homes where there is no father. After applying, there is a screening process, and a case worker makes the assignment.

BOYS AND GIRLS CLUBS OF GREATER DALLAS, INC. (821-2950). Boys and Girls Clubs have seven branches in the metro area, and two of these locations have swimming pools. Youngsters ages 6-18 pay $4 for a yearly membership, and there are no other fees so disadvantaged youth can participate. They meet after school Tuesday-Friday and on Saturday during the school year and on Monday-Friday in the summer. Activities include a variety of sports, tutoring, computers, arts and crafts, woodshops, creative arts, and game room activities.

CAMP FIRE GIRLS AND BOYS (521-CAMP). The Lone Star Council of Camp Fire now accepts both boys and girls in the program. The club tries to meet the emotional, social, and physical needs of today's kids through camping, community service, and self-care programs. Boys and girls who are 5 years old may join, and both day camp and resident camp are offered. **White Rock Day Camp** is a popular summer camp by the lake that plans canoeing, archery, outdoor cooking, and nature crafts for ages 6-15. They also learn safety and survival skills. Camp Fire operates **Kidtalk**, which is a telephone line answered by volunteers for children who are home alone or worried about something and need someone to talk to (522-1144 or TDD 522-1188).

GIRLS INCORPORATED OF METROPOLITAN DALLAS (359-7266). Four centers are operated for girls, ages 6-18, by

Girls Inc. There is a $4 membership fee but no fees for activities. The purpose is to provide after-school care and build self-esteem to help prevent pregnancy and substance abuse and help girls learn how to deal with other challenges. Programs include Operation Smart to help girls excel in science and math and Job Shadowing in which a girl follows a role model who has a job that interests her. In conjunction with the Parks and Recreation Dept., summer day camp is offered for both boys and girls with the weekly fee based on family income.

GIRL SCOUTS OF AMERICA (823-1342). The headquarters of the Tejas Girl Scout Council are located in Dallas, and this twenty-county council has more than 32,000 members. With an emphasis on community service, the Girl Scouts are actively involved in projects to help the community, in outdoor activities, and in wellness education. Girls may begin the program at age 5 as Daisies. Troops are available for girls with special needs, and some literature is printed in Spanish.

INDIAN GUIDES AND PRINCESSES. A YMCA program originally designed to bring boys and girls and their fathers closer together, this group sometimes involves moms, too. Separate tribes, the Indian Guides and Indian Princesses usually meet once a month in members' homes, and participate in two or three campouts which are often held at Camp Grady Spruce at Possum Kingdom Lake. These groups may form in kindergarten, and most continue through the second or third grade. Boys and their dads may later join Pathfinders and then Trailblazers. This group is more expensive than Scouting. Fathers and daughters or sons select Indian names and sometimes do Indian crafts at the meetings. Even fathers who are very reluctant campers look forward to the campouts and the friendship of the other dads and the time with their children. The general YMCA number is 954-0500.

YMCA (954-0500). The YMCA has around fifteen branches in the metroplex area, and participants in the programs may buy memberships. There are additional fees for classes, camps, and other programs, but the fees are reduced for members. Some of the activities and services include full day and after school on-site child care, programs for preschoolers, sports lessons and teams, babysitting while parents participate in classes, summer day and resident camps, Christmas and spring break camps, and Indian Guides and Indian Princesses.

YOUNG LIFE (265-1505). Young Life is a nondenominational Christian organization offered to youth in grades 7-12. The main group meeting is held for students at junior highs and high schools by grade levels twice each month at a designated location. Some groups have Campaigners which is a smaller group that meets in members' homes during the weeks that there is not a general meeting. The purpose is to strengthen Christian values and provide good, clean fun and fellowship for teenagers. Some groups go on day trips and campouts. Their leadership is usually young adults who are positive role models.

YWCA (826-9922). The YWCA consists of six branches, the Women's Resource Center, and a child care center at UTA. Memberships are offered, and members receive a discount on activity fees. The Ross Avenue and Richardson YWCAs have indoor pools and offer lessons, free swim, and after-hours rental. Activities such as tumbling, dance, art, swimming, and karate are offered for children as well as special needs classes. All-day Summer Fun camps are also planned, and child care is provided for over 4,000 youngsters in Dallas County. The Women's Resource Center provides individual and group counseling for individuals and families, legal services, parenting classes, job development services, single parent support groups, and community leadership programs for young women. You do not have to have a YWCA membership to apply for these services, and the fee is based on a sliding scale.

PLAYGROUNDS

One activity of which youngsters never tire is time at the playground, and thankfully, this activity is free. The metroplex area has seven fantastic playgrounds designed by New York architect Robert Leathers, who consults with children about what they would like in a playground before designing it. His castle-like wooden playgrounds are listed below:

Armstrong Park, 200 James Collins, Duncanville
Friendship Park, 525 Polo, Grand Prairie
Grimes Park, 600 East Wintergreen, DeSoto
Kidd Springs, 711 East Canty, Oak Cliff
Prestonwood Elementary, 6625 LaCosa, Dallas
Victoria Park, Northgate and Pleasant Run, Irving
Waggoner Park, 2122 N. Carrier, Irving

Baby swings may be found at Armstrong, Grimes, Victoria, and Waggoner Parks. At Armstrong Park's **Kidsville and Safety Town** (780-5074), youngsters can ride their bicycles and tricycles down a miniature "street" which has traffic signs and railroad crossing. A trip to **Kidd Springs** might include a walk through the oriental gardens nearby.

Toddlers especially enjoy the small, picturesque playground at **Central Square** on Swiss Avenue by the Wilson Block near downtown. A larger preschool playground is at **Lake Highlands North Recreation Center** at Church Rd. and White Rock Trail. Both have sandy floors, so a pail and shovel would be a plus. Playgrounds for both preschoolers and older children are at **Lakewood Park**, 7100 Williamson; **Ridgewood Park**, Trammel and Fisher; Richardson's **Huffines Park**, 1500 Apollo Road; Richardson's **Cottonwood Park**, Cottonwood and Belt Line; Garland's **Audubon Park**, Oates and O'Banion (site of Surf n' Swim); and Highland Park's **Prather Park**, Lexington and Drexel.

The following are some more highly rated parks: **Caruth Park**, Hillcrest and Greenbriar; **Cherrywood Park**, Cedar Springs at Hedgerow; **City Lake Park**, Lakeside and Parkview, Mesquite (allow catch-and-release fishing in the city lake); **Gussie Waterworth Park** next to City Hall in Farmers Branch; **Martha Pointer Park** on Scott Mill Road and **Kid's Corral** in **Mary Heads Carter Park** on Kelly Blvd. in Carrollton; **Willowdell Park**, 12225 Willowdell, east of Central and north of Forest, and

Kid's Country across from Coppell City Hall. Another large wooden castle-like playground is **KidsQuest** at DeBusk Park, 1625 Gross Rd. at LBJ in Mesquite.

Special needs playgrounds include the **Scottish Rite Hospital Playground**, 2222 Welborn, which is primarily for hospital use; Oak Cliff's **Fantasy Landing**, which is wheelchair accessible in **Kiest Park** at 3080 S. Hampton; Farmer's Branch's **Oran Good All Children's Playground** (Lion's Playground), 2600 Valley View; Grand Prairie's **C.P. Waggoner Park** on North Carrier Parkway near Northwest 19th, **Friendship Park** on Polo Road, and **Nance James Park** at 2000 Spikes Street which is used by Dalworth Elementary School; and Plano's **Enfield Park** at Legacy Drive and Alma. Call the parks and recreation center of the city in which the park is located for particular information about suitability.

RANCHES AND HORSEBACK RIDING

Head up the family and move 'em out to a dude ranch for a day of western fun Texas style or maybe just an hour-long trail ride through beautiful woods with a picnic afterwards. Families who enjoy ranch life and would like to stay a week should contact two towns in the Hill Country, Wimberley (512/847-2201) and Bandera (512/796-3045), for a list of their dude ranches. Closer to the metroplex are some ranches and equestrian centers that offer horseback riding for about $12-15/hour, western and English riding lessons, stables for boarding horses, and more fun through hayrides, barbecues, camps, and swimming pools. It is important to call first to make reservations. Most have a brochure.

Southfork Ranch, made famous by the television show *Dallas*, is open for tours, shopping, and special events. Call 972/442-7800.

DUDE RANCHES

Chisholm Trail Ranch (817/638-2410). Chisholm Trail Ranch is a 2,100-acre ranch with a bed and breakfast lodge, horseback riding, camping, fishing, hiking, barn dances, and more for families and groups near Rhome, Texas. The lodge has four bedrooms that can accommodate about eight to fifteen people, and another small cottage sleeps four. The ranch also rents domed tents and teepees. The horseback riding is primarily for adults, but a pony for children is available.

Double D Ranch (972/289-2341). Double D Ranch has a general admission fee which includes use of a picnic area, paddleboat rides, pony rides, mini-golf, petting zoo, playground, and pond fishing (bring bait and gear). Trail rides for ages 8 and up and hayrides are extra. Children under 3 are free. Although they work mainly with groups, sometimes there will be space for families. Group rates include more activities. Double D is located in Mesquite southeast of LBJ and Lake June Rd. on Eastgate.

Texas Lil's Diamond A Ranch (Metro 817/430-0192). Texas Lil's features "A Day At A Dude Ranch," a one-day getaway which includes a souvenir bandana, one-hour horseback ride on a three-mile scenic trail, petting zoo, fishing and hiking, an all-u-can-eat barbecue lunch, playground, swimming, hayride, golf driving range, and unlimited soft drinks. Texas Lil's is northwest of Dallas in Justin.

Rocking L Ranch (903/560-0246). Horseback riding at the Rocking L is about $12, but for an additional grounds fee, cowpokes may fish, swim, picnic, and play games in the recreation room. Hayrides are also offered. Three rooms and a bunkhouse that sleeps 65-70 people are available for use except during the summer when the resident horsemanship camp is held for ages 7 and up. Birthday parties are also welcome. This ranch is east of Dallas, near Terrell.

Wagon Wheel Ranch and Stables (Metro 817/462-0894). At Wagon Wheel Ranch, guided horseback riding over 300 acres is available as well as night rides, hayrides, barbecues, picnics, lessons, and ponies for birthday parties. The ponies may be ridden there or taken to another location. Wagon Wheel Ranch is northwest of Dallas in Coppell.

HORSEBACK RIDING, RIDING INSTRUCTION, and DAY CAMPS

Capricorn Equestrian Center (972/530-1124). Lessons, horse shows, special events, birthday parties, summer day camps. Located in North Garland. 1105 E. Blackburn.

Jolabec Riding Stables (972/562-0658). Horseback riding in wooded area, picnic tables. Located north on Preston at Highway 380.

Las Colinas Equestrian Center (972/869-0600). Horse shows such as annual Mercedes Grand Prix series and AGA Grand Prix, boarding, lessons. Located at 600 Royal, Las Colinas, Irving.

Merriwood Ranch (972/235-5177, 972/495-4646). Lessons, horse shows, summer day camp (instruction in riding and swimming, tennis, volleyball). Located in North Garland. 2541 Big Springs Rd.

Palmerosa Ranch (972/222-2732). Hayrides and cookouts, boarding, English and western lessons, birthday parties for young 'uns with Welsh ponies to ride (may take to another location). Located at 5790 Lumley in Mesquite.

Adventures at Samuell Farm (670-8551). Horseback riding, birthday parties, picnics, lessons. Located at 100 East Hwy. 80 and Belt Line in Mesquite.

THERAPEUTIC HORSEBACK RIDING

Equest (827-7100, 368-7100). Therapeutic Horsemanship. 2909 Swiss Avenue, Dallas.

TROT—Therapeutic Riding of Texas (972/296-6334). Rollin' C Ranch, 1916 Westmoreland, DeSoto.

LAKES, STATE PARKS, AND RECREATION AREAS

Texans gravitate to the area lakes and state parks year round for fishing, camping, and water sports. They provide public boat ramps, fishing piers, picnic areas, campsites, and marinas that rent boats and sell bait. Beautiful wooded areas inspire hikers and other nature lovers, and spotting wildlife is pure delight for all ages.

For information about the facilities at the state parks, write Texas Parks and Wildlife Department, 4200 Smith School Road, Austin, Texas 78744, or call 1-800/792-1112, for their brochure called "Information: Texas State Parks." They sell a $50 Conservation Passport, which is good for one year, that offers unlimited entrance to state parks and a discount on overnight facility fees as well as a discount on the *Texas Parks and Wildlife Magazine* rates.

Park entrance fees range from $1 to $5 per person, and children 12 and under are admitted free. Overnight camping ranges from $7-$18. Facilities, which range from primitive campsites to rustic cabins, may be reserved eleven months in advance by calling a central reservation number, 512/389-8900. The central cancellation number is 512/389-8910. For information about other Texas campsites, call the Texas Association of Campground Owners, 800/657-6555, for their booklet called "RV and Camping Guide to Texas," or you may contact the Corps of Engineers or Park Superintendent at the lake you wish to visit. Be sure to contact the lake during rainy seasons to see if flooding has closed facilities.

Many park areas have a day use and overnight camping fee, and campers pay both each day. Some parks operated by the Corps of Engineers and those privately owned also charge an additional fee for use of boat ramps and beaches. Some entrance fees are per carload and some per person. Call 800/460-9698 for a home boater course.

Bonham State Recreation Area, Rt. 1, Box 337, Bonham 75418 (903/583-5022). 261-acre park with 65-acre lake. Picnic and campsites, overnight group facility and day use group facility, playgrounds, boat ramp, boat dock, fishing pier, swimming allowed. Texas Hwy. 78 south one mile to FM 271. Then go east about 2 miles.

Cedar Creek Lake (Chamber of Commerce, 903/432-3152). 38,000-acre reservoir. Commercial campsites, public boat ramps, marinas with boat rental, fishing, skiing, sailing, swimming allowed, golf courses. Chamber Isle-small, public park with boat ramps, picnic tables, and swimming located between Seven Points and Gun Barrel City on the south side of 334 (small fee). R.H. Lee Park located on FM 3062 (fee). Sunny Glenn Marina Fishing Pier on Hwy. 198, 903/489-0715. Champion Miniature Golf and Batting Cages on Hwy. 198 between Gun Barrel City and Mabank (903/887-3673). To reach Cedar Creek, take 175 south. Exit SH 274 south. Go 9 miles to Seven Points. Take 334 east towards Gun Barrel City. The lake is about 70 miles southeast of Dallas.

Cooper Lake and State Park (Corps of Engineers, 903/945-2108). 22,740 acres. New lake with state park being developed (903/395-3100). It features the most facilities for handicapped visitors. Call about Doctor's Creek Unit and the South Sulphur Unit. South Sulphur has campsites, screened shelters, and 15 cabins for rent. Equestrian area and hiking trail. Located 75 miles east of Dallas between Commerce and Cooper, Texas.

Daingerfield Lake and State Park, Rt. 1, Box 286-B, Daingerfield 75638 (903/645-2921). 80-acre lake surrounded by 551 pine-covered acres. Lighted pier, swimming area, boat ramp (5 mph), canoe/paddleboat/rowboat rental, three cabins, fifty-two campsites, group facility for twenty people. Take I-30 to Mt. Pleasant, exit Ferguson Rd., go east on Hwy. 49 for about 18 miles.

Grapevine Lake, Rt. 1, Box 10, Grapevine 76051 (817/481-4541). 7,380-acre reservoir. Seven public parks with boat ramps and camping facilities, fishing, swimming, picnicking. Silverlake

Park offers a visitor center, boat rentals, fishing supplies, and swimming (Silverlake Marina, Metro 817/481-1918). Oak Grove Park has pontoon boat rental (Scott's Landing Marina, 817/481-4549). Take I-635 to Hwy. 121 and go west to 121 and Fairway Drive. Get a lake map for parksites. Ask about the summer boating lessons for children by the U.S. Coast Guard Auxiliary. The Grapevine Sailing Club offers lessons (Metro 817/821-0383).

Joe Pool Lake, P.O. Box 941, Cedar Hill, Texas 75104 (972/291-3900). Joe Pool Lake is a 7,470-acre reservoir with an 1,800-acre state park (354 campsites) and 1,700 acres of other park land (over 200 campsites) maintained by the Trinity River Authority. **Loyd Park**, 221 campsites, group campsites, showers, fishing piers, two playgrounds, four-lane boat ramp with dock, softball field, hiking trails, October Forest of Fear hayride and haunted trail. **Lynn Creek Park**, two four-lane boat ramps, beach, 81 picnic sites, three group sites, playground, restrooms, amphitheater on shore with lawn seating for more than 1,000. **Lynn Creek Marina** (Metro 817/640-4200) rents ski boats, jet skis, fishing boats, a fishing barge, and party barges at 5700 Lake Ridge Pkwy. Take I-20 west to Great Southwest exit. Go south. Southwest becomes Lake Ridge. The Oasis Restaurant (817/640-7676) is a floating restaurant at the marina which is located a very short distance past the exit for Lynn Creek Park on Lake Ridge Road. Food for the ducks and large carp is available at the marina store. **Cedar Hill State Park**: $5 per person/12 and under free, eight boat launching lanes and two fishing jetties, 355 wooded campsites, two group pavilions, four playgrounds, swimming beach, picnic sites, twelve comfort stations, perch pond for kids. **Penn Farm Historic Site**: gift shop (FM 1382). **Joe Pool Marina and Park Store**: ski boat rentals, wave runners, paddle boats, enclosed fishing barge, and a 21-foot party barge. Located 10 miles southwest of Dallas, FM 1382.

Lake Arlington, Green Oaks Blvd., south off Loop 303, Arlington (972/451-6860, Lake Patrol). 2,275-acre lake. Boating, fishing, picnics. Arkansas Lane Park, 6300 W. Arkansas. Bowman Springs Park, 7001 Poly Webb Road.

Lake Bonham Recreation Area, P.O. Box 305, Bonham 75418 (903/583-8001). 1,200-acre city lake, 87 campsites. Boating, fishing, skiing, swimming, mini-golf, 9-hole golf. From 75 North, take 121 exit to Bonham, in Bonham take 82 East (go to the right off 121), turn left on 78 North, turn right on FM 898, turn right on FM 3 to the welcome sign, and turn left into the park.

Lake Lavon, P.O. Box 429, Wylie 75098 (972/442-5711, 972/442-3141). 21,000-acre reservoir northeast of Dallas, 20 public parks. **Collin Park**: swimming, boat ramps, camping. **Lavon Boat Rental** (972/442-2628) at Collin Park Marina (972/442-5755) rents motorboats, jet skis, pontoons; lessons in skiing. To reach **Collin Park Marina and Campgrounds**, take US 75 to Parker Rd. (2514) and turn right. Turn right onto 1378 south and then take County Rd. 727 to Collin Park.

Lake Ray Hubbard, Rockwall, Garland (972/205-2750, ext. 2761). 22,745-acre lake. Fishing, sailing, skiing (no swimming beaches). **Harbor Bay Marina** (exit Ridge Rd. from I-30): fishing barge, $6/person (972/771-0095). **Marina Del Ray** (2413 Rowlett, exit Belt Line off I-30): rents small fishing boats, Seadoos, pontoon barge; fishing on the bank; fishing dock, $4/adults, $2.50 children 12 and under (972/240-2020). **North Texas Sailing School** at Chandler's Landing Yacht Club (Hwy. 740, 501 A Yacht Club Drive): 20-ft. boats, skipper available, lessons, renter must pass check-out (972/771-2002). **Captain's Cove Marina** (5965 Marina Dr.) rents pontoon boats (972/226-7100). Exit Ridge Rd. from I-30 for public boat ramps next to the highway. *Texas Queen* riverboat offers excursions and dinner cruises (972/475-1767). City of Rockwall Lakefest, mid-June. Fireworks July 4.

Lake Ray Roberts, Denton (817/458-3978, 434-1666). 29,350-acre new reservoir. **Isle Du Bois State Park** (817/686-2148), 1,397 acres off FM 455 east of the dam. 115 multi-use campsites with water and electricity, fourteen equestrian campsites, lighted boat ramp, beach area, picnic sites, group picnic pavilions, lighted fishing pier, 12 miles of dirt trail, 4.5 miles of paved trail (part is handicapped accessible) playgrounds; Johnson Park, north shore, 1,514 acres. When completed, over 4,000 acres in parklands and large wildlife management area.

Lake Texoma, Project Manager, Denison Dam, Rt. 4, Box 493, Denison 75020 (903/465-4990): 89,000-acre lake in Texas and Oklahoma. Fifty parks, 100 picnic areas, marinas, fishing, boating, skiing, **Cross Timbers Hiking Trail** (14 miles), tours of the powerhouse dam (1 P.M.), **Hagerman Wildlife Refuge** (903/786-2826). **Eisenhower State Park**, Rt. 2, Box 50K, Denison 75020 (903/465-1956): 457 acres, fishing piers, Eisenhower Yacht Club Marina, 4.2-mile hiking trail, thirty-five screened shelters, forty-eight campsites with water, fifty trailer campsites, forty-five campsites with water and electricity, sandy beach, picnic areas, group recreation hall, pavilion. Take US 75 to 1310. Go west to Park Road 20 and park entrance.

Texoma marinas/resorts: Grandpappy Point Marina—sailboat charters and lessons, cabins, RV hookups, rental ski boats, wave runners, pontoon boats, located just outside Denison (1-800/969-9622); **Loe's Highport**—yachts, volleyball and basketball courts, beach, located on Highport Rd. in Pottsboro (903/786-9542); **Walnut Creek**—boat ramp and rental, store, located in Gordonville (903/523-4211); **Cedar Mills**—campground, boat charters, cabins, RV and trailer hookups, sailing school, store, and restaurant (open Wed.-Sun.), located in Gordonville (903/523-4222); Resorts: **Tanglewood Resort Hotel and Conference Center** located in Pottsboro (1-800/833-6569). Denison Chamber of Commerce, 903/465-1551. **Lake Texoma Resort Park** (800/654-8240). Located 10 miles west of US 69 on SH 70 between Durant and Kingston, Okla. Lodge, 92 guest rooms; 67 cottages; 500 campsites; group camp for 160 people; 18-hole golf course; indoor recreation and fitness center; stables; full-service marina; Funland with bumper boats, go-carts, miniature golf; park naturalist and planned activities. See "Day Trips" for more things to do around Denison.

Lake Whitney, P.O. Box 5038, Laguna Park Station, Clifton 76634-5038 (817/694-3189): 23,560-acre reservoir with fourteen federal parks and **Lake Whitney State Park**, marinas, tour of dam, fishing, swimming, boating, scuba diving. Lake Whitney State Park, P.O. Box 1175, Whitney 76692 (817/694-3793): 1,315-acre park, two-hour drive southwest, seventy-eight campsites, recreation hall, boat ramps, lighted airstrip, hiking and mini-bike trails, ask about swimming beach and screened shelters (problems with flooding). **Juniper Cove Marina** fishing barge (817/694-3129). From I-35, exit Hillsboro and take Hwy. 22 west to Whitney. Follow signs west three miles on FM 1244.

Lewisville Lake, 1801 N. Mill St., Lewisville 75057 (972/434-1666). 23,280-acre lake. Fourteen parks. Fishing, skiing, swimming, sailing, camping. **Lake Park** operated by the City of Lewisville (972/219-3550): swimming, boat ramps, camping, and fishing barge to the northwest (972/436-9341). Take I-35 north. Exit Justin Rd. (407) and take a right to Lake Park Rd. Fee, $3. **East Hill Park** operated by the Corps of Engineers (972/434-1666) swimming, fishing, ramps, yacht rentals at Pier 121 Marina (972/625-2233). **Parasail Dallas** at Eagle Point Resort (972/357-SAIL). **Hidden Cove Park** (formerly Lewisville State Park) Rt. 2, Box 353H, Frisco, TX 75034: 721 acres. Operated by The Colony. Fifty campsites, thirty-eight screened shelters, three pavilions, enclosed dining hall that seats 100 at water's edge, playground, picnicking, ramps, swimming in day use area. Daily entrance fee. Take Hwy. 423 to Hackberry Rd. Park is at the end of the road.

Mountain Creek Lake, Grand Prairie (972/660-8100). Used primarily by TUE for the power generating plant, Mountain Creek Lake is fairly shallow and is used by fishermen in small boats. **Mountain Creek Park**, operated by Grand Prairie Parks and Recreation Dept., has a pavilion with four picnic tables, jogging trail, boat dock, small playground, and nearby municipal golf course, but no restrooms or water (SE. 8th St. to Marshall Drive east to lake). Dallas Parks maintains some of the lake shore (670-6880).

Possum Kingdom Lake, P.O. Box 36, Caddo 76029 (254/549-1803). 20,000-acre lake. Campsites, marinas, scuba diving to 150 feet, swimming, boating. **Possum Kingdom State Park:** 140 miles west of Dallas, 1,724 acres, official state longhorn herd, 116 campsites, six air-conditioned and heated cabins, lighted fishing pier, boat ramp, playgrounds, swimming area, park store, restrooms, showers, wildlife. In peak season tent and popup camper rentals. Ask about the kids' fishing rodeo in late March or April. Take US Hwy. 180 to Caddo. Drive 17 miles north on Park Road 33.

Purtis Creek State Park, Rt. 1, Box 506, Eustace 75124 (903/425-2332). 355-acre lake. Fifty-nine campsites with water and electricity, twelve primitive campsites with water nearby, two-lane boat ramp, two docks, 50-boat limit with wake speed restriction, picnic sites, playground, hiking trail, fishing for bass on "catch and release" basis but may keep catfish and crappie, two lighted fishing piers, two rearing/trout ponds. Swimming area. No water skiing or sailing. Near Cedar Creek Lake. From Dallas, go east on Hwy 175 to Eustace. Turn left (north) on FM 316 for 2.5 miles to park.

5. Festivals and Special Events

Around Dallas there is always something to celebrate. The theme for the festival might be related to cultural heritage, history, physical fitness, the arts, nature, sports, or technology and products. Whatever the reason for the gathering, appreciative crowds show up for the fun, and very often worthy service and health organizations benefit from the proceeds. It is a good idea to call or watch for newspaper announcements about the festivals because all may not be held annually, or they may change months and/or locations. Keeping current telephone numbers for information is also difficult. If the number listed is out-of-date, try calling the visitor center of the city in which the event takes place, and their personnel can probably give you some information. Please look in Chapter Three for performing arts festivals and in Chapter Four for sporting events.

JANUARY

Kidfilm, AMC Glen Lakes Theater, Central and Walnut Hill (821-6397). Kidfilm, an international children's film festival sponsored by the USA film festival, takes place on a Saturday and a Sunday afternoon.

Martin Luther King Jr., Birthday Events. Look for special events and parades announced in the newspaper at places such as SMU, Martin Luther King Jr. Recreation Center, South Dallas Cultural Center, and other area colleges and community centers as well as the Museum of African-American Life and Culture.

FEBRUARY

African-American History Month Activities. Check the newspapers throughout this month for special activities at museums, bookstores, galleries, recreation centers, colleges, and performing arts centers.

Texas Rangers Mid-winter Banquet and Carnival, Arlington Convention Center, 1200 Stadium Dr., Arlington (817/273-5222). Outstanding players are honored at this annual banquet and carnival.

Dallas Boat Show, Dallas Market Hall, 2200 Stemmons (655-6181). Motorboats and sailboats, exhibits, water sport products and services, and the trout fishing tank fill Market Hall during this show. It's fun even if you don't plan to buy. Admission is about $6, adults, and $3, children. Discount coupons are usually in the newspaper.

Valentine's Day Events. Many of the public libraries plan special activities for Valentines, and the Arboretum sometimes offers free admission for sweethearts. Look for the special "Hearts and Flowers" market at Farmers Market, downtown.

MARCH

North Texas Irish Festival, Fair Park (670-8400). Forty musical groups on eight stages, Irish food and drink, performance workshops, jugglers, magicians, and Urchin Street Children's Faire highlight this celebration of the Irish held on an early March weekend.

Lone Star Cat Club Cat Show, Dallas Convention Center, 650 S. Griffin (349-9652). For more than twenty-six years, cats have competed for prizes at this event. Adoptables are also available.

Dallas Blooms, Dallas Arboretum and Botanical Garden, 8617 Garland Rd. (327-8263). The opening of Dallas Blooms signals that springtime has arrived in Dallas. The event lasts about one month, and the beautiful flowers are breathtaking every year.

Metroplex Doll Club Doll Show, Arlington Convention Center. More than 80 dealers converge on the Convention Center for this annual doll show that includes a display of Madame Alexander dolls.

Home and Garden Show, Market Hall (749-5491). Gorgeous flowers, exhibits, workshops, and children's events are featured at the Home and Garden Show.

Downtown Dallas St. Patrick's Day Parade, intersection of Commerce and Griffin to Ervay, west on Pacific to West End (939-2701). This mid-afternoon celebration features marching bands, floats, clowns, and more. About 4 P.M. the West End Festival on the Plaza begins with more family entertainment, live music, and food.

Hoop-It-Up Spring Warmup, Fair Park near Hall of State (972/392-5700). Three-on-three outdoor basketball tournament on weekend.

Greenville Avenue St. Patrick's Day Parade, on Greenville from Blackwell to Yale (368-6722). A very informal, enthusiastic parade of inventive "floats" and bands is planned annually for Greenville Avenue.

Texas Storytelling Festival, Denton, Texas. Civic Center Park on the weekend.

Dallas New Car Auto Show, Dallas Convention Center (939-2700).

Very Special Arts Festival, Plano Centre, 2000 E. Spring Creek. Held on a Sunday afternoon, this free arts festival is tailored for children with special needs and includes hands-on artwork, various performing arts groups, free refreshments, and a goody bag to take home.

Dino Day, Museum of Natural History, Fair Park (421-DINO). In celebration of dinosaurs, a parade and costume contest, films, scavenger hunt, and artwork are featured each year.

Spring Breakout, Six Flags (Metro 817/640-8900, Ext. 507). Look for special events in addition to regular Six Flags fare.

Texas Kennel Club Dog Show, Dallas Convention Center (972/606-3638). More than 130 breeds participate in this All-Breed Dog Show and Obedience Trial.

APRIL

Imagination Celebration, Dallas Museum of Art and the Trammell Crow Center Lower Pavilions (823-7601). This is a performance and visual arts festival for all ages. Both school-aged and professional performance groups entertain throughout the day. Workshops, hands-on art, and storytelling are also part of the festival, which is held on a Saturday in early April. Drinks and snacks may be purchased. Admission is free.

Texas Heritage Day, Old City Park, 1717 Gano (421-5141). Experience frontier life through basket weaving, paper marbling, spinning, butter churning, square dancing, tours of historic buildings, and many other activities.

Ennis Bluebonnet Trails, Pierce Park, 112 N.W. Main, Ennis (875-2625). Follow a map guiding you to brilliant fields of bluebonnets during mid to late April. Arts and crafts, food, antique show, and more add to the festival. Call 1-800/452-9292, which is the Texas Dept. of Transportation hotline for information on where to spot beautiful wildflowers.

Spring Break Family Fun Fair, Infomart (748-9631). Lots of family fun takes place through weekend activities, such as face painting, fashion shows, Channel 8 and radio personalities, taste testing, product exhibits, petting zoo, and Kidsport Aerobics.

Scarborough Faire, FM 66 and I-35E, Waxahachie (972/938-1888). At Scarborough Faire, an English Renaissance village, families watch knights in armour competing, feast on hearty foods, marvel at the falconer and his birds of prey, watch jugglers and sorcerers, enjoy a variety of performing artists, and browse in village shops. The festival takes place on weekends and Memorial Day from latter April-mid-June.

The Learning Fair, Northpark Center (363-0732). Sponsored by the Brain/Behavior Center, the fair brings together both public and private agencies to provide services for the learning disabled. Counselors, educators, and parents are at thirty-five booths, and entertainment is scheduled. FREE.

Galleria Primavera, Galleria, LBJ and Dallas Parkway (972/702-7100). Garden exhibits, music, and ice skating events are scheduled in the shopping mall during one week in April.

Easter Egg Hunts: Dallas Arboretum and Botanical Gardens, Sandy Lake Amusement Park, Farmers Branch Historical Park, Garland Easter Eggstravaganza, Las Colinas, recreation centers, Prestonwood Town Center, West End Marketplace. Easter Bunny: Casa Linda, Valley View Center, downtown Carrollton, Highland Park Village. Parties: Recreation Centers and libraries. Zoo parade and scavenger hunt. Sunrise service: Check with the Biblical Arts Center.

Easter Brunches with Special Celebration: Check with Cafe America, Doubletree Hotel at Campbell Centre, Harvey Hotel-Plano, Lawry's The Prime Rib, Sheraton Grand at D/FW, Hoffbrau Steaks, Embassy Suites Park Central Area, Sheraton Park Central, Westin Galleria, Arboretum.

Arbor Day/Earth Day Celebrations: Dallas Museum of Natural History, Dallas Nature Center, Grapevine Treefest, Heard Museum, state parks, Arboretum, Farmers Branch Mallon Park.

Plano Roundup, Bob Woodruff Park, Plano. Arts and crafts, fun run, horse demonstrations, barn dance, chili cookoff, and a children's area are "rounded up" for this celebration.

KSCS Country Fair, Texas Stadium (972/438-7676). Concerts and rodeo.

Irving Heritage Fair, Heritage Park, 2nd and Main, Irving (972/259-1249). Demonstrations of historic crafts, food, arts and crafts, music, and dancing take place on Saturday.

Art Fiesta, Old Downtown Carrollton (972/416-6600). Arts and crafts, food, children's activities, and music entertain visitors at this annual festival.

DeSoto Cityfest, Grimes Park, DeSoto (972/224-3565) Games, arts and crafts, and music add to the fun at Cityfest.

Prairie Dog Chili Cookoff and World Championship of Pickled Quail Egg Eating, Traders Village, Grand Prairie (972/647-2331). In addition to the chili cookoff, enjoy music, more food, and the flea market.

Richardson Wildflower and Music Festival, US 75 and Campbell Rd., Richardson (972/234-4141). Taste of Richardson, music, 5K, flowers.

Mesquite Rodeo Parade and Celebration, Mesquite (972/285-8777, 1-800/833-9339). This annual parade kicks off rodeo season, which runs from April to September. It features horses, floats, bands, stagecoaches, and drill teams on a Saturday afternoon.

Cardboard Boat Regatta, River Legacy Park, Arlington (817/860-6752, 800/342-4305).

MAY

Dallas International Bazaar in Addison, 15650 Addison Rd. (1-800/Addison). This festival features international food, crafts, and entertainment from 50 nations, Friday-Sunday.

Cinco de Mayo Celebrations: Greenville Avenue, Fair Park (midway, music, food), Traders Village, Samuell-Grand Recreation Center, Pike Park. Riofest: sponsored by radio stations KESS and KSSA and held at Trinity River Bottom, Commerce and Industrial (630-8531).

Artfest, Fair Park (361-2011). Artfest is a lively, colorful weekend celebration of the arts which includes the work of 300 jury-selected artists, Artfest for Kids, outdoor concert stages with a variety of musical entertainment, and food. Artfest Week includes a variety of activities around town.

Lakewood Love Run, Lakewood First Interstate Bank (651-9611). To benefit the SPCA, the Lakewood Love Run is for pets and their parents. Featured activities usually include a Celebrity Run, 5K with animals allowed, one-mile "pets and parents" fun run/walk with dogs on leash, pet tricks and best outfit contests, and more.

Boy Scouts Annual Scout Show, Williams Square, Las Colinas (637-1480). The largest Scout event in Texas, the Circle 10 Council Show is highlighted by more than 500 booths with demonstrations, games, and exhibits. Other activities include outdoor cooking, crafts, and boat rides.

Kid's World Exposition and Marketplace, Market Hall. Shopping, educational exhibits, games, costumed characters, contests, and hands-on art are planned for families during the weekend.

Texas Black Invitational Rodeo, (565-9026). The best of America's black cowboys and cowgirls participate in rodeo events.

Folklore Festival, Farmers Branch Historical Park, 2540 Farmers Branch Lane (972/247-3131). The festival begins with a 5K run and continues with an antique car rally, stuffed animal parade, tour of historic buildings, exhibits of historic crafts, folk arts and crafts, and food during the weekend.

Playfest, Crescent Theater (978-0110). Playfest is a fundraiser for the Dallas Children's Theater, and the fun includes excerpts from plays, carnival games, and more. Admission is free, and tickets are purchased for activities.

Mother's Day Weekend and Brunch, Dallas Arboretum and Botanical Garden (327-8263). The Arboretum plans a special weekend for Mom and the family each year. Reservations are required for brunch.

Mother's Day Concerts: Connemara in Plano (521-4896) and Greater Dallas Youth Orchestra at the Meyerson (528-7747).

Spring Flower Festival, Farmers Market, 1010 S. Pearl, Downtown (939-2808). Farmers Market celebrates spring with flowers, music, arts and crafts, games, and more.

Main Street Days, Main Street Historic District, Grapevine (Metro 817/481-0454). Plans for this celebration include arts and crafts, music, food, carnival rides, and a street dance.

Grand Prairie Western Days and Rodeo, various locations, rodeo at Traders Village (972/647-2331, 972/264-1558). Highlights at this celebration of our western heritage include a P.R.C.A. Rodeo, downtown parade, arts and crafts, 5K, and food.

Cottonwood Art Festival, Cottonwood Park, Belt Line at Cottonwood Dr. in Richardson (972/234-4141). Visitors may browse and purchase artwork by local artists.

Asian Festival, Artists Square. Music, dance, food, arts and crafts, martial arts.

Garland World Bazaar, Heritage Park, Garland (972/205-2749). International crafts, food, and entertainment round out the festivities at this annual function.

Come 'n Get It Canine Disc Championship. Bring a chair and a picnic and watch the competition. The Ashley Whippet Junior Touring Team usually gives a demonstration. Refreshments are available. Check with Dallas Parks and Recreation for location.

JUNE

Rainbo Bread IronKids Triathlon, Lake Highlands Recreation Center, Church Rd. at White Rock Trail (443-9901, Ext. 5450). For more than eight years, children ages 7-14 have participated in this nationally organized triathlon, which includes swimming, cycling, and running and benefits Boys Clubs of Greater Dallas and the Kidney Foundation. IronKids has a "Parent/Child Fitness Program" booklet which has an introduction by Kenneth H. Cooper, M.D. For more information about this program, write to IronKids, P.O. Box 660217, Dallas, Texas 75266-0217. Check annually for date and location.

Canalfest, Las Colinas, Irving (972/869-1232). Canalfest is a celebration which features bands, arts and crafts, car shows, water and boat shows, food, and the Great American Race in which more than 100 vintage cars participate in a transcontinental race and cross the finish line at Canalfest.

Dairy Day, Old City Park (421-5141). This festival in honor of the dairy industry includes milking demonstrations, dairy products to eat and drink, animals, games, and other activities.

Juneteenth Festivals: City Hall Plaza is the site of the Juneteenth Celebration, which offers music, cultural arts, crafts, food, and games for all ages. Fair Park's (670-8400) celebration takes place at Starplex and the Band Shell and includes a parade, food, music, and other entertainment.

Pioneer Heritage Festival, Samuell Farm, Mesquite (670-7866). This celebration of pioneer life features an antique tractor and engine show, arts and crafts, music, pioneer demonstrations from timber framers to candle making to branding, chuckwagon, hayrides, guided horseback rides, fishing, and petting zoo area.

Texas Scottish Festival and Highland Games, Maverick Stadium, UTA. The weekend festival includes bagpipe and drumming competition, Scottish food, Scottish and Celtic athletic events, children's games, and a dog show.

Lakefest, Rockwall (972/771-7700). Sponsored by the City of Rockwall, Lakefest is held on the shore on the south side of Lake Ray Hubbard, just north of Chandler's Landing near Dockers at I-30. Festivities include a decorated and lighted boat parade, fireworks show, Flag Day ceremony, jet ski and sailing demonstration, carnival, and stage entertainment.

Dad's Day at the Arboretum, Dallas Arboretum and Botanical Garden (327-8263). Barbecue, horseshoes, croquet, and entertainment are planned in Dad's honor for Father's Day. Call for a lunch reservation.

Hoop-It-Up, West End Downtown (972/392-5700). This three-on-three basketball tournament is for children and adults, and wheelchair teams are included. Each team plays at least three games, and the entry fee is around $90.

Land O' Lakes Arts and Crafts Show, Lake Park at Mill, Lewisville. At this lakeside festival, more than 100 artists and crafters gather, and special events for children usually include pony rides, petting zoo, and side street circus. Musical entertainment and food for all is offered.

Lakeside Artfest, Lakeside Park, Duncanville (709-ARTS). Arts and crafts, food, entertainment, clowns, magicians, face painters, and lots more fun at the park on Hill City St. is planned for this summer festival.

Riverfest Arlington, River Legacy Park, 701 N.W. Green Oaks between Davis and Cooper, Arlington, or on the grounds of The Ballpark in Arlington. From Friday evening through Sunday, Riverfest entertains visitors with arts and crafts, fun run, musical performances, critters, horseshoe pitching and other activities. Proceeds go to the River Legacy Foundation and the Junior League of Arlington.

Fritz Park Petting Farm Parade and Carnival, Fritz Park, 312 E. Vilbig, Irving (721-2716). The parade in honor of the opening of the Petting Farm usually forms at Senter Park (900 S. Senter) on a Saturday morning in early June and proceeds to Fritz Park for the carnival. The Petting Farm is open in June and July.

JULY

July Fourth Celebrations: Dallas and almost all surrounding cities plan festivities and fireworks to celebrate America's independence. Contact your chamber of commerce for their celebration plans if they are not listed here. Fireworks are illegal within the city limits without a permit because they are a fire hazard. Please check in Chapter Three for performing arts festivals on the Fourth.

Freedom Fest, Fair Park (670-8400). July 4th festivities begin around noon at Fair Park with entertainers on stage, all-American games, children's activities, and a fireworks finale at the Cotton Bowl.

Old-Fashioned Fourth at Old City Park, 1717 Gano (421-5141). This old-fashioned celebration includes an all-join-in parade, contests, dance, music, games, and tours.

Park Cities, Highland Park Town Hall, 4700 Drexel, to University Park Town Hall, 3800 University (521-4161). For more than thirty years, this Fourth of July parade has delighted residents because they join in the parade. They ride on floats, bicycles, antique cars, and go-karts and march in bands. Snowcones and hot dogs are awaiting them at the end of the line at Goar Park.

Star Spangled Fourth of July, Downtown Garland (972/205-2749). This colorful celebration includes food, crafts, C&W entertainment, children's activities, and fireworks.

Star Spangled Spectacular, Clark Recreation Center, Plano (972/424-7547). Patriotic festivities, food, music, and fireworks finish the day.

Kaboom Town, Addison (972/450-6200). An incredible display of fireworks at the corner of Arapaho and Quorum is simulcast with patriotic music on KVIL radio station on July third.

Las Colinas, Williams Square (972/252-7476). Concerts and fireworks. Parade at Rock Island and O'Connor, Irving.

Richardson Fourth of July, sometimes at Richland College (972/234-4141). Richardson's celebration usually begins in the early evening with demonstrations by groups, such as kite flyers and remote-controlled car clubs. Adding to the fun are performing arts entertainment, clowns, and face painters. Check to see if the Richland pool and planetarium are also open for the celebration. Fireworks end the evening with a bang.

Recreation Centers' July 4th Celebrations: Check with local recreation centers for special events. Lake Highlands North

Recreation Center holds an annual neighborhood parade for all family members.

Ringling Brothers Barnum & Bailey Circus, Reunion Arena. This favorite three-ring extravaganza is anticipated each July. There is usually a designated Family Night when the admission is less expensive.

Taste of Dallas, West End Historical District (748-4801, 720-7717). During this delicious event, restaurants present samples of their best fare. Outdoor entertainment and a children's area are included in the well-attended festivities.

AUGUST

Balloon Fest, Paschall Park, Mesquite (972/285-0211). This colorful hot air balloon festival begins on Friday at dusk with a "Balloon Glow" if it is not too windy. The rest of the activities are held at Paschall Park. Balloon races, food, music, a carnival, and more add to the fun. A shuttle is usually provided from Town East Mall.

Cultural Fest, Fair Park (670-8400). This is a multiethnic celebration which includes artists and craftsmen, entertainment, children's activities, and food.

SEPTEMBER

Labor Day Parade and Jaycee Jubilee, Central Park, Garland (205-2749). In honor of Labor Day, the Jaycees plan a downtown parade, a festival with crafts, a carnival, and the Junior Miss Garland Program over a four-day period.

Pepsi KidAround, Park Central, LBJ and Coit, Rd. Planned for ages 2-10, this benefit festival features puppets, music, painting, storytellers, crafts, and more.

Grapefest, Main Street, Grapevine (Metro 817/481-0454). Grapevine honors its namesake in this festival, which includes wine tasting and judging, vintage cars, "GrapeFair," and children's "GrapeGames."

Aqua Days on the Mandalay Canal, Las Colinas, Irving (972/869-1232). The Mandalay Canal is the site for a water festival featuring music, water exhibitions, boat show, arts and crafts, clowns, and dancers.

Return to Rural America, Pioneer Park, Carrollton (972/245-0319). This festival highlights life outside the big city with games and crafts, exhibits, petting zoo and pony ride, produce stands, and demonstrations.

National Championship Indian Pow-Wow, Traders Village, Grand Prairie (972/647-2331). Tribes and spectators gather annually for the weekend pow-wow which features Indian dancing and competition, food, arts and crafts, exhibits of teepees, and more entertainment.

Montage, Dallas Arts District. Montage is a fundraising festival celebrating the performing arts. Various individuals and groups perform on different stages. Also included are artists' booths and food.

Oktoberfest, Arapaho and Quorum, Addison (972/450-6200). German food, carnival, and children's entertainment are featured in this fall celebration.

Greek Food Festival, Holy Trinity Greek Orthodox Church. Weekend festival offering Greek food, cookbooks, music, and crafts draws appreciative crowds annually.

Family Fun Festival, Heard Museum and Wildlife Sanctuary, McKinney (972/562-5566). Nature activities, crafts, games, wagon rides, nature trails, animals, and food entertain families at this annual Fun Festival.

Kidsport Triathlon, Eastfield College, 3737 Motley, Mesquite. A triathlon for kids and special events for disabled kids is joined with a family festival.

Great Fountain Plaza Festival, Richardson Civic Center, Central and Arapaho (972/234-4141). Family games and entertainment.

Cultural Fest, Artist's Square. This is a multiethnic celebration which includes artists and craftsmen, entertainment, children's activities, and food.

Oak Cliff's Tour of Homes and Arts Festival, Kidd Springs Park, 711 W. Canty. A tour of six homes and a family festival which usually includes a parade, arts and crafts show, entertainment, and children's events is fun for all on a September weekend.

Western Week, Rodeo Grounds on Mill St., Lewisville (972/436-9571). A parade, country fair, and rodeo add up to down-home fun during Lewisville's Western Week.

Plano Hot Air Balloon Festival, Bob Woodruff Park, Park and San Gabriel, Plano (972/422-0296). Hot air balloon races, arts and crafts, and music are featured during this colorful weekend event.

Cityfest International, Plano (972/424-2254). This cultural arts festival celebrates the food, performing arts, and crafts of many nations.

Texas Heritage Crafts Festival, Six Flags Over Texas, Arlington (Metro 817/640-8900). More than 200 craft folks set up shop at Six Flags on two weekends in September. Live music and food as well as demonstrations of almost-forgotten pioneer crafts add to the entertainment.

Family Festival, University of Dallas, 1845 E. Northgate, Irving (972/721-5165). To launch the school's charity week, they sponsor a family carnival with games, prizes, and food.

OCTOBER

State Fair of Texas, Fair Park (565-9931). See Chapter One for highlights of Texas' three-week fair, including concerts, midway, exhibits, food, contests, game booths, parades, Pan American

Livestock Exposition, rodeo competition, and much more. The State Fair is Dallas' second most popular attraction.

Smith's "The Pumpkin Patch" (940/365-2201). This three-acre pumpkin patch, located in Aubrey near Denton, is open for pick-your-own pumpkins right out of the patch. This is great fun for groups such as Scouts.

Great Dallas Duck Race. A benefit for Junior Achievement and the Boys and Girls Clubs of Greater Dallas, the race consists of a 1/8-mile course for more than 20,000 rubber ducks. Participants may adopt a duck for a suggested donation of $5, and prizes are awarded to the parents of the ducks first crossing the finish line.

Autumn at the Arboretum, Dallas Arboretum and Botanical Garden (327-8263). The Arboretum, coated in many brilliantly colored flowers, lures native Dallasites and visitors alike to the month-long celebration of plants and gardening. Demonstrations, plant sales, special exhibits, and entertainment are scheduled for the entire family.

Texas-OU Cotton Bowl Football Game, Fair Park (565-9931). This annual football clash is held on Saturday afternoon during the State Fair. Fans gather for all sorts of celebrations on Friday night, and the winners continue to celebrate throughout the weekend.

Vineyard Fair, Howell Street between McKinney and the Crescent on Cedar Springs. A benefit for the Creative Learning Center, the Vineyard Fair draws thousands of shoppers who browse at booths stocked by artisans, sample food and wine, and listen to live musical entertainment.

Oktoberfest, Traders Village, 2602 Mayfield, Grand Prairie (972/647-2331). Oktoberfest is a European-style festival featuring oompah music, German food, beer garden, and dancing.

Fall Harvest Festival, Dallas Farmer's Market, 1010 S. Pearl, Downtown (670-5880). This celebration of fall's bounty includes music, Pumpkin Junction, fresh produce, and exhibits on Saturday and Sunday.

Country Fair, Downtown Carrollton Square, Broadway off Belt Line (972/245-5610). An early parade kicks off activities such as games, food, and arts and crafts at this old-fashioned celebration. Ask about the parade route.

Harambee Festival, Martin Luther King Community Center, 2922 MLK Blvd. (670-8355). This all-day festival showcases African-American culture.

Haunted Gardens, Dallas Arboretum (327-8263). The Arboretum plans scary trails for older children and not-so-scary events for younger ones. This event is usually held on three evenings near Halloween for goblins, ages 6-12.

Fright Nights, Six Flags Over Texas, Arlington (Metro 817/640-8900). A variety of creepy creatures gather for a Halloween celebration at Six Flags.

Singe Halloween at the Palace of Wax, Ripley's Believe It or Not/Palace of Wax, 601 E. Safari, Grand Prairie (972/263-2391). Halloween event for older children.

Boo at the Zoo, Dallas Zoo (946-5154). Very special activities are planned for Halloween fun.

Samuell Farm Haunted Trail, I-20 and Belt Line, Mesquite (670-7866). A few days before Halloween, Samuell Farm begins its haunted trail and barn, hayrides, carnival games, and petting zoo area.

Halloween in the Park, Farmers Branch Historical Park, Farmers Branch Lane at Ford Rd. (972/247-4607). A haunted house, hayrides, carnival, and more treats are presented for the entertainment of spooks of all ages.

Haunted House and Spook Hike, Dallas Nature Center (296-1955).

Haunted Houses: Begin checking the Friday "Guide" section in the *Dallas Morning News* from mid-October through Halloween for listings of organizations who offer haunted houses, carnivals, and other Halloween events. *dallas child* and *Dallas Family* magazines also list Halloween activities that are appropriate for children in their October issues. The March of Dimes presents haunted houses at multiple locations. Some events are too frightening for young children. Call first if you have questions about suitability.

NOVEMBER

American Indian Arts Festival and Market, Artists Square Downtown. More than seventy-five different tribes and pueblos from across the nation are represented in this cultural festival. Thursday night is Youth Cultural Awareness Night for school-aged children. The market is on Saturday and Sunday.

Dallas YMCA Turkey Trot, Downtown Dallas City Hall (954-0500). This annual 3.5-mile run showcases the downtown area and benefits a shelter for homeless and abused teenagers. A family tent has activities for children.

Senior Citizens Craft Fair, Automobile Building, Fair Park (670-8400). Family members of all ages will appreciate the talents behind the handmade items at this benefit craft fair sponsored by the Junior League of Dallas.

Minyard Food Fest, Dallas Market Hall (393-8513). Visitors annually savor the entertainment at the food festival whose goal is to raise consumer awareness of food products and benefit the North Texas Food Bank. Around 400 exhibit booths, cooking demonstrations, live music, and autograph sessions with sports celebrities are a delight to food lovers of all ages. Check annually for month scheduled.

Dallas Video Festival, Dallas Museum of Art (651-TVTV). Presented by the Video Association and the Dallas Museum of Art, this video festival is an exhibition of more than 250 screenings produced by independent media artists for adults and children, and it is scheduled from Thursday-Sunday on either the first or second weekend in November. Parents and children enjoy the kid-vid programs and hands-on workshops offered on Saturday and Sunday. Some of the videos are made for children, and some are made by children.

Christmas Activities: Check the newspapers toward the end of November because some tree lightings and special events begin the last weekend of November.

DECEMBER

Tree Lightings, Parades, and Carriage Rides: Most of the city halls and some of the shopping, entertainment, and community centers such as the Galleria, Crescent, and West End have breathtaking tree lightings to celebrate the Christmas season. Some, like Dallas, Carrollton, Allen, Richardson, and Grapevine, include parades. Call your chamber of commerce for specific dates and times. The Dallas Holiday Tree Lighting and Parade takes place at City Hall Plaza and includes a visit from Santa, Santa's Village, choirs, dancers, Christmas critters, and refreshments. Carriage tours of lights are usually offered at Highland Park Village and the West End.

Although Dallas rarely has a white Christmas, it truly is a "wintery wonderland" of holiday entertainment for families as the following festivities will attest. Also, look for special musical and theatrical events in Chapter Three's "Performing Arts Festivals."

Adolphus/Children's Christmas Parade, Commerce and Griffith, Downtown Dallas (918-1035). More than 160,000 people come out to cheer on the annual parade featuring floats, bands, antique cars, horses and riders, clowns, favorite characters and celebrities. Check the newspapers or call for the route.

Swiss Avenue Home Tour and Festival, Swiss Avenue at Munger (220-9630). Held on a weekend, the home tour includes eight homes and an English garden. Other activities which have grown up around the home tour are a parade at Triangle Park, antique and craft sale, carriage rides, and musical entertainment.

Winterfest, Mandalay Canal, Las Colinas, Irving (972/869-1232). Fifty thousand lights twinkle along the canal in a holiday festival that features a winter wonderland of entertainment, including Santa Cruises. Festivities continue through New Year's Eve.

Christmas at the Arboretum, Dallas Arboretum (327-8263). The December celebration at the Arboretum offers a tour of the DeGolyer mansion decorated for Christmas, workshops for children, an outdoor market, and entertainment provided by handbell choirs, chorale singers, and more.

Christmas in the Branch, Farmers Branch Historical Park, Ford Rd. at Farmers Branch Lane (1-800-BRANCH9). Christmas in the Branch begins early in December with Dickens in the Park which features horse-drawn carriage rides, tour of historical buildings, bells, and choirs. A Christmas Lighting Display Driving Route leads visitors from City Hall into the park. Authentic English teas and demonstrations of Christmas Past are also part of the celebration. Call for a calendar.

Kwanzaa. This celebration of African culture includes the principles of unity, creativity, faith, collective work, responsibility, cooperative economics, and self-determination. The Kwanzaa seasonal events are usually held at many locations around town including the following: Paul Quinn College, St. Phillip's School and Community Center, Martin Luther King Jr. Recreation Center, Lincoln High School, and the South Dallas Cultural Center.

Galleria Wonderland Express, Galleria, I-635 and Dallas Parkway (972/702-7100). A benefit for the Ronald McDonald House in Dallas, the Wonderland Express is a magical collection of twelve "O" gauge trains with 350 cars and 2,500 feet of track that travel through miniature scenes created realistically in minute detail. The nearby Wonderland Forest is comprised of dozens of trees, twinkling lights, and animated characters. This fantasy collection is open daily except Thanksgiving and Christmas on the third level. Sponsors and volunteers are needed each year.

Candlelight Tour at Old City Park, 1717 Gano (421-5141). The beauty of this annual event never dims. Special activities include tours of decorated historic buildings, musical entertainment, children's tent, surrey rides, refreshments, and holiday shopping on a weekend in mid-December.

Jingle Bell Run, Meyerson, 2301 Flora (692-0203). Festive costumes of all descriptions for individuals, groups, and their pets are in vogue for the annual Jingle Bell Run benefiting the Carter Blood Care Center. A 5K run, one-mile fun run, pooch parade and costume contest, and treats at Santa Land are planned for all ages.

Holiday in the Park, Six Flags Over Texas, Arlington (Metro 817/640-8900, Ext. 517). Held mainly on weekends from November-January, Holiday in the Park offers exciting holiday shows, an exhibition of beautifully decorated trees, carolers and other musical groups, rides, and sledding on a hill of snow.

Christmas in Heritage Park, 4th & Austin, Garland (972/272-9160). The Junior League of Garland presents an annual craft bazaar, Santa Claus, music, food, and children's entertainment.

Samuell Farm's Christmas, I-30 and Belt Line, Mesquite (670-7866). Samuell Farm's holiday entertainment usually includes activities such as "Santa's Peppermint Trail," hayride, and crafts.

Lantern Light Tours, Heritage Farmstead Museum, Plano (972/424-7874). Special holiday foods, music, crafts, and decorated two-story Victorian farmhouse capture the holiday spirit for visitors at the Lantern Light Tour.

Dickens Downtown Christmas, Historic Downtown Plano, East 15th (972/422-0642, 972/424-7547). Held in conjunction with the Christmas Tree Lighting in Haggard Park, this holiday celebration includes live music, strolling jugglers and costumed characters, refreshments, caroling, and a visit from the jolly old elf.

Dallas Farmers Market Anniversary Celebration, 1010 S. Pearl (670-5880). For more than fifty years, the Dallas Farmers Market has supplied fresh produce and plants to residents of Dallas. Look for holiday musical entertainment, Christmas trees, their new calendar, baskets of nuts and fruits for gift giving, arts and crafts, poinsettias, and special events.

Christmas at the Cabins, M.T. Johnson Plantation Cemetery and Historic Park, 621 Arkansas Ln. (north side), Arlington (817/460-4001). Festive holiday activities are planned each year around the historic cabins and schoolhouse.

"Star of Bethlehem" Planetarium Shows: The re-creation of the Star of Bethlehem and the Christmas story are presented at area planetariums such as Richland College, St. Mark's, and The Science Place.

Santa's Appearances: Confusing as it may be to little children, Santa seems to be everywhere they go. Most shopping malls, larger shopping centers, Christmas festivals, recreation center holiday parties, and parades keep Santa very busy in Dallas. Some malls and large department stores offer Breakfast with Santa and other special decorations and activities, such as the puppet shows and chorale singers at Northpark, the model trains at the Galleria and Richardson Square Mall, and the spectacular holiday tree in the center of the ice rink at the Galleria.

6. Day Trips

Sometimes the best way for a family to get to know one another better is to leave home in the family car to a new or favorite destination for the day where they can play and learn new things together away from the hectic routine at home. The destinations outlined in this chapter are within a one to two-hour driving time. If you have time to plan enough ahead, writing the town's chamber of commerce for tourist information and talking with friends who have been there for ideas about what to do and what to take adds to the enjoyment of the trip. When using this guide, remember to call ahead because attractions open and close regularly.

When traveling with children, it is helpful to make a stop by the bookstore or public library for some favorite books, books-on-tape, or book-and-cassette combinations. Some older kids like to take along a battery-powered booklight in case some of the travel time is at night as well as their own personal cassette player with headphones. Sing-along cassettes, snacks, drawing kits, and travel-sized games also help to pass the time peacefully. Some moms pack a "surprise bag" with play items that the children have never seen before. Including an "S & S" (stop and stretch) time about midway during travel helps to work out the wiggles. Always take a first aid kit that has bandages and something for insect bites. If you will be outdoors, insect repellent and sunscreen are good ideas. Also, remember the camera because there will very likely be some moments to capture.

BONHAM

Bonham was settled by a former Arkansas sheriff, Bailey English, in 1837, and was named for James Butler Bonham, a defender of the Alamo. A statue of James Bonham is on the courthouse square. The Bonham Area Chamber of Commerce address is 110 East First, Bonham 75418 (903/583-4811). Be sure to call to verify hours and days.

FANNIN COUNTY MUSEUM OF HISTORY, One Main St. at First (903/583-8042). This museum houses nine rooms of historical artifacts of Bonham and Fannin County in the restored 1900 Texas and Pacific Railway Depot. A brochure that maps out a five-mile walk/drive tour is available here. Also, the depot is home for the Red River Art Gallery and the Chamber of Commerce. Hours are April 1-Sept. 1: Tuesday-Saturday, 10-4; Sept. 2-March 1: Tuesday-Saturday, 12-4. *Admission:* free.

FORT INGLISH MUSEUM AND PARK, US Hwy. 82W at Chinner (903/583-3441). Located near the Sam Rayburn Library, Ft. Inglish is a replica of the fort built by Bailey Inglish to protect the ten pioneer families that he brought with him from Indian raids. In the museum are historic documents, weapons, tools, clothing, and other artifacts of the lives of the pioneers. Three log cabins were moved here and restored. Hours during April 1-September 1 are Tuesday-Friday, 10-4, and Saturday and Sunday, 1-4. Admission is free, but donations are appreciated. Closed Monday.

SAM RAYBURN LIBRARY AND MUSEUM, P.O. Box 309, Bonham, Texas 75418; US Hwy. 82W at Elphis (903/583-2455). Housed here are books, records, gifts, a collection of gavels, a replica of the speaker's office in Washington, a complete collection of the *Congressional Record* and other memorabilia of "Mr. Sam" and his more than forty-eight years in office, seventeen years as Speaker of the House. *Hours:* Closed Monday. Tuesday-Friday, 10-5; Saturday, 1-5; Sunday, 2-5. *Admission:* free.

SAM RAYBURN HOUSE, Rt. 3, Box 308, Bonham, Texas 75418; US Hwy. 82W west of the Rayburn Library (903/583-5558). Originally built by Sam for his parents in 1916, the two-story, fourteen-room white house was primarily occupied by Sam and his sister and contains their furnishings and clothes. A commemorative event is held each January 6 in Sam's honor. He was buried in 1961 at Willow Wild Cemetery, West 7th and TX Hwy. 121. Note: The house recently underwent restoration due to a fire in 1997. *Hours:* Closed Monday. Tuesday-Friday, tours at 10 and 11 A.M. then on the hour from 1-4 P.M.; Saturday tours on the hour from 1-5. Sunday tours are 2-5. Winter hours may change. Groups should make reservations. *Admission:* free.

BONHAM STATE RECREATION AREA and LAKE BONHAM RECREATIONAL AREA feature lakes and outdoor activities. See Chapter Four under "Lakes, State Parks, and Recreation Areas."

EVENTS: May-Bois D'Arc Festival on third weekend; July-Kueckelhan Ranch Rodeo on Wednesday-Saturday during last week; September-Greater Dallas Bicyclist Association Bicycle Rally during second week; October-Fannin County Fair held Thursday-Saturday during the last week; December-Christmas Parade on the first Saturday. Trades Day is first weekend following the first Monday of each month.

DIRECTIONS: US Hwy. 75 N 60 miles to TX Hwy. 121 E. Approximately 75 miles northeast of Dallas. It is about a thirty-minute drive from Bonham to downtown Denison, which is the next entry.

DENISON

The MK&T Railroad gave birth to Denison in 1872 as land was purchased and a town was mapped out, and the new town was named after Katy Vice President George Denison. Former President Dwight D. Eisenhower's father was a Katy Railroad employee, and Ike was born here on October 14, 1890. Another important event in Denison's history occurred when Denison Dam was constructed across the Red River, creating Lake Texoma, which covers 89,000 acres in Texas and Oklahoma. Brochures for historical driving and walking tours of Denison, an official Texas Main Street City, are available from the Denison Area Chamber of Commerce whose address is 313 West Woodard Street, Denison 75020 (903/465-1551).

EISENHOWER'S BIRTHPLACE, 208 East Day St. at Lamar; from Crockett, go west at Nelson. Dwight David Eisenhower, a five-star general of the army and two-term U.S. president, was born in this house and lived here three years until his family moved to Abilene, Kansas. A family quilt and a portrait of an American Indian by President Eisenhower are the only Eisenhower contributions to the house, but the furnishings represent the 1890s. Guided tours are given daily Monday-Saturday 10-4, and Sunday 1-5 March-November. Closed on Sunday December-February. A pavilion with picnic tables and handicap accessible restrooms as well as a headquarters which houses the visitor center, gift shop, and office are across the street. Guided "Ike Hikes" of the ten-acre park may be scheduled by calling 903/465-8908. Park entry fee is adults, $2, ages 6-12, $1. Call the Chamber of Commerce for current information (903/465-1551).

GRAYSON COUNTY FRONTIER VILLAGE, Loy Lake Park (903/463-2487 or 903/465-9447). Located in a wooded area that has a lake, picnic areas, and hiking trail, the Frontier Village includes log cabins and farm machinery and a museum filled with artifacts dating back to the 1840s. Arts and crafts shows are in May and November. *Hours:* Wednesday-Saturday, 1-5 beginning April 1-August 30. *Directions:* Loy Lake Park is located southwest of Denison. From south of Denison on US 75, take exit 67, Loy Lake exit.

KATY DEPOT, 100 block of East Main (903/463-7729). Built in 1902, the MK&T Depot was an active part of life in Denison for many years. The restored depot now houses businesses, shops, a restaurant which is open for lunch, and a small railroad museum. The park in front looks much like it did in 1911. The museum hours are Monday-Saturday, 10 A.M.-1 P.M. and 2-4 P.M. (903/463-6238).

HAGERMAN NATIONAL WILDLIFE REFUGE, Rt. 3, Box 123, Sherman 75092-4564 (903/786-2826). The refuge includes 11,319 acres of habitat for 280 species of migratory birds. Visitors birdwatch, picnic, take pictures, hike, and look over interpretive panels at the Visitors Center. The peak time to see migrating waterfowl is from October-March. Shore birds are often most prevalent in mid-summer. Boat fishing is allowed from April-September within the refuge that surrounds the Big Mineral arm of Lake Texoma, but camping, skiing, and swimming are prohibited within refuge boundaries. Remember your binoculars and camera. A leaflet for a self-guided auto tour is in the headquarters. *Refuge hours:* daylight hours, daily. *Office hours:* Monday-Friday, 7:30-4; weekends, 8:30-4 if volunteers are available. *Admission:* free. *Directions:* From US 75 at Sherman, go west on FM 1417 and turn right into the refuge. Call first about lake level.

EISENHOWER STATE PARK and LAKE TEXOMA, Rt. 2, Box 50K, Denison 75020 (903/465-1956 from 8 to 5). For information about this 457-acre park on Texas' third largest reservoir, please look in Chapter Four under "Lakes, State Parks, and Recreation Areas."

Events: March-Art and Wine Renaissance; April-Texoma Lakefest Regatta; May-Memorial Day Parade; July-Western Week; September-Aerobatics and Air Show; October-Main Street Fall Festival; December-Tour of Homes and Christmas Parade. *Directions:* Denison is approximately 75 miles north of Dallas on US 75.

FORT WORTH

Will Rogers said something to the effect that "Fort Worth is where the West begins. Dallas is where the East peters out." Ft. Worth's western heritage is very much alive in Sundance Square, the Stockyards, western art museums, Log Cabin Village, Will Rogers Memorial Center, and annual celebrations. Ft. Worth began as a frontier outpost in 1849 to help protect incoming settlers from renegade Indian raids. Cattle drives ran through Ft. Worth on the Chisholm Trail after the Civil War. Cowboys stopped here to load up on provisions on the way to Abilene, Kansas, and stopped to spend their money and have a good time on the way home, which produced a very rowdy area of town called "Hell's Half Acre." Townspeople worked hard, including their own physical labor, to get the railroad tracks to Ft. Worth and succeeded, and their town became known as "Cowtown." Cattle were shipped to Ft. Worth, and the business of meatpacking thrived at the Stockyards. The arrival of the military bases, the discovery of oil, and the use of trucking to replace railroads all impacted the development of Ft. Worth as well as an increase in interest in the arts influenced by philanthropists Amon Carter and Kay Kimball.

To receive information about Ft. Worth, write or call the Convention and Visitors Bureau, 415 Throckmorton, Ft. Worth, 76102 (800/433-5747 or 817/336-8791). If you are just driving in, stop at the Visitor Center at the Stockyards, 130 East Exchange Ave., and select brochures of places that interest you as well as a map of the Stockyards. You might stay there and enjoy what the Stockyards has to offer or go downtown to the Historic Sundance Square to begin your tour at Fire Station No. 1. Ft. Worth Transportation Authority, "The T," offers a VisiTour bus pass. For $3, visitors have unlimited travel on the regular city bus service. Call 817/871-6200 for information. The Events Hotline number is 817/332-2000. Call for details of special events.

SUNDANCE SQUARE. The old and new blend in the historic Sundance Square in Ft. Worth's central business district. The Square is defined by West 2nd St., Houston, West 4th, and Commerce. Brick streets and restored turn-of-the-century buildings add to the charm of this area named for outlaw Sundance Kid who, along with Butch Cassidy, often entertained himself at the disreputable Hell's Half Acre. Shops, restaurants, the Caravan of Dreams, Casa's Theater on the Square, movie theater, the Sid Richardson Collection of Western Art, Fire Station No. 1, and other points of historical interest make Sundance Square a great place to begin your tour of Ft. Worth. As you walk around the square, be sure to notice the clock, which was made in 1893, outside Haltom's Diamonds at Main and East 3rd, the trompe l'oeil ("to fool the eye") artwork of Richard Haas in the Chisholm Trail mural on the southwest side of Main and 3rd, and the suit of armor high above the Knights of Pythias Hall at Main and 3rd. Historical markers around the square explain important buildings and events. The Nancy Lee and Perry R. Bass Performance Hall is a five-level horseshoe-shaped auditorium that seats 2,000. The opera, symphony, and ballet are among the groups that perform in this European-style opera house.

FIRE STATION NO. 1, Second and Commerce (817/732-1631). Built in 1873, Fire Station No. 1 now houses a free walk-through exhibition called *150 Years of Fort Worth* which chronicles the history of the land and people who lived in Texas and the Ft. Worth area. *Hours:* Daily, 9 A.M.-7 P.M.

SID RICHARDSON COLLECTION OF WESTERN ART, 309 Main Street (817/332-6554). This museum houses the private collection of oilman Sid Richardson (1891-1959). Many paintings of Frederic Remington, such as *The Buffalo Runners*, *Ambush*, and *Bear Hunting*, are displayed. Paintings of buffalo hunters and Indians as well as bronzes by Charles M. Russell are also showcased. Saddles, vests, and chaps with beautiful leather and silver artistry are on exhibit. The museum has a gallery brochure for children that contains a visual scavenger hunt. Housed in a replica of an 1895 building, the museum also has a bookstore. *Admission:* Free. *Hours:* Tuesday-Wednesday, 10-5; Thursday-Friday, 10-8; Saturday, 11 A.M.-8 P.M.; Sunday, 1-5. Closed Monday and major holidays.

CARAVAN OF DREAMS, 312 Houston St. (817/877-3000). The Caravan of Dreams is a 250-seat performing arts center and a nightclub. Atop the roof is a geodesic dome which houses a cactus garden including 200 species of cacti from five deserts. It may be toured for free by appointment.

─────── **MUSEUMS AND EXHIBITIONS** ───────

In Ft. Worth's Cultural District within walking distance of one another are the Amon Carter Museum, The Fort Worth Art Museum, the Kimball Art Museum, and the Fort Worth Museum of Science and History. The Visitor Information Center for the Cultural District is located in the rotunda of the Museum of Science and History. Admission is free at all of these museums, and groups must schedule their visits with each museum. Handicapped access is available at all of the listed museums.

AMON CARTER MUSEUM, 3501 Camp Bowie at Montgomery (817/738-1933). The collection by artists, such as Thomas Cole,

Georgia O'Keefe, Winslow Homer, Frederic Remington, and Charles M. Russell, within this museum was assembled by the late publisher and philanthropist Amon G. Carter Sr. and represents 150 years of American art. Tours are held daily at 2 P.M. Bookstore. *Admission:* free. *Hours:* Tuesday-Saturday, 10-5; Sunday, 12-5. Closed on major holidays. For tours, ask for extension 222.

THE CATTLEMAN'S MUSEUM, 1301 West 7th St. between Summit and Henderson (817/332-7064). The spirit of longhorns, cattle drives, and cowboys is relived through interactive monitors located in the West Texas town setting, the "talking longhorn" entrance diorama, a wall explaining cattle breeds, branding iron room, and other exhibits that tell the story of the cattle and ranching industry. *Admission:* free, donations welcome. *Hours:* Monday-Friday, 8:30-4:30.

FORT WORTH MUSEUM OF SCIENCE AND HISTORY, 1501 Montgomery St. at West Lancaster (817/732-1631 or Metro 817/654-1356). This museum is extremely popular with families who enjoy both permanent and changing exhibits on fossils, Texas history, the history of medicine, computer technology, and human physiology. **Kidspace** is an indoor discovery area designed for children ages 6 and under. Children especially like the hands-on exhibits and classes at the exceptional Museum school. Museum store. *Admission:* adults, $5; children 3-12, $3; and seniors, $4. *Hours:* Monday, 9-5; Tuesday-Thursday, 9 A.M.-8 P.M.; Friday-Saturday, 9-9; Sunday, 12-8.

- The **Noble Planetarium** presents astronomy shows for $3.

- The **Omni Theatre** consists of an 80-foot diameter domed screen which surrounds viewers and gives them the feeling of being part of the action. Popular programs include *Everest*, *Alaska*, and *The Greatest Places*. Some shows may be too intense for very young children or upsetting to those with intense motion sickness. Call about suitability if you have questions. *Admission:* adults, $6; children and seniors, $4. *Hours:* Multiple showings daily. Call for times. Advance tickets may be purchased at the museum box office or Ticketmaster locations. This is recommended for popular show times.

KIMBALL ART MUSEUM, 3333 Camp Bowie, west of University (817/332-8451 or Metro 817/654-1034). The Kimball Art Foundation was established in the 1930s by Kay Kimball who left his art collection and fortune to the foundation in 1964 to build an art museum. Outstanding collections in the museum span 3,000 years. There are works of Egyptian, Asian, Mesoamerican, and African origin and others from Western Europe. The collection of Asian arts is particularly remarkable, featuring Japanese screens, hanging scrolls, Chinese paintings, and sculptures of various origins. Tours, the Buffet restaurant, and a bookstore are available as well as a noncirculating library by appointment. Kimbell Treasure Hunts sheets may be picked up at the Information Desk on the lower level. *Admission:* free except for special exhibits. Free parking is available off Arch Adams Street. *Hours:* Tuesday-Thursday, 10-5; Friday, 12-8; Saturday, 10-5; Sunday, 12-5.

MODERN ART MUSEUM OF FORT WORTH, 1309 Montgomery St. at Camp Bowie (817/738-9215). Celebrating its 100th anniversary in 1992, Fort Worth's first art museum houses a collection of modern and contemporary American and European art, including paintings, sculptures, photography, and works on paper. Adult and children's art classes and workshops as well as a free lecture series are offered. You may wish to browse in the museum store. *Admission*: free. Wheelchair accessible. Free parking. *Hours:* Tuesday-Friday, 10-5 (10-9 on Tuesday, February-April and September-November); Saturday, 11-5; Sunday, 12-5.

THE MODERN AT SUNDANCE SQUARE, 410 Houston Street (817/335-9215). The Modern at Sundance Square is an annex of the Modern Art Museum of Fort Worth. It houses changing small-scale exhibitions and a larger branch of the museum store. Works from the museum's collection of modern and contemporary American and European painting, sculpture, and photography are exhibited regularly. *Admission:* free. Wheelchair accessible. *Hours*: Monday-Thursday, 11-6; Friday-Saturday, 11 A.M.-10 P.M.; Sunday, 1-5.

PATE MUSEUM OF TRANSPORTATION, P.O. Box 711, Ft. Worth 76101 on US Hwy. 377, between Fort Worth and Cresson, Texas (817/396-4305). Just outside Ft. Worth on the highway that leads to Granbury is the Pate Museum where the history of transportation is visualized through their collection of classic, antique, and special interest automobiles such as the Pierce Arrow and Packard, as well as a collection of aircraft which ranges from helicopters to transports to jet fighters. An unusual item on exhibit is a Minesweeper Boat 5 because few museums display a sea-going vessel inland. The museum also has a mock-up of a nose cone of a space capsule (817/332-1161). The museum is about a twenty-minute drive south of Ft. Worth, and from the museum it is only about a fifteen-minute drive to Granbury. *Hours:* 9 A.M.-5 P.M., Tuesday-Sunday. Closed Monday. *Admission:* free.

──────── **HISTORICAL SITES** ────────

LOG CABIN VILLAGE, 2100 Log Cabin Village Lane and University (817/926-5881). Located across from the Zoo in a heavily wooded section of Forest Park, Log Cabin Village consists of seven authentic log homes originally built in the mid 1800s. Staff and volunteers who dress in period costumes are on the grounds daily to demonstrate pioneer crafts and answer questions. *Admission:* adults, $1.50; children (4-17) and seniors $1.25; children under 4 free. School programs, $2-$5 per person by reservation only. *Hours:* Tuesday-Friday, 9-5.; Saturday, 10-5; Sunday, 1-5.

STOCKYARDS HISTORIC DISTRICT, North Main and 130 E. Exchange (Visitor Center, 817/625-9715 or Metro 972/988-6877; North Ft. Worth Historical Society, 817/625-5082). Anyone who wishes to recapture the spirit that was the West if only for a few hours must visit the 125-acre Stockyards, especially during a festival such as Pioneer Days or Chisholm Trail Roundup. A stop at the Visitor Center, located toward the end of East Exchange (east of Main Street), would help you get your bearings in this ten-block historic district. A map of the Stockyards and brochures covering most major attractions in the Ft. Worth area are available there. They also offer walking tours of the Stockyards and Billy Bob's Texas for a fee.

With the arrival of the railroad in 1876, Ft. Worth became the shipping destination for cattle, and the Union Stockyards Company was built. The Fort Worth Stockyards Company bought the company out in 1893 and held the first livestock show three years later. Meatpackers, Armour & Company and Swift & Company, moved in around 1902, and construction of the present Livestock Exchange Building began. Today, the meatpackers are gone, and the 100 acres of stock pens have been reduced to fifteen acres. Visitors enjoy the major livestock buildings, shops, museum, sculptures, horse-drawn carriage rides, and restaurants. The Fort Worth Mounted Patrol has its barns at 131 E. Exchange. Covered picnic tables are located in a little park west of Main at 26th and Ellis, and some family spots for meals are the Old Spaghetti Warehouse, Booger Red's, and the Star Cafe. Nearby are Cattleman's Steakhouse and Joe T. Garcia's.

Stockyards Station, a 50,000-square-foot facility, houses the Visitor Center, galleries, restaurants, and retail stores. Stockyards Trails are walking tours of the historic district and Billy Bob's Texas (Metro 988-6877 or 817/625-9715). Each Saturday from Memorial Day to Labor Day, live entertainment is offered in the Stockyards Beer Garden. The **Wild West Amusement Park**, open from March-October, has rides for ages 2 and up.

- The **Livestock Exchange Building** houses businesses and a museum that contains memorabilia from the 1986 Sesquicentennial Wagon Train Collection. It's toward the back of the main hall on the left (817/626-7921). *Admission:* free. *Hours:* Monday-Saturday, 10-5.

- **Cowtown Coliseum** was the site of the world's first indoor rodeo in 1918. It is open daily from 8 A.M.-5 P.M. The Ft. Worth Championship Rodeo is held every Saturday night from early April to mid-September at 8 P.M. Recently, a bull and barrel racing event has been added on Sunday afternoons at 2 P.M. during approximately the same season. For information about the rodeo or special events, call 817/625-6427 or toll free 888/COWTOWN.

- The **Stockyards Hotel** was built in 1907 and restored in 1984, and it offers 52 rooms. You might peek in or stay for lunch at the restaurant called Booger Red's Saloon and Restaurant next door to see the saddle bar stools, the five ceiling fans that are turned by one belt, and the mounted buffalo head and horns of the longhorn. The story of Booger Red is framed on the wall. A children's menu is offered, but service is not fast. Stockyards Hotel: 109 E. Exchange (817/625-6427 or 800/423-8471).

- **Billy Bob's Texas** claims to be the "World's Largest Honky-Tonk." Under a 100,000-square-foot roof are top name entertainment, dance floor, pro-bull riding every Friday and Saturday, gift shop, arcade, and restaurants. Tours are available through the Visitor Center. Call Metro 817/589-1711 or 817/642-7117 for information or tickets. Location: 2520 Rodeo Plaza.

—— PARKS, GARDENS, AND WILDLIFE ——

BOTANIC GARDEN
3220 Botanic Garden Blvd.
Ft. Worth, Texas 76107 • 817/871-7686, 817/871-7673

Located across from Trinity Park, the Botanic Garden consists of several different gardens on 109 acres. The **Rose Garden** contains more than 3,400 roses, which peak in late April and October. Lush tropical plants fill the 10,000 square foot **Conservatory**. Exotic begonias are housed in the **Exhibition Greenhouse;** flowering plants such as colorful phlox and salvia are highlights of the **Perennial Garden**; and experimental perennials bloom in the **Trial Garden**. The leaves release the scents in the **Fragrance Garden**.

The beauty and tranquility of the **Japanese Gardens** will be a delight to all family members. This 7.5-acre hilly garden features beautiful pools and waterfalls, a teahouse, pagodas, and other structures emphasizing simplicity and harmony. Children enjoy feeding the large Koi, the imperial carp. A gift shop is available. No tripods for cameras are allowed (817/871-7685).

Admission: Admission to the grounds is free. **Japanese Gardens:** Adults, $2 weekdays; $2.50 weekends; children 4-12, $1; children under 4, free. **Conservatory:** adults, $1; children, 50 cents.

Hours: Grounds open daily, 8 A.M.-11 P.M. **Japanese Gardens:** April-October, 9 A.M.-7 P.M. daily; November-March, 10-5 Tuesday-Sunday. Closed Monday. **Conservatory:** April to October, Monday-Friday, 10-9; Saturday, 10-6; Sunday, 1-6. November to March, Monday-Friday, 10 A.M.-9 P.M.; Saturday, 10-4; Sunday, 1-4. Gift shop open 10-4 in the Japanese Gardens.

HERITAGE PARK, East Belknap at Houston, behind the Tarrant County Courthouse. Heritage Park, a small park on a bluff, has refreshing waterfalls and water walls. It is safest to visit this park in the daytime. At the bottom of the bluff is an eight-mile asphalt trail for bicycling, walking, jogging, or skating alongside the Trinity River.

FORT WORTH NATURE CENTER AND REFUGE
Rt. 10, Box 53 or 9601 Fossil Ridge
Ft. Worth, Texas 76135 • 817/237-1111

Classes, workshops, story hours, and festivals are held in this 3,500-acre protected habitat for buffalo, deer, many varieties of birds, and more wildlife. It's the largest city-owned nature center in the US. Visitors may stop by the visitor center for information about hiking on twenty-five miles of trails, and guided trailwalks are offered by appointment. A boardwalk over a marshy area allows a closer look at waterfowl. Picnic tables are available for families but not groups. Gift shop. *Admission:* free. *Hours:* Tuesday-Saturday, 9-5; Sunday, 12-5; closed Monday. *Directions:* Take TX Hwy. 199 (Jacksboro Hwy.) two miles past the Lake Worth Bridge.

FORT WORTH WATER GARDEN, 1502 Commerce and 15th Street (817/871-5700). This 4.3-acre water garden designed by Phillip Johnson has five water pools called Cascade, Wet Wall, Quiet Water, Aerated Pool, and Active Pool, and children love the steps leading down to the pools. Many pretty trees shade the area, which is across the street from Tarrant County Junior College and near the Convention Center. This is certainly worth a visit, and it is free. Water displays are between 10 A.M. and 10 P.M. daily.

FORT WORTH ZOO

1989 Colonial Parkway at University south of I-30
Ft. Worth, Texas • 817/871-7050 or 817/871-7051
www.fortworth.com

The Fort Worth Zoo, which opened in 1909, features more than 5,000 animals in natural habitats on 58 acres. Frequently guests are only separated from the animals by a river or waterfall and are often face-to-face with the animals through large viewing windows. Featured exhibits include the World of Primates, a 2.5-acre indoor exhibit which simulates a tropical rain forest, and Asian Falls, which features waterfalls, hills, trees, and an elevated boardwalk. Below the boardwalk are Sumatran tigers, Malayan sun bears, and a white Siberian tiger. Added recently are the Fufi-Film Komodo Dragons, Penguin Island, and Meerkat Mounds. Zootique Gift Shop, strollers for rent, and concessions are available.

Another treat for families is the **Forest Park Train**, which is a miniature steam train that carries visitors into Trinity Park on a ride that lasts about forty-five minutes. Summer hours: noon-5, Tuesday-Sunday; closed Monday (817/336-3328). Fee.

The Zoo is across the street from Log Cabin Village and not far from the Botanic Garden.

Hours: 10-5 daily, weekend hours extended seasonally.

Admission: Adults, $7; children, ages 3-12, $4.50; and seniors (65 up), $3. Wednesday is half-price day. Portraits of the Wild Art Gallery, $1.

Directions: From I-30, exit at University and turn left on Colonial. Continue about one-half mile.

——— MORE ENTERTAINMENT ———

BURGER'S LAKE, 1200 Meandering Rd. (817/737-3414). Near Carswell Air Force Base, this spring-fed lake provides great summer entertainment for families on the two sandy beaches. Kids can slide into the lake on a water slide, dive from the diving board, or swing in from a trapeze. There is plenty of shallow water for little ones. Twenty acres are available for picnicking, and there are picnic tables, a concession, and a volleyball court. Recommended items to bring are lawn chairs and floats. A discount is available for groups, and no alcohol or pets are allowed. *Summer-Labor Day hours:* 9 A.M.-dark, daily. *Admission:* $8; children 6 and under, free.

CASA MANANA, 3101 W. Lancaster at University near the Will Rogers Memorial Center (817/332-2272). Casa Manana is a theatre-in-the-round with 1,800 seats that is covered by a geodesic dome. Families enjoy musicals, concerts, and plays. Children's theatre is very active as well as a theater school for all ages.

QUEEN MARIA
P.O. Box 136534
Lake Worth, Texas 76136 • 817/238-9778

Watch the sun set on shimmering Lake Worth as you dine aboard the *Queen Maria* paddle wheeler. Guests board at 6:45 P.M. on Saturday evenings in the summer for the two-hour dinner cruise. Reservations are necessary. Charter cruises are available.

The dining room is enclosed and air-conditioned, and the open top deck is partially covered with a canopy. The Fort Worth Nature Center is about two miles farther.

Admission: Adults, $30; children, ages 3-12, $15, under 3, free.

Directions: Take Hwy. 199 out of Ft. Worth to a quarter mile past the Lake Worth bridge. Make a U-turn and come back to the boat on the right by the bridge. The boat can be seen from the highway.

TANDY CENTER SUBWAY and ICE RINK. The Tandy Subway may be boarded at a fourteen-acre parking lot located on the banks of the Trinity River near Forest Park Blvd. and W. 2nd St. and Heritage Park. The world's only privately owned subway provides a free seven-minute round-trip ride that goes underground for a short time to Tandy Center located a few blocks away (817/390-3011). While at Tandy Center, located at 200 Throckmorton St. between Third and Weatherford, you might shop, skate, or browse in the downtown library. The Tandy Ice Rink is in One Tandy Center (817/878-4800). Group rates are available, and there is a shop and snack bar. The tri-level mall invites shoppers to spend time in more than fifty shops and restaurants (817/390-3720).

TARANTULA TRAIN, 2318 Eighth Ave. and 140 E. Exchange, Stockyards Ft. Worth, Texas • 817/625-RAIL or 800/952-5717

Once aboard the *Tarantula* train, you can easily imagine what passenger train travel was like not that many years ago when great "Iron Horses," like the 1896 Steam Engine #2248 that now pulls the three beautifully restored passenger cars, crossed the country full of passengers who had not even dreamed of air travel. The seats in each railcar have backs that move across so you can face others in your party or always be facing forward when the train is backing up. Rich mahogany wood, shining brass, and ten ceiling fans in each car add to the beauty. The cars are heated in winter, and the fans and open windows cool it in summer. When the whistle blows, passengers begin a nine-mile, one and one-half hour round trip that crosses the Trinity and follows the old Chisholm Trail toward 8th Ave. and then returns to the Stockyards. The Stockyards Depot has a turnstile. The scenery is not terrific along much of the trip, but the atmosphere is not to be missed. Dusk is a beautiful time to ride because the lights come on downtown and are reflected in the Trinity River. Passengers may also board at the station in Grapevine for a round trip.

A small restroom is located in each car, but no food, drink, or gum is allowed. Picking up your tickets early is a good idea. If you love the ride, write or call the Ft. Worth mayor to let her know. Birthday parties may be arranged.

Hours: Change with the season, and special times may be added for holidays.

Admission: Round trip: adults, $10, children ages 3-12, $5.50; under age 3, $3; and seniors, $8. One-way tickets are less. Grapevine tickets are more.

SPECIAL EVENTS

Southwestern Exposition and Livestock Show • 3rd Friday in
   January/17 days
The Last Great Gunfight • Febuary 8
Cowtown Marathon • Last Saturday in February
Cowtown Goes Green • Mid-March
Cowtown Coliseum Rodeo • April through September
MAIN ST. Arts Festival • Early April
Cinco de Mayo Celebration • Last weekend in April
Mayfest • First weekend in May
SW Bell Colonial Golf Tournament • Mid-May
Chisholm Trail Roundup • 2nd full weekend in June
Juneteenth • Mid-June
Shakespeare in the Park • June/July
Pioneer Days • Late September
Oktoberfest • 1st full weekend in October
Fort Worth Air Show • October
Parade of Lights/Christkindl Market • Weekend after
   Thanksgiving
First Night Fort Worth • New Year's Eve

GLEN ROSE

To study the relevant history of Glen Rose, you would literally have to return to the age of the dinosaurs, because they have fascinated scientists and 3-year-olds alike with the large three-toed footprints they left behind in the bed of the lazy Paluxy River which flows through the town. Settlers moved into the area known for its wild roses in the 1870s, and the county seat was established here. Glen Rose citizens were also known for their use of petrified wood as a building material, and some examples of its use are still around. Another claim to fame for a while in the 1920s and 1930s was the use of sulphur water for medicinal purposes in the bathhouses.

Today the town is still built around the rock courthouse, and no one seems in much of a hurry, which is one of its many great appeals. From Highway 67, exiting on Highway 205 will take you past **Oakdale Park**, which is the site of many wonderful festivals and a large public swimming pool, past a great swimming area on the Paluxy called the Big Rocks, which you will easily recognize, and into the heart of the square. While in town, stop by the Somervell County Museum, located at Elm and Vernon, and soak up local history through the varied collections of fossils and pioneer memorabilia (open weekends until summer). When we were there, for a small fee you could purchase an authentic dinosaur hunting license (just in case).

The Glen Rose Motor Inn (254/897-2940) offers rooms and a swimming pool, and Oakdale Park (254/897-2321) rents cabins. Campgrounds are at Oakdale Park, along the Brazos, and in Dinosaur Valley State Park if your family is having too much fun to go home at the end of the day. Oakdale Park also rents canoes and tubes. Hideaway Country Log Cabins rents five cabins located on a 150-acre property, which also has a swimming pool. They are located 16 miles NW of Glen Rose (254/823-6606). Low Water Canoe Rental, located about 3 miles east on FM 200, also has rentals (254/897-3666). Just as you approach the city limits on Hwy. 67 is the Expo Building, which includes facilities for conventions and reunions as well as a rodeo arena and equestrian center. Contact the Chamber of Commerce, P.O. Box 605, Glen Rose, Texas 76043 (254/897-2286 or toll free 888/346-6282). The drive takes about two hours.

COMANCHE PEAK NUCLEAR PLANT, Visitor Information Center, Texas Utilities Generating Co., P.O. Box 1002, Glen Rose, Texas 76043 (254/897-2976). As you pass Cleburne and get closer to Glen Rose, the terrain becomes hilly, and you can see for miles. Look to your right for the two white domes, which are Comanche Peak's nuclear reactors. Please read under "Science" in Chapter Two for more details about tours of the plant. **Squaw Creek Lake** (254/573-7053), which is around four miles north of Glen Rose off Hwy. 144, is a 3,300-acre lake that services the power plant but is also used for recreation, including scuba diving. *Directions:* To reach the plant from Hwy. 67 exit on FM 56 and go north. The visitor center is about one-half mile inside the front gate.

DINOSAUR VALLEY STATE PARK
P.O. Box 396
Glen Rose, Texas 76043 • 254/897-4588
(reservations only, 512/389-8900)

The Paluxy River, which is a tributary of the Brazos River, runs through this heavily wooded state park which is best known for the tracks left in the river bed by dinosaurs about 110 million years ago. The visitor center is located just inside the park, and friendly rangers will accept the admission fee and answer questions. They often will be down at the river explaining the history of the region to interested groups. A little further down the road on the right are the two life-sized replicas of the Brontosaurus and the Tyrannosaurus rex which were donated to the park after the New York World's Fair Dinosaur Exhibit in 1964-65. Very young children who are not too sure the dinosaurs are really extinct might look at this on the way out instead of in. On the left is a shaded picnic area with some playground equipment. The best tracks are on the road to the left, and park signs guide you. Steps lead down to the river, and it is somewhat steep.

Wearing beach shoes (not flip-flops) or old tennis shoes with some tread on the bottom is best. You can walk across the river bottom on large, exposed rocks, but they can be slippery. The river is usually shallow enough to see the tracks, but in times of heavy rainfall, calling ahead would be a good idea. Two necessary tools for youngsters from 2 to 72 are a small plastic bucket with a handle and a small aquarium fish net. The guppies and tadpoles flourish in the nooks and crannies among the rocks, and trying to catch them is great fun. If not already in a swimsuit, remember a change of clothes because a slip into the water is very likely. Sunscreen is a must. Shaded campgrounds are available here as well as restrooms with showers. A small amphitheater provides some interesting summer entertainment, and there are both nature and hiking trails. *Hours:* Open daily from 8-10 for day use and overnight also for campers. *Admission:* State park admission is adults, $5, 12 and under, free. Camping is additional. *Directions:* From US Hwy. 67, south of Glen Rose, take FM 205 to Park Road 59.

FOSSIL RIM WILDLIFE CENTER
2155 County Rd. 2008
Glen Rose, Texas 76043 • 254/897-2960

Endangered species are always the focus at this 2,700-acre private wildlife reserve. Excited kids can already spot ostriches as you pay to enter the park. You will get an audiocassette tape that will narrate the safari and you will probably want to buy cups of food to feed the exotic animals while driving through. More food may be purchased at the Nature Store, which is about midway through the 10-mile drive. The terrain is hilly, and there are lots of dense cedar and small shrubbery, so a pair of binoculars and sharp eyes will help in spotting more recalcitrant species. Taking snapshots or videos is also fun.

An interesting nature store, restaurant, restrooms, short hiking trail, picnic tables, and a petting zoo pasture that all will enjoy are located at the midpoint. The overlook view of the countryside is spectacular here, and spring and fall are particularly beautiful times to visit. All proceeds go toward wildlife conservation efforts. A guided tour, behind-the-scenes tour, and conservation camps are offered.

Hours: Best to call ahead because they change with the season, but summer hours are usually 9-6:30.

Admission: Adults, $12.95; children, ages 3-11, $9.95; under age 3, free; seniors, ages 62 and over, $11.95. Group rates are available with reservations.

Directions: On Hwy. 67 south of Glen Rose, drive about three miles. Signs will direct you to the preserve. A new bed and breakfast called The Lodge at Fossil Rim has opened for overnight stays (254/897-4933).

TRES RIOS
P.O. Box 2112
Glen Rose, Texas 76043 • 254/897-4253

Once a YWCA camp, Tres Rios is now privately owned and offers air-conditioned, rustic cabins and motel-type rooms of various sizes in a wooded area. At the entrance is a store with groceries and fishing supplies. The camp was named for the three rivers, Brazos, Squaw Creek, and Paluxy, that meet beside it. Tres Rios offers canoe and tube rentals, a swimming pool, volleyball area, a 9,000 square foot pavilion, and camping areas. There is no beach on the Tres Rios side of the river. Call for special events.

Directions: From Hwy. 67 east of Glen Rose, exit south on County Hwy. 312 (old Hwy. 67). Signs will direct you. Fees vary depending on type of accommodations.

TEXAS AMPHITHEATER
P.O. Box 8
Glen Rose, Texas 76043 • 254/897-4509 or 800/687-2661

On Saturday evenings from June through October, the life story of Jesus unfolds in an outdoor contemporary musical drama, *The Promise*, which is produced on a 65 x 100 square foot tri-level stage that has a six-story archway towering above it. Parts of the

The Promise may be a little intense for very young children. Texas Amphitheater also hosts a Spring Concert Series and special events on July 4 and Labor Day. Just in case some Texas-size mosquitoes decide to attend the festivities, some insect repellent and no perfume or lotions are good ideas.

Hours: Friday and Saturday; arrive at 8 P.M. for the 8:30 performance.

Admission: Adults, $19, $16, $12; children, $8. Call for reservations.

Directions: Driving in on Hwy. 67, pass Hwy. 144. Turn right at the sign ¼-mile on the right (Bo Gibbs Dr.). Go 1½-miles. Turn right on Texas Drive. A concession is available.

SPECIAL EVENTS: April - Celtic Festival, Oakdale Bluegrass Picnic, Sunrise Services, Tres Rios Bluegrass Festival; **May -** Oakdale Splash Weekend, Oakdale Bluegrass Jamboree, Art on the Square; **June -** Dinosaur Days Downtown; **July -** Fourth Celebration, Oakdale Bluegrass Pickin' Under the Stars/Fiddlers' Carousel; **September -** Oakdale Camper's Jamboree, Labor Day Concert, Tres Rios Fall Bluegrass Festival; **October -** Oakdale Bluegrass Reunion, Tres Rios Southwestern Bluegrass Festival, Halloween on the Square; **December -** Christmas on the Square.

TEXAS STATE RAILROAD
RUSK/PALESTINE

TEXAS STATE RAILROAD
P.O. Box 39
Rusk, Texas 75785 • 800/442-8951 in Texas
or 903/683-2561

Steam rises and the whistle blows as the 1896 iron horse pulls out from the Palestine Depot carrying its passengers on a 50-mile round-trip excursion through the East Texas Piney Woods. Aboard the train, passengers visit unhurriedly, tour the different cars, and visit the concession for soft drinks and ice cream. If small children are aboard, bringing some small games and toys would be a good idea. Older children might enjoy a game or deck of cards. Bring a camera to take pictures at the depot as children talk to the engineer and fireman and tour the engine cab. At the mid-point the two trains pass each other as one heads toward Rusk and the other to Palestine.

Flowers and blooming dogwoods are beautiful in the spring, and fall is breathtaking as the leaves change colors. Picnicking at the Rusk Depot is lots of fun, and families may bring their own food or buy fast food at the concession, which also has souvenirs. You might bring a little extra to feed the ducks on the lake at the Rusk Depot. Passengers then board for the return trip. The Palestine park offers water-only campsites, picnic tables, pavilions, and a playground. At Rusk there are full hookups for campers.

Hours: Spring schedule is Saturday and Sunday from mid-March to late May; Summer schedule is Thursday-Monday from late May to late July; Fall schedule is Saturday and Sunday from August to early November. The train leaves the Palestine Depot at 11 A.M. and returns at 3 P.M., and the gates for boarding trains are opened 45 minutes before train departure. Seating is on a first-come-first-served basis, so families would need to arrive at least by 10 A.M. Reservations are recommended.

Admission: Round trip prices: adults, $15; children, ages 3-12, $9. One-way tickets: adults, $10; children, $6. Group discounts are available.

Directions: Palestine is about 120 miles from Dallas, which is approximately a three-hour drive. Take I-45 south to Corsicana. Go southeast on US Hwy. 287 to Palestine, then take US Hwy. 84 east about four miles (Rusk is 27 miles farther east on Hwy. 84). Rusk State Park is two miles west of Rusk off Hwy. 84.

MUSEUM FOR EAST TEXAS CULTURE
400 Micheaux Ave.
Palestine, Texas 75801 • 903/723-1914

Located in a former high school built in 1915, this historical museum houses a replica of a classroom in a country school as well as railroad memorabilia. Their latest renovation is an 1856 log dogtrot cabin, which is in the gym area. The museum is in John H. Reagan Park, which has picnic tables and a playground. *Hours:* Monday-Saturday, 10-5; Sunday, 1-4. *Admission:* adults, $1; children ages 3-12, 50 cents; under 3, free. *Directions:* The museum is located about three miles from the Texas State Railroad. Take Hwy. 84 east to Loop 256 and continue east on Hwy. 84 to Crockett Road. Go one block and turn right on Micheaux.

TEXAS DOGWOOD TRAILS and DAVEY DOGWOOD PARK, located just north of Palestine on North Link Street off US Hwy. 155, Palestine Convention and Visitors Bureau, P.O. Box 2828, Palestine, Texas 75802 (903/723-3014). Each year for three weekends in March and April, the dogwood blossoms and Palestine itself open for visitors to enjoy. In the 400-acre Davey Dogwood Park, visitors may drive or walk through the beautiful, white-blossomed trees. Other festivities include a parade, arts and crafts, melodrama dinner theater, tours of Victorian homes, carriage rides, fishing tournaments, and more. Other special events include Hot Pepper Festival in October and a Christmas Parade and Pilgrimage in early December. The Convention and Visitors Bureau offers information about walking and driving tours of Palestine. A stop by Eilenberger Bakery at 512 N. John is a treat (800/831-2544). The **National Scientific Balloon Facility** is located five miles west on Highway 287N to FM 3224. Look under "Science" in this guide for more information.

OTHER PLACES OF INTEREST

Engeling Wildlife Refuge, located twenty miles west of Palestine on Hwy. 287, is home for a great variety of animals including deer, wild hogs, birds, fox, squirrel, and rabbits. Fishing is free in Catfish Creek, and camping is allowed (903/928-2251). **Lake Palestine**, a 22,500-acre lake located twenty miles north of Palestine, offers boating, swimming, and other water sports. Camping areas and motels are around the lake.

TYLER

Called "The Rose Capital of America," Tyler's Municipal Rose Garden and annual Texas Rose Festival in mid-October bring thousands of visitors there each year. The sandy soil is particularly adapted to growing azaleas, pine trees, peaches, and blueberries, also. See the "Farmers Markets and Pick Your Own" section of Chapter Two for those in the Tyler area.

Tyler was named in the mid-1800s for US President John Tyler, who penned his name on the joint resolution which enabled Texas to be admitted as a state. Once the center of the booming oil business in East Texas, Tyler now focuses more on gardening and other types of agriculture and forestry as major industries since the oil business has declined. One third of the commercially grown rose bushes in the world originate in Smith County. Besides the beautiful gardens, Tyler offers a variety of activities for visitors in lakes, museums, and a zoo. For more information, contact the Tyler Area Chamber of Commerce, 407 N. Broadway, P.O. Box 390, Tyler, Texas 75710 (903/592-1661, 800/235-5712). Tyler is about a two-hour drive east on I-20.

BROOKSHIRE'S WORLD OF WILDLIFE MUSEUM AND COUNTRY STORE
1600 W.S.W. Loop 323, P.O. Box 1411
Tyler, Texas 75710-1411 • 903/534-2169

In honor of Brookshire Grocery Company's founders, Wood and Louise Brookshire, the museum highlights more that 250 mammals, fowl, reptiles, and aquatic species from North America and Africa. The African exhibit also includes artifacts such as handmade jewelry and woodcarvings. A life-sized replica of a 1920s grocery store, the Country Store is stocked with old-time goods, antique toys, and antique merchandising equipment. A 1926 Model T Ford and a 1952 big red fire truck are outside on the grounds as well as a picnic area, covered pavilion, and playground. Groups of fifteen or more should call two weeks in advance for reservations for guided tours.

Hours: Tuesday-Saturday, 9-noon and 1-5 with the picnic area and playground open through lunchtime; closed on major holidays.

Admission: Free

Directions: Take I-20 east and turn south on Hwy. 69. Go southwest on Loop 323 to the Old Jacksonville Highway and turn right. It is located just past the Distribution Center.

CALDWELL ZOO
2203 Martin Luther King Blvd., P.O. Box 4280
Tyler, Texas • 903/593-0121

The openness of the natural habitats with different species of animals grazing on the lush grasses together are most impressive to visitors at the Caldwell Zoo. Animals from around the world as well as native Texas critters and fowl are offered for viewing. A favorite spot is on the veranda of the snack shop where visitors can still see much of the zoo. A picnic area is available. Be sure to visit the hands-on displays in the education center and stop by the petting corral area.

Hours: October 1-March 31, 9:30-4:30; April 1-September 30, 9:30-6 P.M.; open daily except some major holidays.

Admission: FREE. All facilities are wheelchair accessible. No radios or pets allowed.

Directions: Take I-20 east to Tyler and go southeast on US Hwy. 69. Turn left (east) on MLK Blvd., and the zoo is on the left.

CARNEGIE HISTORY CENTER
125 S. College at Elm
Tyler, Texas • 903/593-1847

Housed in the former Carnegie Public Library building, the History Center features exhibits of artifacts of Tyler and Smith County as well as Civil War artifacts which were uncovered from the large prisoner of war camp that was located in Tyler.

Hours: Wednesday, 12-4; Thursday, 1-5; Friday-Saturday, 12-4.

Admission: FREE

THE DISCOVERY SCIENCE PLACE
308 N. Broadway, Tyler, Texas • 903/533-8011

The Discovery Science Place is a hands-on science museum for children. In the tunnels of Discovery Mountain, kids learn about bats, earthquakes, volcanoes, and more. On the ship *Awakening*, discover the wonders of wind, solar power, magnetism, and navigation. The many fun, hands-on exhibits will be worth the trip.

Hours: Tuesday-Saturday, 9-5; Sunday, 1-5.

Admission: Adults and children $3.50 for one exhibit, $5 for both exhibits; 2 and under, free; 10% discount for seniors.

MUNICIPAL ROSE GARDEN
1900 West Front (Hwy. 31) at Rose Park Drive
Tyler, Texas • Rose Garden Center 903/531-1212
Rose Museum 903/597-3130

The beauty of 30,000 plants exhibiting more than 500 varieties of roses on fourteen acres is indescribable from May to November. In the one-acre **Heritage Rose and Sensory Garden** located in the southwest corner, varieties that date back to 1867 are showcased. Another garden features approximately 168 camellias. The **Rose Museum Complex**, which covers 30,000 square feet and includes a visitor center, is located at Rose Park Drive and West Front. The Rose Garden is the site of part of the Texas Rose Festival, including the Queen's Tea where the public can meet the Texas Rose Festival Queen and enjoy refreshments. Also included in the four-day festival are a parade, coronation, dance, art show, arts and crafts fair, rose show, and tours of rose fields.

The **Whistle Stop Ranch Railroad Museum** is open Saturday and Sunday during the Rose Festival and Azalea Trail and other times by appointment (903/894-6561).

Hours: Garden Center, Monday-Saturday, 9-5; Sunday, 1-5.

Admission: The Municipal Rose Garden is free, and it is open all day every day. Call about fees and hours for the museum.

TYLER MUSEUM OF ART
1300 S. Mahon
Tyler, Texas 75706 • 903/595-1001

Located on the east side of Tyler Junior College on Mahon at Fifth, the Tyler Museum of Art features changing exhibits of nineteenth- and twentieth-century contemporary art focusing on regional artists. Another highlight is a permanent exhibition of photographs of the East Texas region. *Hours:* Tuesday-Saturday, 10-5; Sunday, 1-5. *Admission:* free.

TYLER STATE PARK
789 Park Road 16
Tyler, Texas 75706 • 903/597-5338

Playing on a 400-foot sandy beach, swimming and fishing for channel catfish and black bass in the 64-acre spring fed lake, and hiking are some of the outdoor entertainment offered at this 994-acre state park in the piney woods. A nature trail, mountain bike trail, concession, restrooms with showers, and rentals of boats, canoes, and paddleboats during the summer season are also available. Boats are limited to 5 MPH. Picnic tables and camping areas that have some screened shelters are accessible from the main road.

Hours: Day use, 8 A.M.-10 P.M.; overnight for camping.

Admission: $3 for adults, 12 and under free; camping additional.

Directions: From I-20, go two miles north on FM 14 to Park Rd. 16.

SPECIAL EVENTS: Azalea and Spring Flower Trail, late March-mid-April; Tyler Heritage on Tour, early April; East Texas Fair, late September; Texas Rose Festival, mid-October.

ON THE WAY: Two colorful and energetic towns very much worth a visit are just a little past midpoint between Dallas and Tyler. The town of **CANTON** on the south side of I-20 is well known for its **First Monday Trade Days**. See the "Shopping" section of Chapter Two for details. A historical park has opened in **EDGEWOOD**, which is just north of I-20. Exit on Hwy. 859. The two-block area called **Heritage Park** contains two log cabins, cafe, general store, bandstand, blacksmith shop, farm implement museum, log barn, one-room schoolhouse, barbershop and public bath, early Americana museum, caboose, depot and water tower, church house, and gift shop. Call the Edgewood Historical Society (903/896-4326) for tour group information. The park is usually open on Tuesday, 10 A.M.-noon; Wednesday, Friday, and Saturday 10-4. *Admission:* adults, $2.50; children, $2.

Just about thirty minutes east on US 80 before it joins I-20 is **TERRELL**, which also has some sites of historical interest. Please see "Historic Terrell" in Chapter Two.

WACO

Indians, outlaws, and Texas Rangers were early inhabitants of Waco, Texas. The Rangers built an outpost called Fort Fisher where the Texas Ranger Museum is located today. A Spanish explorer first mapped "Waco Village" in 1542, and a trading post was established in 1844. The Chisholm Trail came through Waco at the Suspension Bridge, which is now only open to foot travel. Dedicated in 1870, the 475-foot bridge across the Brazos River is located at University Parks Drive near the Convention Center with Indian Spring Park on the west bank and Martin Luther King Park on the east bank. A riverwalk runs from there at Washington Ave. to the Texas Ranger Museum and beyond, and it is an enjoyable walk unless heavy rains have caused water to close part of it. The railroad came to town in 1871, and Waco has continued to thrive. For more information about Waco, call the Tourist Information Center, which is located in Fort Fisher, I-35 and University Parks Drive, Exit 335B, at 800/WACO-FUN or

254/750-8696. A twenty-four-hour tourist information recording that cites special events for the month is 254/752-WACO. From Dallas, go left (east) on University Parks. The Visitor Center can been seen from I-35. Tours of the city may be taken on Mule Drawn Wagon Tours (May-Sept., Monday-Friday). Call 254/750-8696 or 254/836-4845. Visitors may also ride the Brazos Trolley to main attractions (254/753-0113) or try a riverboat excursion on the *Brazos Princess*.

BAYLOR UNIVERSITY, Exit 335 B off I-35 to University Parks Drive. The Wiethorn Information Center to the right at the main entrance has visitor parking and permits (254/710-1921). A map of Baylor may also be obtained at the Waco Visitor Information Center at Fort Fisher, which is a short distance north of the campus. Chartered in 1845, Baylor has become the world's largest Baptist university. One of the first stops should be at **Bear Plaza** for a look at the Baylor Bear in his fancy lair. Hopefully, he will be awake and know that he had visitors. Bear Plaza is across Waco Creek from the Baylor Book Store between 1200 S. 5th and 7th Streets.

- The **Armstrong Browning Library** contains the world's largest collection of material related to Robert Browning, one of the greatest British poets of the Victorian Age. The library also contains major manuscript collections of his wife Elizabeth Barrett Browning, John Ruskin, Charles Dickens, and Ralph Waldo Emerson. What children will appreciate are the fifty-six stained-glass windows that illustrate the poems and themes of the Brownings and the Pied Piper window in the Sturdivant Alcove. The museum is located on 700 Speight Ave. between 7th and 8th Streets (254/710-3566). *Hours:* weekdays, 9-noon, 2-4; Saturday, 9-noon. *Admission:* Free. Donations appreciated.

- **Strecker Museum**, the oldest continuously operating museum in Texas, has exhibits which include geology, botany, reptiles, birds, mammals, and early man's physical struggles and cultural advances up through the pioneers in Central Texas. A very large fossil marine turtle is a highlight of the visit for many children as well as the live museum habitats and the gift shop. The museum is located on S. 4th Street and Speight in the Sid Richardson Science Building. *Hours:* Tuesday-Friday, 9-noon and 1:30-4; Saturday, 10-4; Sunday, 2-5 (254/710-1110). *Admission:* free.

CAMERON PARK, 4th and Herring Streets (254/750-5980). Cameron Park features 680 acres with wooded picnic sites and various forms of wildlife. Miss Nellie's Pretty Place is a wildflower preserve, and across the street is a children's playground with access for handicapped children. The park fronts on the Bosque and Brazos Rivers and is the location of the zoo.

CAMERON PARK ZOO (formerly Central Texas Zoological Park). Herring and 1701 N. Fourth Street (254/750-8400). The zoo features both exotic and native wildlife. Highlights include Gibbon Island, Treetop Village and African Savanna, bald eagles, reptile house, educational facilities, and the Texas Heritage area, which includes longhorns, buffalo, and javelina. A total immersion Herpetarium facility features snakes, lizards, turtles, and amphibians from all over the world. Children have fun in the naturalistic play area. *Summer hours:* Monday-Saturday, 9-5, Sunday, 11-5. *Admission:* Adults, $4, children 4-12, $2.

DR PEPPER MUSEUM AND FREE ENTERPRISE INSTITUTE, 300 South 5th Street, Waco, Texas 76701 (254/757-1024). Dr Pepper, the oldest major soft drink in America, was first mixed in Morrison's Old Corner Drug Store by Dr. Charles C. Alderton and was served in 1885. The present museum, a tribute to the "Pepper Upper," houses memorabilia in the former Artesian Manufacturing and Bottling Company established in 1906 which manufactured and distributed Dr Pepper as well as several other soft drinks. With new construction on the second and third floors, the Museum doubled in space open to the public in 1997. There is a scaled re-creation of the Old Corner Drug Store complete with talking animatron of Doc Alderton. Bottling equipment, containers, and the well exhibit completes the first floor. The second floor exhibits concentrate on marketing and advertising, featuring a popular video of 20 years of Dr Pepper commercials. The W.W. "Foots" Clements Free Enterprise Institute offers educational programs to scheduled groups. A 51-seat theater offers guests a place to view the *Tour 19* Free Enterprise video. The museum also features a gift shop and an old-fashioned soda fountain that serves Dr Pepper and Blue Bell Ice Cream. *Hours:* Monday-Saturday, 10-4; Sunday, 12-4. From Memorial Day to Labor Day open until 5. *Admission:* Adults, $4; students, $2; seniors $3.50; preschoolers, free. Advance reservations are required for groups of ten or more. Group discount, 10%.

GOVERNOR BILL AND VARA DANIEL HISTORIC VILLAGE, 1108 S. University Parks Drive, I-35, Exit 335B (254/710-1110). Located on thirteen acres just east of Ft. Fisher Park on the Brazos River, more than twenty wood-framed buildings re-create an 1890s farming community in Texas and help visitors to understand the life of the river town where there was no electricity, water came from wells and creeks, and wood-burning stoves provided heat. *Hours:* Tuesday-Friday, 10-4; Saturday-Sunday, 1-5; tours on the half hour. *Admission:* Adults, $3; seniors, $2; children, K-12, $1; Baylor students, free.

LAKE BRAZOS AND LAKE WACO. Lake Brazos is a town lake at the confluence of the Brazos and Bosque Rivers, which is the site of festivals, boat racing, and rowing regattas. **Lake Waco** is completely within Waco city limits and offers unsupervised swimming, boating, camping, fishing, skiing, and other recreational activities (254/756-5359). Lake Waco's **Airport Park** off Airport Road has drinking water and restrooms, camping (fee), boat ramp, and a marina with bait and fishing barge. The swimming beach and shower house are before you get to the camping area, and there is no fee. Day use hours are 6 A.M.-11 P.M.

LION'S PARK, 1716 N. 42nd (254/772-4340). Lion's Park offers a variety of family entertainment in its facilities which include swimming pool, picnics, tennis, miniature golf, playground, small amusement park with eight rides for children, and miniature train. Call for current hours as they change with the season.

TEXAS RANGER HALL OF FAME MUSEUM, P.O. Box 2570, Waco, Texas 76702-2570 (254/750-8631). A visit to Waco might begin by exiting 335B off I-35 to visit the Texas Ranger Hall of Fame, which is on the left of the highway. This is also the location of the Visitor Information Center and Fort Fisher Park. Baylor University is just across the street to the south. Every hour, there is a twenty-minute slide and sound show in the auditorium toward the rear of the museum, which is a great way to help everyone understand the settlement of Texas territory and the role of the Texas Rangers. The collection of firearms and other weapons is most impressive. There are also life-sized dioramas of scenes in the lives of the Rangers as well as collections of Indian, Mexican, and pioneer artifacts. *Museum hours:* Daily, 9-5, except Thanksgiving, Christmas, and New Year's Day. *Admission:* adults, $3.75; children, $1.75. *Tourist Center hours*: 8-5, Monday-Saturday; 9-5, Sunday.

Taking the road along the south side of the Visitor Center leads to the Historic Village and the Sports Hall of Fame. Fort Fisher Park, which is next to the museum, offers camping and screened shelters (254/750-8630). Tourist information: 254/750-8696.

TEXAS SPORTS HALL OF FAME, 1108 S. University Parks Dr. at I-35, Exit 335B (254/756-1633). Located just east of Fort Fisher Park, the Texas Sports Hall of Fame honors more than 350 favorite sports heroes through a collection of memorabilia and interactive exhibits. Included in the museum are the Texas High School Sports Hall of Fame and the Texas Tennis Museum and Hall of Fame. *Hours:* Daily, 10-5; summer 10-6. *Admission:* adults, $4; seniors, $3.50; students, ages 5-12, $2.

EVENTS: April-Brazos River Festival; **Summer** - Summer Sounds Concerts and Brazos Nights Concerts at Indian Spring Park; **May** - Car Show at Fort Fisher; **July** - Brazos Boat Races; **August** - Texas Folklife Festival; **October** - Heart O' Texas Fair and Rodeo; **December** - Christmas on the Brazos.

OTHER PLACES OF INTEREST NEARBY: Texas Safari Wildlife Park, 35 miles to Clifton (254/675-3658); SummerFun USA Water Park, 1410 Waco Rd., Belton (254/939-0366); Southwest Outlet Center, 104 N.E. Interstate Highway 35, Exit 368A or B, Hillsboro (254/582-9205).

7. Resources

—— SPECIAL EVENTS AND ——
TICKET/RESERVATION HOTLINES

Arts District Event 24-hr. Information Line 953-1985
Artsline/24-hr. Line 522-2659
ARTTIX Ticket Reservations 871-2787
Dallas Events Hotline/24-hr. Line 746-6679
Dillard's Box Office 800/654-9545
General Cinema Movie Reservations/Ticketmaster . . 373-8000
Half-Price Tickets 696-4253
Irving Art Centre's Artsline 972/252-ARTS
KISS-FM Information Line 972/263-1061
Mandalay Canal at Las Colinas Event Line/24-hr. . 972/869-1232
Metroplex Events Information 800/METROPLEX
MovieFone/Movie Information 972/444-FILM
Parks and Recreation Special Events 670-7070
SPCA Events Line . . . . 651-9611 Ext. 160
Tennis Reservations/Neighborhood Courts 670-8745
Ticketmaster 373-8000
USA Film Festival 821-NEWS

—— CONVENTION AND VISITOR'S BUREAUS ——

DALLAS CONVENTION AND VISITOR'S BUREAU

Two locations downtown offer a friendly, "Hi, y'all!" to visitors to the Dallas area as well as natives who keep up with the latest entertainment. The most current *Dallas: Official Visitors Guide*, a publication of the DCVB, is there as well as countless brochures of great places to visit. The Hotline, 746-6679, lists special events, business, and relocation information, and you may request a visitor's packet. Locations: 1030 Northpark Center; DCVB Offices, Renaissance Tower, 1201 Elm St., 20th Floor (746-6677). For more information about Big D, write the Dallas Convention & Visitors Bureau, 1201 Elm St., Suite 2000, Dallas, Texas 75270.

DALLAS/FORT WORTH AREA TOURISM COUNCIL

This council publishes a free, informative guide to Dallas, Fort Worth, and surrounding cities called the *Official Visitors Guide to the Dallas/Fort Worth Area* which is available at the Dallas Visitors Bureau locations or by contacting the council at P.O. Box 836571, Richardson, Texas 75083-6571 (972/680-8580). Some coupons are located in the back of the magazine.

—— STATE DEPARTMENT OF HIGHWAYS —— AND PUBLIC TRANSPORTATION

The Travel and Information Division, P.O. Box 5064, Austin, Texas 78763-5064, publishes a free, helpful guidebook to Texas cities, called *Texas State Travel Guide*, which gives general information as well as information about attractions in the area. Toward the end of the book are descriptions of Texas lakes, parks, forests, rocks, flowers, birds, and tourist bureaus.

Addison
P.O. Box 144, Addison 75001 (972/416-6600, 800/ADDISON)

City of Arlington Convention and Visitors Bureau
921 Six Flags Drive, Box A, Arlington 76004 (800/342-4305, 817/640-0252)

Duncanville Chamber of Commerce
300 E. Wheatland, Box 380036, Duncanville 75138 (972/298-6128)

Farmers Branch Office of Economic Development and Tourism
4100 McEwen, Box 819010, Farmers Branch 75381 (972/243-8966 or 800/BRANCH9)

Garland Convention and Visitors Bureau
200 Museum Plaza Drive, Garland 75040 (972/272-7551)

Grand Prairie Convention and Visitors Bureau
605 Safari Pkwy., Suite A-6, Grand Prairie 75050 (972/264-1558, 800/288-8386)

Grapevine Convention and Visitors Bureau
One Liberty Park Plaza, Grapevine 76051 (817/424-0561 or 800/457-6338)

Irving Convention and Visitors Bureau
3333 N. MacArthur, Suite 200, Irving 75062 (972/252-8484 or 800/2-IRVING)

Lancaster Chamber of Commerce
1535 N. Dallas, Box 1100, Lancaster 75146 (972/227-2579)

Lewisville Chamber of Commerce/Visitors Bureau
233 West Main, P.O. Box 416, Lewisville 75067 (972/436-9571)

McKinney Chamber of Commerce
1801 W. Louisiana, Box 621, McKinney 75070 (972/452-0163)

Mesquite Chamber of Commerce and Visitors Information
617 N. Ebrite, Box 850115, Mesquite 75185 (972/285-0211)

Metrocrest Chamber of Commerce
Addison, Carrollton, Coppell, Farmers Branch 1204 Metrocrest, Carrollton 75006 (972/416-6600)

Plano Chamber of Commerce
1200 E. 15th Street, Plano 75074 (972/424-7547)

Richardson Chamber of Commerce
411 Belle Grove, Richardson 75080 (972/234-4141)

—— PUBLICATIONS——

Dallas newspapers:

Dallas Business Journal
4131 N. Central Expressway, Suite 310 Dallas, Texas • 696-5959

Dallas Examiner
424 Centre St. Dallas, Texas • 651-7066

The Dallas Morning News
P.O. Box 655237 Dallas, Texas 75265 • 745-8383, 800/431-0010

Oak Cliff Tribune
4808 S. Buckner Dallas, Texas • 943-7755

Park Cities News
8115 Preston Dallas, Texas • 369-7570

Park Cities People
6116 N. Central Expressway Dallas, Texas • 739-2244

The White Rocker News
10809 Garland Road Dallas, Texas • 327-9335

Community newspapers serving nearby cities:

Arlington Citizen Journal • 817/261-1191
Coppell Gazette • 972/393-7424
Duncanville Suburban • 972/298-1234
Fort Worth Star-Telegram • Metro 817/429-2655
The Garland News • 972/272-6591
Irving News • Metro 817/695-0500
The Mesquite News • 972/285-6301
Metrocrest News • 972/418-9999
Plano Star Courier • 972/424-9504
Richardson News • 972/234-3198

Neighborhood newspapers and newsletters (distributed FREE in restaurants, libraries, newsstands, etc.):

*Advocate/Lake Highlands-East Dallas-
    Lakewood* • 823-5885 ext. 212
ARTimes in Irving • 972/252-7558
Las Colinas People • 972/717-0880
Richardson Today • 972/238-4270

Foreign language newspapers:

Dallas Chinese Times • 972/907-1919
El Hispano Newspaper • 357-2186
Korea Times in Dallas • 972/243-0005
Novedades • 943-2932

Books:

Camper's Guide to Texas, by Mickey Little, Third Edition, Gulf Publishing, Houston, 1990.

The Children's Pages: A Dallas Resource Book for Parents, Lauren Publications, Carrollton, TX (447-9188), 1995.

Dallas, by Judith M. Garrett and Erika Sanchez, 2nd edition, Texas Monthly Press, 1992.

Dallas/Fort Worth Restaurants: 1996 Update, by Ron Ruggless and Susan Safronoff, ZAGAT Survey, New York, 1996.

Dallas Outdoor Recreation Guide, by Gail Hawk, Hawk Publishing, Garland, 1993.

Dallas: Shining Star of Texas, by Jim Donavan and Carolyn Brown, Voyager Press, Stillwater, MN, 1994.

Dallas Uncovered, by Larenda Roberts, Republic of Texas Press, Plano, 1995.

Directory of Children's Services and Needs, Special Needs, Child Care, Counseling, Crisis, Health, Parenting Services, published by Save the Children/Dallas (824-8800), 1991.

DISCOVER Dallas/Fort Worth, by Virginia and Lee McAlester, Alfred A. Knopf Publisher, 1988.

A Guide for Seeing Dallas County History, by the Dallas County Historical Commission, 1987 (trail booklet available at the Hall of State).

A Guide to Dallas Private Schools, by Lynn Magid, Private in Print, (214/386-0956).

Hiking and Backpacking Trails of Texas, by Mickey Little, Fourth Edition, Gulf Publishing, Houston, 1995.

Mother's Manual for Summer Survival, by Kathy Peel and Joy Mahaffey (Tyler, Texas moms), Focus on the Family, 1989.

Natural Wonders of Texas: A Guide to Parks, Preserves, and Wild Places, by Paul Cooke and Sunita Cooke, Country Roads Press, Castine, Maine, 1995.

Roadside Geology of Texas, by Darwin Spearing, Mountain Press, Missoula Montana, 1991.

Short Trips In and Around Dallas, by Laura Trim, LDT Press, 1985.

Texas, by Robert R. Rafferty, Texas Monthly Press, 1989.

Texas Family Style, edited by Ann Ruff, Second Edition, Lone Star Books, Houston.

Texas Festivals, by Dawn Albright, Palmetto Press.

Texas Off the Beaten Path, by June Naylor Rodriquez, Globe Pequot Press, Old Saybrook, Conn., 1994.

Texas Parks and Campgrounds, by George Oxford Miller, Third Edition, Texas Monthly Press, Austin, 1995.

Texas Water Recreation, by Ann Ruff, Taylor Publishing Co.

Texas Wildlife Viewing Guide, by Gary L. Graham, Falcon Press.

Texas Zoos and Animal Parks, by Ann Ruff, Taylor Publishing Company, 1990.

Weekends Away: Camping and Cooking in Texas State Parks, by Sheryl Smith-Rodgers, Eaken Press, Austin, 1993.

Magazines:

D Magazine, 939-3636. D is a monthly magazine with information about Dallas personalities, events, and restaurants.

dallas child and *Baby Dallas*, Lauren Publications, 972/447-9188. This monthly parenting magazine offers helpful articles about child-raising, kid-friendly restaurants, and exciting places to go, and it is offered for free at libraries, children's stores, and day cares or by subscription.

Dallas Cowboys Official Weekly, Southwest Professional Sports Publications, Inc., 556-9900. Each week this football news magazine highlights games, coaches, plays, and players.

Dallas Family, Family Publications, Inc., 521-2021. This monthly parenting magazine has articles about raising healthy children, creating good relationships, entertaining children, educating them, being a good consumer, and selecting child care. There is a very informative events calendar for the month.

Dallas/Ft. Worth Health and Fitness Magazine, Health & Fitness Publishing, Inc., 972/490-8880.

Dallas Observer, New Times, Inc., 637-2072. Offered free in newsstands or by subscription, this weekly news magazine includes features about controversial personalities, political and other news, a community calendar of events, and live music and concert information. The calendar does include events for children, but it also contains romance ads that are not for children.

The Dallas Weekly, Admast Publishing Co., 428-8958. This weekly magazine serving the African-American community offers news articles, features, sports, community calendar, and more information about health, education, and youth. It is offered free at some locations, or readers may subscribe.

Dallas Woman, Women's Publishing Group, 4230 LBJ Freeway, Suite 105, 490-9880. Women's issues in and out of the working world are addressed.

Texas Highways, State Department of Highways and Public Transportation, 512/465-7408. Wonderful things about Texas landscape, wildlife, history, and communities are photographed and featured in this colorful monthly magazine.

Texas Monthly, Texas Monthly, Inc., Subscription Service Center, P.O. Box 7090, Red Oak, Iowa (in Dallas 871-7717). *Texas Monthly* features interesting people, places, restaurants, and news statewide.

Texas Parks & Wildlife, Texas Parks and Wildlife Dept., 800/792-1112. The nature photography is beautiful in this monthly magazine featuring fascinating facts about wildlife and endangered or threatened species and activities, such as where to fish, swim, and hike, in the state parks.

———— TELEPHONE SERVICES ————

SOUTHWESTERN BELL GREATER DALLAS YELLOW PAGES (A-L)

The introductory pages of the *Yellow Pages* are a very helpful guide to the Dallas area. They provide telephone numbers of attractions, service organizations, events, and hospitals as well as maps of seating inside major arenas and a map of Fair Park. A zip code directory is also included.

Time of Day Service 844-6611
Road Conditions/Closings/Wildflowers/Jobs 374-4100
Weather Information for Travelers and Recreation . . . 787-1701

—— TOP 20 PLACES TO GO ——

Amusement Parks: Celebration Station, Sandy Lake, Putt Putt,
    Malibu, Mountasia, Twin Rivers
Children's Theater: Dallas, Garland, Plano, Richardson
Dallas Aquarium
Dallas Arboretum and Botanical Garden
Dallas Museum of Art
Dallas Museum of Natural History
Dallas Public Library—Downtown
Dallas Zoo
Indoor Playparks: Discovery Zone, Planet Pizza
Las Colinas: Mustang Sculptures, Shopping, Water Taxis
Mesquite Championship Rodeo
Old City Park on Festival Days
Playgrounds/Recreation Centers/Pools
Samuell Farm/Adventures at Samuell Farm Horseback Riding
The Science Place and Planetarium/IMAX Theater
Six Flags Hurricane Harbor
Six Flags Over Texas

State Fair of Texas
The Studios at Las Colinas
West End Marketplace/Tilt, CityGolf, Planet
    Hollywood, Dallas World Aquarium

—— FREE ACTIVITIES FOR FAMILIES ——

African American Museum at Fair Park
Animal shelters
Arlington Museum of Art
Art galleries
Arts and crafts malls
Bachman Lake
Bath House Cultural Center *
Biblical Arts Center *
Bike trails
Bolin Wildlife Exhibit
Bookstores
Children's Medical Center miniature trains
City Hall and Plaza activities
Christmas Tree Lightings
College campuses
College theater performances *
Collin Co. Youth Park & Museum
Comanche Peak Nuclear Plant
Connemara Conservatory
C.R. Smith Aviation Museum
Dallas Arboretum *
Dallas Firefighter's Museum: Old Tige
Dallas/Fort Worth Airport
Dallas Horticulture Center
Dallas Museum for Holocaust Studies
Dallas Museum of Art *
Dallas Museum of Natural History *
Dallas Nature Center *

* During limited hours these attractions are free to the public, or
  admission is free with fees for special exhibits or designated activities.

Disc golf
Dog shows
Downtown Dallas Historical Plazas
Downtown Historical Squares
Downtown Dallas Underground
Farmers Branch Historical Park
Farmers markets
Festivals and art fairs
Fishing
Flea markets and trade days
Fritz Park Petting Farm in Irving
Goliad Place in Rockwall
Grand Prairie Historic Homes
Heard Museum and Wildlife Sanctuary *
Historic, self-guided trails
History of Aviation Collection-UTD
International Museum of Culture
Interurban Railway Depot in Plano
Jesuit Dallas Museum
Kite flying and Frisbee tossing at the park
Lakes
Landmark Museum of Garland
Libraries
Magic shops
Meadows Museum at SMU
Mustang exhibit and Canal Walk at Las Colinas
Nature preserves, parks, greenbelt areas
Nature stores
Nature trails
Nurseries
Old Post Office Museum in McKinney
Outdoor concerts in the park
Owens Spring Creek Farm
Parades
Pate Museum of Transportation

* During limited hours these attractions are free to the public, or
  admission is free with fees for special exhibits or designated activities.

Perry Homestead Museum in Carrollton
Pet stores
Planetariums
Playgrounds
Recreation centers *
Shakespeare in the Park
Shopping malls
Silent Wings Museum in Terrell
Skating, outdoors
South Dallas Cultural Center *
Spectator sports-youth and amateur games
Sports for family play-tennis, basketball, softball, badminton,
    ping pong, volleyball
Symphony and community bands, outdoor concerts
Telephone Pioneer Museum of Texas
Tennis on neighborhood courts
Tours of the Working World
Trammel Crow Pavilions and Sculpture Garden
Union Station
West End Historical District
White Rock Lake

* During limited hours these attractions are free to the public, or
  admission is free with fees for special exhibits or designated activities.

—— BIRTHDAY PARTY IDEAS ——

Air Combat School - older children
Arcade - West End Tilt
Art-A-Rama
Backyard carnival
Barney birthdays
Ballpark at Arlington/Tour and Museum
Batting cages, outdoor and indoor
Bowling lanes
Braum's
Broomball at ice rink

Burger King
Capricorn Riding Academy
Chuck E. Cheese's Pizza
Cooking School
Crafty Kids/Plaster Crafts
Crystal's Pizza
Dallas Children's Theater
Dallas Fun and Fitness Center
Dallas Nature Center
Dallas Puppet Theatre
Discovery Zone
Dollhouse Museum
Dress up party/rental trunk
Eaglequest Golf Park
Eisenberg's Skatepark
FamiliARTS
Festivals
Fire station
Friendze Jewelry Making
Fritz Park Petting Farm in Irving/June and July
GameWorks at Grapevine Mills
Go-kart rides, outdoor and indoor
Granada Theater
Green Oaks Golf Center in Arlington
Gymboree Gymnastic centers
Hard Rock Cafe
Heard Museum and Wildlife Sanctuary
Horseback riding
Ice skating
Indoor soccer centers
Joe Willy's Restaurant
Lake parks
Le Theatre de Marionette
The Little Gym
Magic show
Magic Time Machine Restaurant
Malibu Speedzone

Mandalay Canal Boat Ride and Mustang Sculpture
McDonald's Friendly Red Caboose in Irving
McKinney Avenue Trolley
Mesquite Rodeo
Metroplex Gymnastics
Miniature golf
MJ Designs craft party
Mountasia Golf and games
Movies
Museums
Northpark on Ice
NRH2O Water Park
Old Tige's: Dallas Firefighter's Museum
Olympic Pizza
Paintball - junior high or older
Paint 'N Party
Paint Palette
Paint Yer Pottery
Palace of Wax/Ripley's Believe It Or Not!
Palmerosa Ranch in Mesquite
Petting zoo
Planet Pizza
Planetarium show/IMAX Theater
Playground/picnic
Pony rides
Puppet show
Putt Putt
Restaurant
Rapid Revolution skateboarding and rollerblading, indoor
Rock climbing gym - Exposure, Stone Works
Samuell Farm/horseback riding
Sandy Lake Amusement Park
Scavenger hunt
Science Place/Kids Place
Six Flags Hurricane Harbor water park
Six Flags Over Texas
Skating rinks, ice and roller

Space Walk of Dallas rentals
Spinner's Pizza
Sports event - Cowboys, Mavericks, Rangers, Sidekicks, Stars
Sportsridge Athletic Club
Sports Spectrum Indoor Soccer
Storytellers
Surf 'N Swim
Swimming pool, outdoor and indoor
Tarantula train in Ft. Worth, Stockyards Amusement Park
Texas Stadium tours/games
Theater - children's play
Theater - early morning rental for private showing & breakfast
Tours of the Working World
Twin Rivers Amusement Park
Wagon Wheel Ranch
West End - Tilt, CityGolf, Planet Hollywood, Dallas World
  Aquarium, movies
Whirlyball
YMCA: indoor pool
Zoo

—— RAINY WEATHER IDEAS ——

Adair Baseball World
African-American Museum at Fair Park
Airport/aviation museums
Animal shelter
Arcade—Eaglequest, Celebration Station, Malibu, GameWorks
Art galleries
Biblical Arts Center
Bolin Wildlife Museum
Bookstore
Bowling
Burger King's or McDonald's indoor parks
Cavanaugh Flight Museum in Addison
Children's Medical Center miniature trains
Children's theater
City Hall

Dallas Aquarium
Dallas Firefighter's Museum
Dallas Museum for Holocaust Studies
Dallas Museum of Art
Dallas Museum of Natural History
Dallas Puppet Theatre
Dallas World Aquarium
Dollhouse Museum
Dave and Buster's
Grapevine Mills Outlet Mall
Hall of State
Hardware store
Heard Museum
Hidden Treasures Museum-Northpark Center
Hobby and craft stores
Hotel - elevators, restaurants
Ice cream and yogurt parlor
Indoor archery
Indoor miniature golf - Eaglequest, CityGolf
Indoor play parks - Discovery Zone, Planet Pizza
Indoor tennis
International Museum of Culture
Interurban Railroad Museum/Saturday
Library
Meadows Museum at SMU
Nature store
Palace of Wax/Ripley's Believe It Or Not!
Perry Homestead Museum
Pet store
Planet Pizza
Planetarium show
Rock climbing gym
Science Place
Shopping mall
Silent Wings Museum in Terrell
Sixth Floor Museum
Studios at Las Colinas

Texas State History Museum/Arlington
Tours of the Working World
Toy store
Underground Downtown Dallas
West End Marketplace

Index

A

A Likely Story, 130
A.W. Perry Homestead Museum, 89
ACT II Children's Theatre of
    Addison, 169
Addison, 138, 169
Addison Airport, 119
African-American Museum, 2
Age of Steam Railroad Museum, 3
Air Combat School, 64
Airplanes, 108, 117
American Museum of the Miniature
    Arts, 5
AMTRAK, 121
Animal Adoption Center, 84
Anita N. Martinez Ballet Folklorico
    Dance Studio, 158
Annual concerts and performance
    and film festivals, 176
Antique Sewing Machine Museum,
    87
Arcades, 58, 141
Archery, 189
Arlington, 7, 50-51, 73, 112, 164
    Historical Society, 88
    History, 87
    Museum of Art, 132
Art centers, 131
Art classes, 136
Art galleries, 131
Art museums, 131
Arts District, 113
Arts District Theater, 171
Audubon Society, 68
Auto racing, 187
Auto show, 124
Aviation history, 100, 103-104, 254

B

Bachman Lake, 6
Ballpark in Arlington, The, 7
Baseball, softball, and t-ball, 189
Basketball, 190
Bath House Cultural Center, 60, 133
Baylor's Truett Hospital, 139
Biblical Arts Center, 133
Bicycling, 96, 190
Big Town Farmer's Market, 79
Bird watching, 68
Birthday party ideas, 294
Black Academy of Arts and Letters,
    Inc., 134
Boat show, 123
boats, 123, 262
Bolin Wildlife Exhibit, 85
Bonham, 248
Bonham State Recreation Area, 218
Bookstores, 129, 141
Botanic Garden, 259
Bowling, 191
Brookhaven, 152
Broomball, 197
Brunch, 147
Buses, 120

C

C.R. Smith Museum, 118
Camps, 210, 215
    sports, 207
Canton, 146
Capers for Kids, 170
Carriages, 124
Carrollton, 47, 69, 159
    history, 89

Old Downtown Square, 89
Cars, 112, 124
  vintage, 85
Carter Blood Care Center tour, 106
Casa Manana, 262
Cat show, 82
Cavanaugh Flight Museum, 119
Cedar Creek Lake, 219
Cedar Hill State Park, 220
Cedar Valley, 152
Celebration Station, 10
Chamber Symphony of the
  Metrocrest, 159
Channel 8/WFAA-TV tour, 107
Cheerleading, 192
Children's Chorus of Greater
  Dallas, 160
Children's Medical Center tour, 107
Christmas trees, 80
City of Dallas Farmer's Market, 79
Collections, 143
Collegiate sports, 186
Collin County Youth Park and Farm
  Museum, 100
Collin Creek Mall, 141
Comanche Peak Nuclear Power
  Plant, 77
Community colleges, 151
Computer science, 77
Confederate Air Force, 100
Connemara Conservancy, 67
Convention and visitor's bureaus,
  284
Cooper Lake and State Park, 219
Coppell, 69
Cotton Bowl, 186
Cottonwood Creek Preserve, 69
Craft Guild of Dallas, 134
Creative Arts Center/School of
  Sculpture, 135
Creative Arts Theatre and School,
  170

D

Daingerfield Lake and State Park,
  219
Dallas Aquarium at Fair Park, 10
Dallas Arboretum and Botanical
  Gardens, 12
Dallas Area Rapid Transit, 121
Dallas Black Dance Theatre, 158
Dallas Chamber Orchestra, 160
Dallas Children's Theater, Inc., 170
Dallas City Hall, 90, 108
Dallas Classic Guitar Society, 161
Dallas Convention and Visitor's
  Bureau, 284
Dallas Convention Center, 139
Dallas County Audubon Society,
  Inc., 68
Dallas County Historical Plaza, 91
Dallas County Park and Open Space
  Program, 68
Dallas Cowboys, 114
Dallas Farmer's Market, 79
Dallas Firefighter's Museum: "Old
  Tige," 14
Dallas history, 90
Dallas Horticulture Center, 15
Dallas Jazz Orchestra, 161
Dallas Love Field, 118
Dallas Memorial Center for
  Holocaust Studies, 17
Dallas Morning News, 109
Dallas Museum of Art, 18, 162
Dallas Museum of Natural History,
  21
Dallas Nature Center, 22, 69
Dallas on Ice, 58
Dallas Opera, 166
Dallas Public Library, 126
  tours, 109
Dallas Puppet Theatre, 168
Dallas School of Music, 161
Dallas Summer Musicals, 171

Dallas Symphony Association, Inc., 162
Dallas Theater Center, 171
    tour, 110
Dallas Visitor Information Center, 95
Dallas Visual Arts Center, 135
Dallas Water Utilities tours, 110
Dallas World Aquarium, 24
Dallas Zoo, 25
Dallas/Ft. Worth Area Tourism Council, 285
Dallas/Ft. Worth International Airport, 108, 118
Dance, 158
Dancing, 192
Daughters of the American Revolution House, 91
Day camps, 151
Dealey Plaza, 91
Denison, 222, 250
Dinosaur Valley State Park, 266
Disabled Sports Association, 203
Disc golf, 192
Discovery Zone, 65
Disney Store, 141
Dog show, 82
Dolls, 89, 98, 143
Downtown Dallas, 115
Dr Pepper Bottling Company tour, 112
Duck Creek Greenbelt, 71
Dude ranches, 215

E

Earth Day, 71
Eastfield, 152
Ecology, 76
Edgewood, 272
Eisenhower State Park, 222
El Centro, 153
Elm Fork Preserve, 69

Emergency Animal Clinic, 84
Enchanted Forest Books for Children, 130
Escarpment Preserve, 69
Event and ticket/reservation hotlines, 284

F

Fair Park, 27
FamiliARTS, 176
Farmers Branch Historical Park, 96
Farmers Branch History, 96
Farmers Branch Mustang Trail, 96
Farmer's markets, 78
Farms, 80
Fencing, 193
Festivals and special events, 226
Fine Arts Chamber Players, 162
First Monday Trade Days, 276
Fishing, 193
Flag Pole Hill, 60
Flea markets and trade days, 146
Florence Ranch Homestead, 101
Football, 194
Fort Worth, 252
    Nature Center and Refuge, 260
    Zoo, 261
Fort Worth Dallas Ballet, 159
Fossil Rim Wildlife Center, 267
Free activities for families, 292
Fritz Park Petting Farm, 84
Frontiers of Flight Museum, 31, 118
Fun Fest, 65

G

Galleria, 141
Garland, 56, 71, 75, 84, 97
Garland Civic Theatre's Children on Stage, 172
Garland Opry, 167

General Motors Assembly Plant
tour, 112
Glen Rose, 77, 265
Golf, 194
disc, 192
spectator, 187
Goliad Place, 104
Grand Prairie, 44, 97, 147
Grand Prix, 124
Grapevine, 98
Grapevine Lake, 219
Grapevine Mills Outlet Center, 143
Grapevine Opry, 168
Grapevine Springs Park Preserve,
69
Gray Line Tours, 122
Greater Dallas Youth Orchestra,
163
Greyhound, 122
Gymnastics and tumbling, 196

H

Hagerman Wildlife Refuge, 250
Half-Price Tickets, 156
Hall of State, 32
Hard Rock Cafe, 149
Heard Natural Science Museum
and Wildlife Sanctuary, 34
Helicopters, 117
Heritage Farmstead, 36
Hiking and volksmarching, 196
History of Aviation
Collection-UTD, 103
Hobbies, 143
Home and Garden Show, 71
Horse racing and horse shows, 187
Horseback riding, 215
Hot air balloons, 117, 188
Hotels, 147
Hunting and sporting clays, 196
Hyatt Regency at Reunion, 148

I

Ice hockey, 197
Ice skating, 197, 262
IMAX Theater, 48
Indians, 147
International Museum of Cultures,
92
Interurban Railway Station, 102
Invention Convention, 78
Irving, 38, 55, 99, 112, 114
Irving Heritage District, 99
Isle Du Bois State Park, 221

J

J. Erik Jonsson Central Library, 127
Jesuit Dallas Museum, 136
Joe Pool Lake, 220
J's Art Studio, 136
Junior Players, 172

K

KD Studio Actors Conservatory,
172
Kid Art, 136
Kite flying, 198
KLIF/KPLX Radio Station tour, 113

L

L.B. Houston Nature Area, 72
Lacrosse, 198
Lake Arlington, 220
Lake Bonham Recreation Area, 221
Lake Lavon, 221
Lake Mineral Wells State Park, 86
Lake Ray Hubbard, 123, 221
Lake Ray Roberts, 221
Lake Texoma, 222, 250
Lake Whitney and State Park, 223

Lakes, 6, 47, 60, 86, 123, 133, 218, 219, 220, 221, 222, 223, 224, 250, 269, 272, 276
Lakewood Arts Academy, 136
Lancaster, 100
Landmark Museum, 97
Las Colinas, 38, 99
Las Colinas water taxis, 123
Le Theatre de Marionette, 169
Lemmon Lake Preserve, 70
Lewisville Lake, 223
Libraries, 109, 126
Longhorn sculpture, 139
Love Field Airport, 118

M

M.T. Johnson Plantation Cemetery and Historic Park, 88
Malibu Speedzone, 65
Malls, 141
Martial arts, 198
McCommas Bluff Preserve, 70
McDonald's, 66, 141
McDonald's Friendly Red Caboose, 99
McKinney, 100
    Heard Museum, 34, 101
McKinney Avenue Trolley, 113, 122
McKinney history, 85
Meadows Museum, 137
Meadows School of the Arts, 163, 173
Medieval Times Dinner and Tournament, 151
Mesquite, 10, 45, 70, 101, 142
Mesquite Arts Center, 101
Mesquite Championship Rodeo, 40
Metro Players, 173
Meyerson Symphony Center, 114, 162
Miniature golf, 194
Motor sports—cars, carts, and model planes, 198

Mountain Creek Lake, 223
Mountain View, 153
Mrs. Baird's Bakery tour, 106
Museum for East Texas Culture, 271
Music, 265
Music and chorus, 159
Music Mill Amphitheater, 164

N

National Museum of Communication, 99
National Science Balloon Center, 77
Nature, 67, 269, 272
Nature Center and Refuge, 260
Nature Company, 72
North Lake, 154
North Mesquite Creek Preserve, 70
Northpark Center, 72
NRH2O, 204
Nurseries, 78-79

O

Observatories, 72
Old City Park, 41
Old Downtown Carrollton Square, 89
Opera, 166
Operation Kindness, 83
Opry, 98, 167-168
Orienteering, 199
Owens Spring Creek Farm, 42

P

Paddleboating, 199
Paintball, 199
Palace of Wax, 44
Palestine, 77
Party supplies, 146
Pegasus Plaza, 92

Penn Farm Historic Site, 220
Performing arts, 133
  for children, 156
  variety series, 175
Pet adoption centers, 82
Petmobile Pet Hospital, 84
Pets, 82, 141
Pick your own food, 80
Pioneer Park Cemetery, 90
Pizza, 149
Planet Hollywood, 58, 149
Planet Pizza, 66
Planetariums, 72
Plano, 36, 67, 102, 141
  Interurban Railway Station, 102
Plano Children's Theatre, 174
Playgrounds, 213
Pocket Sandwich Theatre, 174
Possum Kingdom Lake and State
  Park, 224
Prestonwood Town Center, 142
Publications, 286
Pumpkins, 80
Puppetry, 168
Purtis Creek Lake and State Park,
  224

R

Rafting, canoeing, tubing, and
  kayaking, 200, 265
Rainy weather ideas, 297
Recreation centers and youth
  organizations, 210
Recycling and conservation, 76
Religion, 129, 133
Resources, 283
Restaurants, 149
Reunion Tower, 148
Richardson, 42, 103
Richardson Children's Theatre, 174
Richardson Symphony Orchestra,
  164

Richland College, 154
  Planetarium, 72
Ripley's Believe It Or Not!, 44
Riverboats, 123, 262, 276
Rock climbing, 200
Rocketry, 201
Rockwall, 104
Rodeos, 147, 187
Roller skating, 201
Ronald's Playplace, 66
Rootabaga Bookery, 131
Rowlett Nature Trail, 73
Running, 201
Rusk, 269

S

Sailing and motor boating, 201
Samuell Farm, 45
Sandy Lake Amusement Park, 47
Scarborough Faire, 93
Science, 77, 106, 254, 269, 272
Science Fair, 78
Science Place, 48
Science Place Planetarium, 73
Science projects, 78
Scuba diving, 202
Sculpture, 88, 90, 137
Sculpture and murals outdoors,
  137-138
Shopping, 140
  malls, 141
Sierra Club, 74
Silent Wings Museum, 104
Six Flags Hurricane Harbor, 50
Six Flags Over Texas, 51
Sixth Floor, 53
Skateboarding and rollerblading,
  202
Skating, 58
Skiing, water, 202
Snider Plaza, 131
Soccer, 203

Society for the Prevention of
    Cruelty to Animals, 83
South Dallas Cultural Center, 165
Southfork, 215
Special Olympics, 203
Sports, 184
    arena, 185
    camps, 207
    collegiate, 186
    individual, family, and team, 189
    major league, 184
    spectator, 184
Sports and recreation, 184
Sports Hall of Fame, 276
St. Mark's School of Texas
    Observatory, 73
Stamp collecting, 103
Starplex Amphitheater, 164
State Fair of Texas, 27, 91
State parks and recreation areas,
    218, 265, 269, 272
Storytellers, 125
Studios at Las Colinas, 55, 99
Subway, 262
Summer camps, 136
Sunshine Generation, Inc., 165
Surf 'N Swim, 56
Swimming, 204, 262
Swiss Avenue Historic District, 93
Symphony, 114

T

Tanger Outlet Mall, 142
Tarantula train, 98, 263
Telephone Pioneer Museum of
    Texas, 57
Telephone services, 291
Tennis, 206
    spectator, 189
Terrell, 104
Texas Amphitheater, 269
Texas Boys Choir, 165

Texas Committee on Natural
    Resources, 74
Texas Girls Choir, 166
Texas Queen Riverboat, 104, 123,
    221
Texas Stadium, 114
Texas State Department of
    Highways and Public
    Transportation, 285
Texas State Museum of History, 88
Texas State Railroad, 269
Texas Utilities Electric Company
    tour, 115
Texas Wilderness Pow Wow, 74
Thanks-Giving Square, 94
The International Theatrical Arts
    Society (TITAS), 173
Theater, 110, 169, 265
Theatre Three, 175
Ticket/reservation hotlines, 284
TITAS, *See* The International
    Theatrical Arts Society
Tom McCurdy's Fruit Stand, 79
Top 20 places to go, 291
Tour buses, 120
Tours, 76-77, 83, 85, 87, 96, 102
Tours of the working world, 105
Town East Mall, 142
Toy stores, 145
Toys, 131, 141, 145
Trader's Village, 146
Traders Village and RV Park, 147
Trains, 99, 102, 120, 262, 269
    miniature, 88, 107, 143
Trammel Crow Center, 139
Transportation, 116, 254, 262, 269
Tres Rios, 268
Triathlon, 207
Trips, 248
    Bonham, 248
    Denison, 250
    Ft. Worth, 252
    Glen Rose, 265

Texas State Railroad, 269
Tyler, 272
Waco, 276
Trolleys, 120
Truett Hospital/Baylor, 139
Turtle Creek Greenbelt, 74
Tyler, 272
    Caldwell Zoo, 273
    State Park, 275

U

Underground Dallas, 115
Union Station, 95, 121, 148
University of Texas at Arlington
    Planetarium, 73

V

Valley View Mall, 142

W

Waco, 276

Waxahachie, 93
West End Historic District, 58
West End Marketplace, 58
Whirlyball, 66
White Rock Lake, 60, 133
Whole Earth Provision Co., 75
Wild Bird Center, 68
Wildflowers, 75
Wildlife, 85, 250, 259, 265, 269, 272,
    276
Wildlife program, 87
Wildscapes, 86
Wilson Block, 135
Wilson Historic District, 93
Woodland Basin Nature Area, 75

Y

Yellow Rose Touring Company, 123
Young Actors Studio, 175
Young Artist, 137
Youth organizations, 210